New Frontiers in Regional Science: Asian Perspectives

Volume 20

New Frontiers in Regional Science: Asian Perspectives

This series is a constellation of works by scholars in the field of regional science and in related disciplines specifically focusing on dynamism in Asia.

Asia is the most dynamic part of the world. Japan, Korea, Taiwan, and Singapore experienced rapid and miracle economic growth in the 1970s. Malaysia, Indonesia, and Thailand followed in the 1980s. China, India, and Vietnam are now rising countries in Asia and are even leading the world economy. Due to their rapid economic development and growth, Asian countries continue to face a variety of urgent issues including regional and institutional unbalanced growth, environmental problems, poverty amidst prosperity, an ageing society, the collapse of the bubble economy, and deflation, among others.

Asian countries are diversified as they have their own cultural, historical, and geographical as well as political conditions. Due to this fact, scholars specializing in regional science as an inter- and multi-discipline have taken leading roles in providing mitigating policy proposals based on robust interdisciplinary analysis of multifaceted regional issues and subjects in Asia. This series not only will present unique research results from Asia that are unfamiliar in other parts of the world because of language barriers, but also will publish advanced research results from those regions that have focused on regional and urban issues in Asia from different perspectives.

The series aims to expand the frontiers of regional science through diffusion of intrinsically developed and advanced modern regional science methodologies in Asia and other areas of the world. Readers will be inspired to realize that regional and urban issues in the world are so vast that their established methodologies still have space for development and refinement, and to understand the importance of the interdisciplinary and multidisciplinary approach that is inherent in regional science for analyzing and resolving urgent regional and urban issues in Asia.

Topics under consideration in this series include the theory of social cost and benefit analysis and criteria of public investments, socio-economic vulnerability against disasters, food security and policy, agro-food systems in China, industrial clustering in Asia, comprehensive management of water environment and resources in a river basin, the international trade bloc and food security, migration and labor market in Asia, land policy and local property tax, Information and Communication Technology planning, consumer "shop-around" movements, and regeneration of downtowns, among others.

More information about this series at http://www.springer.com/series/13039

Akihiro Otsuka

A New Perspective on Agglomeration Economies in Japan

An Application of Productivity Analysis

Springer

Akihiro Otsuka
Association of International Arts and Science
Yokohama City University
Yokohama, Japan

ISSN 2199-5974 ISSN 2199-5982 (electronic)
New Frontiers in Regional Science: Asian Perspectives
ISBN 978-981-10-6489-0 ISBN 978-981-10-6490-6 (eBook)
DOI 10.1007/978-981-10-6490-6

Library of Congress Control Number: 2017952056

Printed on acid-free paper

This Springer imprint is published by Springer Nature
The registered company is Springer Nature Singapore Pte Ltd.
The registered company address is: 152 Beach Road, #21-01/04 Gateway East, Singapore 189721, Singapore

Preface

This book clarifies the role played by agglomeration economies in regional economies and explores the feasibility of using regional economic growth in declining population areas of developed countries. Where quantitative economic expansion is increasingly difficult, improving productivity is necessary to realize sustainable regional economic growth. One of the sources of agglomeration economies is the creation of technological knowledge (innovation) and its spillover, which is important for determining the competitive advantages of a region. Therefore, in this book, the focus is on agglomeration economies, the driving force behind regional economic growth, and the actual conditions of agglomeration economies in Japan. The effects of agglomeration economies are comprehensively determined by both the effects of their productivity and productive efficiency. As such, the analytical approach proposed in this book uses productivity and productive efficiency analysis methods. Through their application, readers will be able to identify desirable policies for regional economies that promote agglomeration economies and contribute to the realization of regional economic growth.

Many studies have investigated the role played by agglomeration economies in cities and regions in various countries around the world, adopting a traditional analytical approach using the production function. Many researchers have subsequently attempted to improve this approach, directing the stream of research accordingly. However, most of these studies focus on a static approach that assumes perfect competition, and there are few examples that adopt the analytical approach that focuses on the dynamic changes of agglomeration economies. A dynamic analysis is essential to consider economic dynamism, or the sustainable growth of regional economies. Despite this, while a theory of agglomeration that assumes imperfect competition has been constructed in spatial economics, no empirical model assuming imperfect competition as its microeconomic foundation has been constructed. To address this issue, this book proposes a novel analytical method that quantitatively clarifies the dynamic effects that agglomeration economies have on regional economic growth.

The research objectives of this book are as follows. First, it proposes a new approach that uses a productivity analysis method to determine the actual conditions of agglomeration economies in Japan, from the perspectives of both regions and industries. Second, it proposes a novel empirical model that takes imperfect competition into consideration and, thereby more accurately establishes the actual conditions of dynamic external economies, specifically dynamic externalities. Third, it ascertains the impact of agglomeration economies on regional economic growth through productive efficiency using multiple productive efficiency analysis methods.

The main feature of this book is that it proposes numerous new analytical approaches. The first is an analytical approach that uses the Solow residual to deal with the estimation-relation problem of the production function, which has become an issue in the traditional analytical approach of agglomeration economies. This method avoids the problem of endogeneity, which is a weakness of the traditional approach. Second, it reveals a new empirical model that assumes imperfect competition. Since most firms in the market do face imperfect competition, this model more realistically determines the dynamic effects of agglomeration economies. Third, to comprehensively understand the effects of agglomeration economies on productivity changes, it proposes an analytical approach that utilizes stochastic frontier and data envelopment analyses. Applying growth accounting techniques makes it possible to quantitatively ascertain the effects of agglomeration economies on economic growth.

Consequently, readers will be able to learn about novel analytical approaches and see examples of their application through the empirical analysis of agglomeration economies. This knowledge will make it possible to clearly define the roles played by agglomeration economies in the development of regional economies, and to quantitatively understand both the effects of productivity and productive efficiency on regional economic growth. Through these methods and the analytical findings, readers will be able to propose regional economic policies that will benefit economies with declining populations.

The intended readers are mainly graduate students and researchers (scholars) in the field of regional science, but it will also be useful for policy makers. This book is an advanced attempt at introducing new analytical methods to aid in understanding agglomeration economies and to provide examples of their application. To the best of my knowledge, there is no other publication that has comprehensively analyzed this topic with these approaches. Because of its originality, there are few other publications that could compete with it.

This book is organized into ten chapters. Some chapters are previously published journal papers. I would like to thank the editorial board in Regional Studies, Papers in Regional Science, The Annals of Regional Science, The Economic Review (The Keizai Kenkyuu), The Economic Analysis (The Keizai Bunseki), Journal of Applied Regional Science, and Okayama Economic Review for permitting me to reuse these articles. In addition, some chapters of this book have been published as part of a Japanese book. In writing this book, I have received reprint permission from University Education Press Co., Ltd. The original manuscript has been greatly revised and updated. I thank Professor Mika Goto, Professor Toshiyuki Sueyoshi, and Norihiko Yamano as co-authors of some of the original articles for encouraging me to proceed with the research. A draft of the third chapter is published as a discussion paper in the Regional Economics Applications Laboratory (REAL), University of Illinois. I am grateful to Professor Geoffrey J. D. Hewings and the REAL staff for their valuable comments and suggestions. In addition, I would like to thank Professor Shoji Haruna, from whom I have received valuable advice on my research for a long time.

This book was written as a part of a research activity at Yokohama City University. I have received a Grant-in-Aid for Young Scientific Research by Yokohama City University. I would like to thank the founders of Yokohama City University and President Yoshinobu Kubota. This work also has supported by a Japan Society for the Promotion of Science (JSPS) Grant-in-Aid for Scientific Research (KAKENHI) 15K17067. Parts of this book are based on research results from the Central Research Institute of the Electric Power Industry. When I worked at this laboratory, I received helpful comments and suggestions from the laboratory's staff. I would like to thank them.

Finally, I would like to thank my wife Harumi Otsuka for her dedication in supporting me during the writing of this book. I hope this book will be a cornerstone for our future research.

Yokohama, Japan Akihiro Otsuka

Contents

Chapter 1
Introduction and Summary

Abstract This chapter describes the research background three objectives of this book. The first objective is to clarify from multiple perspectives how industrial agglomeration influenced the growth of the regional economy in Japan during the 1980s and 1990s, when globalization of economic activity and the hollowing-out of industries were in progress. The second is to shed light on the industrial agglomeration effects from a dynamic perspective by looking at industrial development. The third objective is to propose a new analytical approach using the techniques of productive efficiency analysis. This book is comprised of ten chapters. A summary of each chapter is described in this chapter.

Keywords Industrial agglomeration • Agglomeration economies • Regional science • Japan

1.1 Research Background

Since the collapse of the bubble economy, the business environment surrounding firms has experienced major changes. The decade of the 1990s is often referred to as "the lost decade" for its unremitting long period of low economic growth. During this period, many domestic firms were unable to escape from the experience of their past successes and felt increasingly trapped. On the other hand, the world economy rapidly expanded its sphere of economic activity during this decade, as it became progressively more borderless in response to technological developments. Along with the development of the world economy, big firms facing global competition internationalized their operations. Japan's foreign direct investment increased from 1.6 trillion yen in 1985 to 10.1 trillion yen by the year 2012, and the trend of globalization has continued.[1] As a result, the production scale of Japan's domestic manufacturing industry has followed a downward trend. After the total shipment value of manufactured goods peaked at 341 trillion yen in 1991, by the year 2010, it had declined to 289 trillion yen. Likewise, while the number of

[1]Bank of Japan, Foreign direct investment, from the *Balance of International Payments Monthly*.

A. Otsuka, *A New Perspective on Agglomeration Economies in Japan*,
New Frontiers in Regional Science: Asian Perspectives 20,
DOI 10.1007/978-981-10-6490-6_1

business establishments hovered at around 430,000 in the 1980s, by the year 2010, there were only 220,000 establishments.[2]

Japan's postwar industrial policy has focused on the relocation of plants from large metropolitan areas to rural areas. Under the slogan of balanced development of the national land, relocation of production functions to rural areas has been done mainly to rectify regional disparities. The purpose of the policy was to create employment by relocating plants to rural areas and to revitalize the regional economy. Large metropolitan areas are responsible for the management function, rural areas are responsible for the production function, and a regional division of production was established. To efficiently carry out the vertical division of production among regions, the Japanese government developed a physical infrastructure including roads, airports, harbors, and telecommunications. The regional economy has developed because of the national land and industrial policy.

From the perspective of the globalization of economic activity, however, there are some doubts about the effectiveness of these regional industrial policies. Currently, an important theme in regional policy is how to raise the competitiveness of regional industries to invigorate the regional economy. Specifically, as the relocation of plants to overseas has progressed, the effectiveness of traditional methods to develop local regions, such as industrial relocation to rural areas in the country, has been lost. Under these circumstances, what is currently required is changing the structure of industrial agglomeration by creating a high productivity sector with the goal of improving the competitiveness of the regional economy while keeping the economic benefits gained through cost competition (Cabinet Office 2004). Recently, with the backing of abundant cash reserves and aiming for growth, a strategy has been emerging to position Japanese domestic plants as the hub of high value-added products.

Globalization of economic activity has further complicated the regional interdependencies by way of intra-firm transactions and intra-industry transactions. Not only have technologies such as microelectronics, new materials, and information systems with a wide range of applications become ubiquitous, it is now possible for firms to obtain their production components, such as source materials, parts, auxiliary services, and capital, from around the world instead of sourcing them locally. Furthermore, since the infrastructure, which is the foundation of society, is well developed in every region, the comparative advantage due to these disparities has also vanished. If firms are to realize sustainable growth under such circumstances, it is necessary for them to extract themselves from cost competition and increase their profitability by pursuing their unique strategies. For this reason, what becomes important is solving the question of how efficiently can comparative advantages be created, rather than simply pursuing "comparative advantages."

In addition to the influence of globalization of economic activities on Japan's economy, there are internal structural problems, including a declining birth rate and

[2]Ministry of Economy, Trade and Industry, *Statistics on business establishments with four or more employees* from the *Census of Manufactures*.

an aging population. The growth rate of regional economies is already in decline because of the adverse effects those internal problems have had on economic activities; for example, a reduced productive-age population can harm the dynamism of society and the smooth procurement of the labor force. In this situation, it is important for regional industries to improve their productivity to achieve higher economic growth per capita. In particular, it is necessary to improve productive efficiency by transforming the industrial structure and by reallocating labor resources from sectors with lower productivity to those with higher productivity.

According to Porter (1990, 1998), constant competition and cooperation among firms generates innovation and accelerates the transfer of technical knowledge among firms. A region's advantage is not determined by how cheap their labor force is or how much capital they possess; it is determined by how efficiently they can innovate and whether they have a system to propagate and internalize their innovations. Thus, there is an expectation that an industrial agglomeration can function as a place for collaboration and will encourage innovation from businesses.[3] In other words, innovation is the source of an industry's competitiveness, and the significance of industrial agglomeration is its ability to create a micro business environment that makes innovation possible. For this reason, research that focuses on the economic impact of industrial agglomeration plays a significant role in strategizing for regional economic growth.

1.2 Outline

1.2.1 Objectives and Feature

The central theme of this book is to propose an approach to analyze the economic impact of industrial agglomeration, and to conduct a quantitative analysis of the industrial agglomeration effects in Japan. The purpose of this research is as follows.

The first objective is to clarify from multiple perspectives how industrial agglomeration influenced the growth of the regional economy in Japan during the 1980s and the 1990s, when globalization of economic activity and hollowing-out of industries were occurring. During the 1990s, Japan experienced a long period of low growth and persistent stagnation of productivity growth. On the other hand, the productivity gap between the highly productive regions and the less productive regions was narrowing. It is necessary to understand how the industrial agglomeration influenced regional disparities. To examine the role industrial agglomeration

[3]In Japan, the formation of new industrial agglomerations, where regional resources such as knowledge and techniques are brought together, has been pursued in each region under various projects such as the "Industrial Clusters Plan" headed by the Ministry of Economy, Trade and Industry, and the "Intellectual Cluster Creation Project" by the Ministry of Education, Culture, Sports, Science and Technology.

plays in regional economic growth, this book proposes a new analytical approach relating to agglomeration economies, and demonstrates how to overcome the limitations of the traditional method.

The second objective is to shed light on the industrial agglomeration effects from a dynamic perspective by looking at industrial development. The main characteristic of this analytical framework is that it sets imperfect competition as its premise. According to Porter, competitive advantage is generated in the process of pursuing a unique strategy, and its source is found in innovation and the differentiation of products. In theory, the formation of agglomerations and developmental processes under conditions of imperfect competition and increasing returns to scale in production technology are clearly identified. In fact, all key national industries form an oligopoly. Even in studies that examined existing markup pricing with firm data from the manufacturing industry, the results indicate that each of the firms faced imperfect market competition. Therefore, to evaluate the industrial agglomeration effects in Japan, it is necessary to set imperfect competition as the micro foundation.

The third objective is to propose a new analytical approach using the techniques of productive efficiency analysis. In previous studies, much effort has been put into detecting the influence of industrial agglomeration on labor productivity, a factor of overall productivity, and many researchers have made improvements in this analysis method. On the other hand, the influence of industrial agglomeration on the productive efficiency of regional economies has not been fully explained in the past, but it can now be understood by applying the techniques of stochastic frontier analysis and data envelopment analysis. Using the techniques of growth accounting, this book demonstrates that industrial agglomeration could potentially improve total factor productivity by improving productive efficiency.

This book adopts the prefecture level as the geographical unit of analysis. There are two levels of the Japanese administrative division. The upper level is called a "prefecture," and there are 47 prefectures. The lower level is called a "municipality," and there are several municipalities within one prefecture. Currently, there are 1718 municipalities in Japan.

Recent studies point out that the effect of industrial agglomeration surpasses the municipality level and extends to a wider area (Burger and Meijers 2016; Camagni et al. 2016). By setting the target to be analyzed to the prefecture level, it is possible to grasp the effect of industrial agglomeration, including the spillover effect between cities, in addition to the agglomeration economies at the city level. In other words, the agglomeration economies at the prefectural level signify aggregated external economies of scale. In this regard, this book is a macroscopic analysis of the agglomeration economies using aggregated data. In addition, this book also proposes an analytical approach that can handle microscopic interpretation using aggregated data.

It is well known that using aggregated data cannot capture the effects of industrial agglomeration occurring at the firm level. However, by using the aggregated data, it is possible to accurately grasp the influence of the agglomeration economies on the entire regional economy. This means that analysis results can be suitably utilized for regional policy planning and evaluation. Furthermore, it is possible to avoid the problem of statistical noise in the microdata at the firm level.

The common problem among prefecture and municipality levels is that in megacities, such as Tokyo and Osaka, the agglomeration economies are spread over several areas. For this reason, setting metropolitan areas according to the range of economic activities becomes important. Unfortunately, unlike in the United States, there are no official statistics for metropolitan areas in Japan. Several Japanese research institutes are developing metropolitan area databases, but most economic data includes various statistical biases, which make it difficult to accurately evaluate the results of econometric analysis for metropolitan areas.

1.2.2 Structure and Summary

This book is comprised of ten chapters. Since each chapter is written to stand alone, the reader will be able to read any chapter independent of the others. However, Chaps. 2, 3, 4, 5, 6, 7, 8, 9, and 10 are each written with several themes, so it would be preferable to read those chapters together by theme. Following is a summary of each chapter.

The first theme of this book, handled in Chaps. 2, 3, and 4, is an empirical approach to agglomeration economies.

Chapter 2 details the role of industrial agglomeration in regional economies, and discusses the issues of existing empirical studies. The role industrial agglomeration plays in regional economies has been well studied, as it has been a subject of discussion for a long time. An abundance of specialized workers, as well as several related industries, can be found in agglomerations. Therefore, it is possible for a firm to achieve high productivity through input sharing, labor market pooling, and knowledge spillovers. Such effects can generally be found in two cases. The first case is where an agglomeration of similar industries generates an increase in productivity. The second is where an agglomeration of different industries generates an increase in productivity. Traditionally, the effects have been measured by external economies of scale, but an analytical approach that uses spatial density to seek the source of external economies has recently been proposed. This chapter reviews these research trends.

Using a traditional approach to agglomeration economies, Chap. 3 sheds empirical light on the relationship between agglomeration economies and regional economic growth, and that relationship's impact on the convergence of regional disparities in productivity. An empirical analysis indicates that agglomeration economies have significant effects on regional economic growth. Furthermore, agglomeration economies contribute to economic convergence in the manufacturing industry, while at the same time contributing to increasing disparities across regions in the non-manufacturing industry. These results suggest that an increase in the share of non-manufacturing industries has the potential to create regional disparities.

Chapter 4 proposes a new approach to measuring agglomeration economies. Under the proposed approach, this chapter uses the Solow residual to measure agglomeration economies, and confirms that agglomeration economies exist in both manufacturing and non-manufacturing industries. Furthermore, this chapter shows that social overhead capital has a positive effect on agglomeration economies. Currently, agglomeration economies are robust only in large metropolitan areas; however, they are present throughout Japan because of the disproportionate allocation of social overhead capital within the nation.

The second theme of this book is an empirical approach on dynamic externalities, which are a new type of agglomeration economies. This theme is handled in Chaps. 5, 6, and 7.

Chapter 5 focuses on the dynamic externalities that are a source of competitive advantages, and reviews the related empirical studies. Knowledge spillover, a core of dynamic externalities, is being widely researched, mainly in the field of industrial organization theory. However, there is little empirical study considering knowledge spillover from the viewpoint of industrial agglomeration. A few studies estimate the extent and type of dynamic externalities, and find evidence consistent with dynamic externalities. Although different data sources have been used, the methodologies are similar. This chapter reviews the main methodologies used to examine dynamic externalities, and discusses empirical analysis issues of previous studies.

Chapter 6 investigates the way dynamic externalities promote industrial growth in Japanese manufacturing industries. In contrast to previous studies, this chapter proposes a novel approach that characterizes dynamic externalities by total factor productivity. Using panel data for Japanese prefectures from 1985 to 2000, this chapter finds evidence of localization (MAR) externalities and urbanization (Jacobs) externalities. However, this chapter does not provide clear evidence that dynamic externalities act as a centripetal force for industrial location.

Chapter 7 examines the effects of dynamic production externalities in emerging industries. An analysis employing four-digit data of Japanese manufacturing industries shows that: (1) Ceramic, stone and clay products, general machinery, and precision instruments and machinery enjoy the advantages generated by being located close to other industries. (2) New manufacturing technology sectors, such as industrial robots, tend to benefit from agglomeration effects, although information technology sectors do not. (3) Most emerging industries do not profit from economies of scale. These findings reveal that emerging industries benefit from industrial agglomeration effects and face market competition.

The third theme of this book, handled in Chaps. 8, 9, and 10, is an application measurement of industrial agglomeration effects.

Chapter 8 examines whether agglomeration economies, market access, and public fiscal transfer have a positive or negative influence on the productive efficiency of Japanese regional industries. To accomplish this research objective, the chapter applies stochastic frontier analysis to a prefecture level Japanese data set, which consists of estimated spatial and industrial economic activities. An empirical result described in this chapter indicates that both agglomeration economies and the improvement of market access have a positive influence on the productive efficiency of Japanese manufacturing and non-manufacturing industries. In contrast, public fiscal transfer has a negative impact on productive efficiency. These findings indicate that many prefectures that are characterized by weak market access and/or high dependence on public fiscal transfer, are often associated with low productive efficiency.

Chapter 9 re-examines the impacts of agglomeration economies and fiscal transfer on productive efficiency in Japanese regional industries. Two popular methodologies are applied to measure productive efficiency: stochastic frontier analysis and data envelopment analysis. The empirical findings are summarized as follows: (1) Agglomeration economies improve productive efficiency. (2) Fiscal transfer negatively influences productive efficiency. (3) Those two findings are observed for aggregated manufacturing and non-manufacturing industries, and for sectors in manufacturing industries. (4) The importance of agglomeration economies for regional industries has increased in recent years. Based on these results, this chapter discusses effective regional policy for Japan.

Chapter 10 analyzes the determinants of regional variations in new firm formation by industry, using the data of Japanese prefectures. The results reveal the following evidence: (1) Market access is the factor that promotes new firm formation in all industries, though the impact on new firm formation is greater in the service industry than in manufacturing industry. (2) Industrial agglomeration contributes to stimulating new firm formation in the manufacturing industry. (3) While average wage is an important factor in the manufacturing industry, it is not significant in the service industry.

1.3 Regional Economic Structure in Japan

The following discussion introduces the regional economic structure of Japan. In Japan, economic activity is largely concentrated geographically. The population of the Greater Tokyo area (i.e., Saitama, Chiba, Tokyo, and Kanagawa Prefecture) accounts for 27.36% of the total national population, and production within this area is 32.30% of total national production (Table 1.1). However, the Greater Tokyo area accounts for only 7.34% of the total national livable land. The population of the Greater Tokyo area is significantly higher than that of the second most populous region, Kansai at 16.25% (this region includes Shiga, Kyoto, Osaka, Hyogo, Nara, and Wakayama Prefecture), and of the third most populous region, Chubu at 13.46% (this region covers Gifu, Shizuoka, Aichi, and Mie Prefectures). In fact, the Greater Tokyo area is roughly equivalent to the total population of the other two regions. Similarly, production in the Greater Tokyo area (at 32.30% of the national figure) is roughly equivalent to the combined total production of Kansai (15.70%) and Chubu (14.14%). Population and overall economic production show similar distributions, since both are highly concentrated in large metropolitan areas.

Table 1.1 Regional structure in Japan (2010)

11 Regions	Inhabited area share (%)	Population share (%)	Production share (%) All industries	Manufacturing industries	Non-manufacturing industries
Hokkaido	18.18	4.35	3.64	1.87	4.07
Tohoku	20.35	9.29	7.86	7.28	7.99
Kita-Kanto	8.36	6.18	6.11	10.00	4.90
Greater Tokyo area	7.34	27.36	32.30	21.39	36.55
Chubu	10.88	13.46	14.14	22.19	11.99
Hokuriku	3.53	2.42	2.42	2.72	2.37
Kansai	6.97	16.25	15.70	16.70	15.05
Chugoku	6.90	5.96	5.60	7.18	5.04
Shikoku	3.97	3.18	2.72	2.84	2.61
Kyusyu	12.55	10.44	8.75	7.65	8.62
Okinawa	0.96	1.11	0.74	0.18	0.82

Source:
Central Research Institute of Electric Power Industry's Regional Economic Database
Note:
Hokkaido: Hokkaido
Tohoku: Aomori, Iwate, Miyagi, Akita, Yamagata, Fukushima, and Niigata
Kita-Kanto: Ibaraki, Tochigi, Gunma, and Yamanashi
Greater Tokyo Area: Saitama, Chiba, Tokyo, and Kanagawa
Chubu: Nagano, Gifu, Shizuoka, Aichi, and Mie
Hokuriku: Toyama, Ishikawa, and Fukui
Kansai: Shiga, Kyoto, Osaka, Hyogo, Nara, and Wakayama
Chugoku: Tottori, Shimane, Okayama, Hiroshima, and Yamaguchi
Shikoku: Tokushima, Kagawa, Ehime, and Kochi
Kyushu: Fukuoka, Saga, Nagasaki, Kumamoto, Oita, Miyazaki, and Kagoshima
Okinawa: Okinawa

Regional distributions of manufacturing and non-manufacturing production differ slightly. Production in manufacturing industries is primarily concentrated in rural areas, while production in non-manufacturing industries is concentrated in large metropolitan areas. For example, 21.39% of total manufacturing production activity occurs in the Greater Tokyo area, while the figure for Chubu is as high as 22.19%. For other areas, production activity also accounts for a higher proportion than the population does: production in Kansai accounts for 16.70% of the total, Kita-Kanto 10.00%, Hokuriku 2.72%, Chugoku 7.18%, and Shikoku 2.84%. On the other hand, production activity in non-manufacturing industries is concentrated in the Greater Tokyo area and accounts for 36.55% of the total, which is a higher proportion than that of the population. That is, the distribution of manufacturing industries diverges significantly from the population distribution, while the distribution of non-manufacturing industries strongly resembles that of the population distribution.

Figure 1.1 also depicts the production share of (a) manufacturing industries and (b) non-manufacturing industries in each prefecture. The two types of industries are

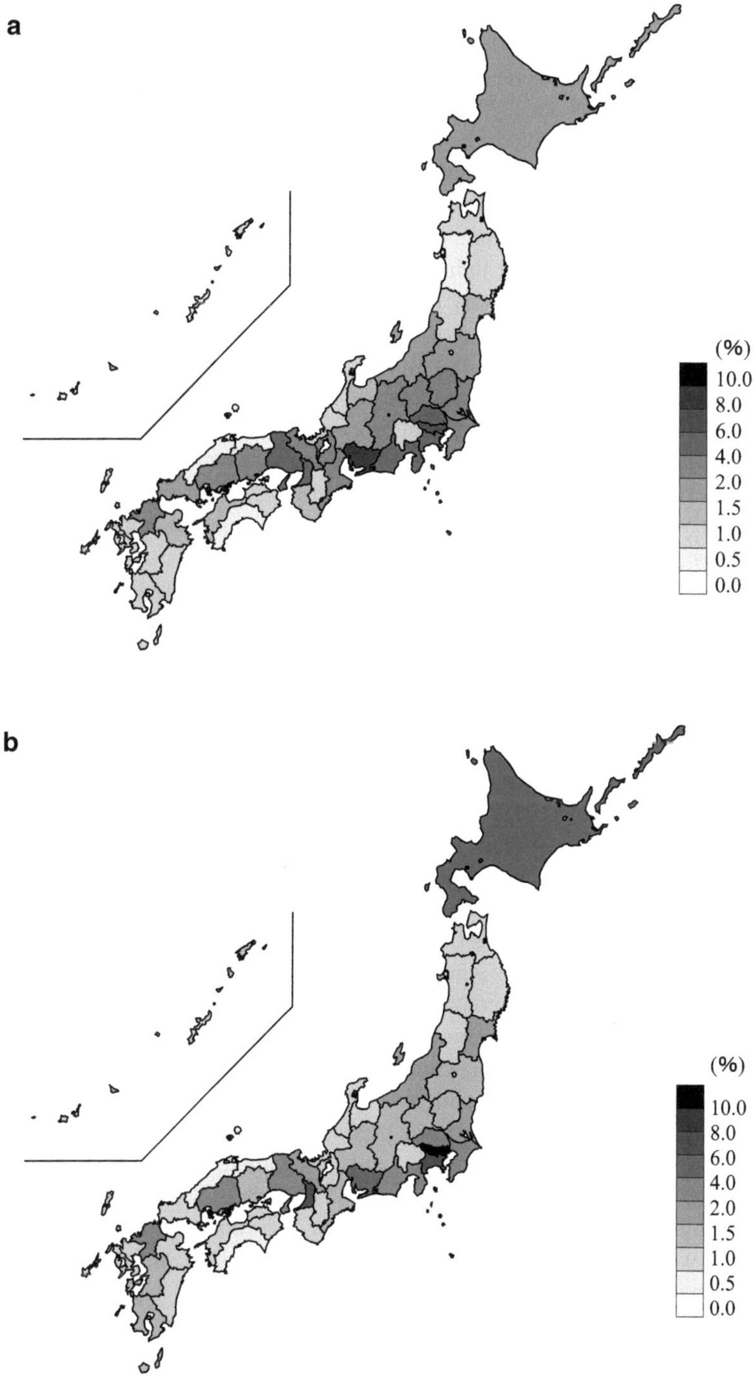

Fig. 1.1 Production share (%) in 2010. (**a**) Manufacturing industries (**b**) Non-manufacturing industries (*Source*: Central Research Institute of Electric Power Industry's Regional Economic Database)

widely distributed in the large metropolitan areas such as the Greater Tokyo area, the Kansai region, and the Chubu region. Manufacturing industries locate in the non-metropolitan areas, such as the Kita-Kanto region and the Chugoku region near the large metropolitan area. This unique feature is the result of past industrial policy, which has promoted the decentralization of manufacturing industries. Meanwhile, the large metropolitan areas in the Greater Tokyo area have a substantial share of the economic production activities in non-manufacturing industries, which includes all types of industries except for manufacturing industries. The service industry is the largest industry in the non-manufacturing sector, and business trends of the service industry influence the distribution of non-manufacturing industries. An important feature of the service industry is that demand in each region depends on the region's population concentration. Consequently, the geographical distribution of non-manufacturing industries is comparable to that of the population. In other words, the greatest proportion of non-manufacturing industries is observed in the Greater Tokyo area where the size of population is very large. This suggests that the economic activity of non-manufacturing industries may rely significantly on agglomeration economies based on the population concentration in each region.

Finally, we observe the growth trend of the regional industrial structure. From the 1980s through the 2000s, Japan's industrial structure shifted from a manufacturing-centric structure to a service industry-centric structure. Looking at the growth in contribution by industry toward Japan's gross domestic product between the years 1980 and 2010, the service industry reached a growth rate of 15.87%, slightly more than the manufacturing industry's rate of 13.69%. These rates indicate that the service industry is now becoming the driver of growth in the national economy. However, when one looks at the regional economies, the regions where the service industry has strong influence are limited to the populous areas such as Saitama, Chiba, Tokyo, and Kanagawa; in all other regions, the manufacturing industry continues to be the driver of the regional economies. Looking at growth contribution by industry to gross prefectural product during the period from 1980 to 2010, there are 25 prefectures where the growth contribution of the manufacturing industry exceeds the growth contribution of the service industry (Fig. 1.2). In the Tohoku region, this includes Aomori, Yamagata, and Fukushima, while in the Kita-Kanto region, Ibaraki, Tochigi, Gunma, Yamanashi, and Nagano are included. Prefectures in the other regions include Toyama, and Ishikawa in the Hokuriku region, Gifu, Shizuoka, Aichi, and Mie prefectures in the Chubu region, Shiga, and Wakayama in the Kansai region, and Okayama, Hiroshima, Yamaguchi, Tokushima, and Ehime in the Chugoku and Shikoku regions, and Saga, Kumamoto, and Oita in the Kyushu region. Most of these regions concentrate on manufacturing. However, with the rise of China and other Asian nations, the manufacturing hub of standard mass-produced goods began to actively shift out of Japan from the 1980s to the 2000s. Despite this, the influence of the manufacturing industry on regional economic growth remains strong, and the manufacturing industry has continued to be the vital force that drives the regional economies.

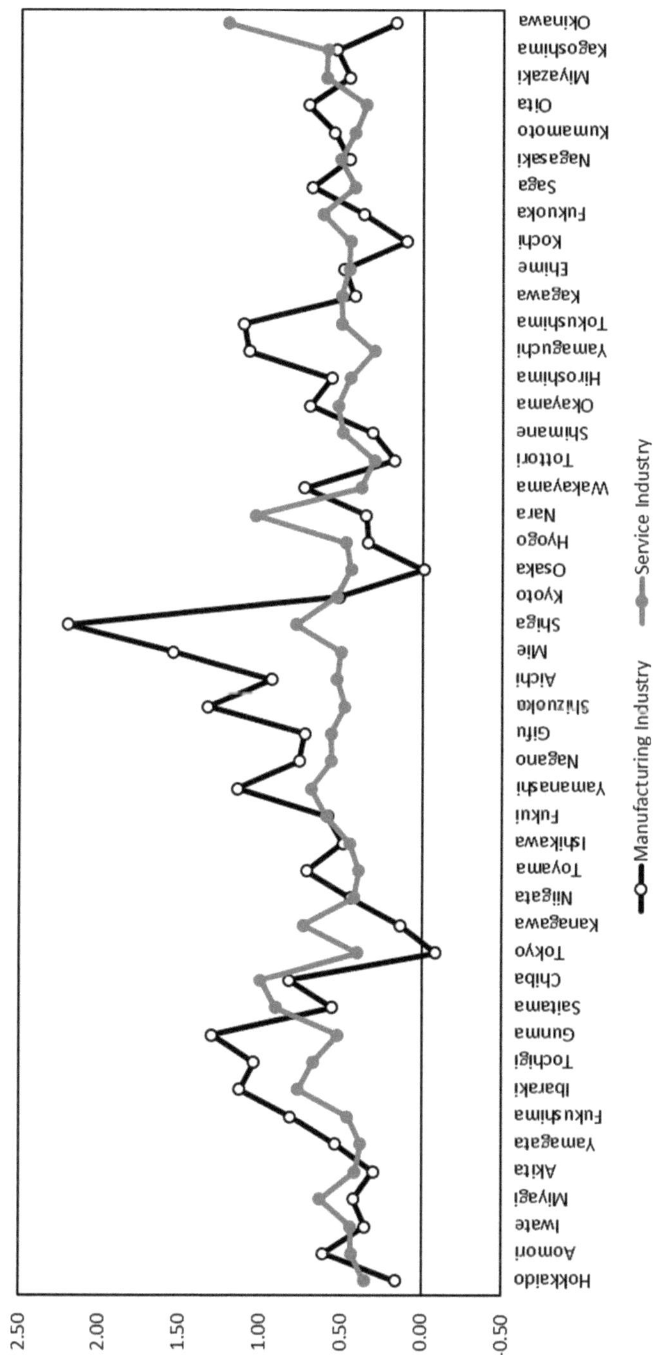

Fig. 1.2 The growth contribution by industry to gross prefectural product (in %, annual rate, 1980–2010) (*Source:* Central Research Institute of Electric Power Industry's Regional Economic Database)

References

Burger MJ, Meijers EJ. Agglomerations and the rise of urban network externalities. Pap Reg Sci. 2016;95(1):5–15.
Cabinet Office. Regional economy 2003. Tokyo: National Printing Bureau; 2004. (in Japanese)
Camagni R, Capello R, Caragliu A. Static vs. dynamic agglomeration economies: spatial context and structural evolution behind urban growth. Pap Reg Sci. 2016;95(1):133–58.
Porter ME. The competitive advantage of nations. New York: Free Press; 1990.
Porter ME. On competition. Boston: Harvard Business School Press; 1998.

Chapter 2
Empirical Knowledge of Agglomeration Economies

Abstract This chapter details the role of industrial agglomeration in regional economies, and discusses the issues found in existing empirical studies. The role industrial agglomeration plays in regional economies has been discussed and empirically studied for a long time. Agglomerations include several related industries, and an abundance of specialized workers. Therefore, it is possible for firms to achieve high productivity through input sharing, labor market pooling, and knowledge spillovers. Such effects can generally be found in two cases: The first case is where an agglomeration of similar industries results in an increase in productivity. The second case is where an agglomeration of different industries results in an increase in productivity. Traditionally, these effects have been measured by external economies of scale, but an analytical approach has recently been proposed that uses spatial density to seek the source of external economies. This chapter reviews these research trends.

Keywords Industrial agglomeration • Agglomeration economies • Regional science

2.1 Introduction

Since Marshall (1890) systematized the classical theory of industrial agglomeration, the reasons that industries agglomerate in specific geographical areas have been explained through "comparative advantage," which emphasizes natural conditions. This explanation has been confirmed by empirical studies as valid. Even with the ongoing globalization of economic activity, comparative advantage continues to be important. However, with the advancement of the industrial organization theory, the idea of international economics was completely overhauled in the 1980s—trade was no longer interpreted as occurring because of comparative advantage but because of specialization based on increasing returns. Thus, "constant returns to scale" and "perfect competition," the premises of the theory of comparative advantage, are gradually becoming meaningless.

The search for a new theory based on "increasing returns to scale" has already been attempted through the discussion on "spatial economics" as described by

A. Otsuka, *A New Perspective on Agglomeration Economies in Japan*,
New Frontiers in Regional Science: Asian Perspectives 20,
DOI 10.1007/978-981-10-6490-6_2

Krugman (1991a), Fujita et al. (1999), and Fujita and Thisse (2002). They explain the self-cumulative nature of industrial agglomeration, which is formed by the relationship among economies of scale, transportation costs, and diversity. Furthermore, according to Porter's (1990, 1998) theories on competition, "industrial clustering" and "competitive advantage" are emphasized in the formation and development of industrial agglomeration. This competition theory includes all aspects of product differentiation and transportation costs, static efficiency, and innovation on the premise of global goods and production factor markets. Dynamic efficiency, such as innovation and the speed of a learning curve, characterizes the theory, rather than static efficiency, such as the level of labor productivity.

This chapter describes the function of industrial agglomeration in a regional economy based on the main theories related to industrial agglomeration. Empirical studies in this field have already been reviewed by Rosenthal and Strange (2004) and Combes and Gobillon (2015). This chapter focuses on the analytical approaches to industrial agglomeration effects, and considers their characteristics and challenges.

The remainder of this chapter is structured as follows: Section 2 describes the factors of industrial agglomeration and their effects. Section 3 identifies the traditional analytical approach in empirical studies, and discusses topics to be further analyzed. Section 4 introduces a new analytical approach to analyzing industrial agglomeration. Finally, the conclusion and additional issues that must be examined and considered in future empirical studies are provided in Sect. 5.

2.2 Theoretical Background

It is well known that the simple neoclassical framework is incapable of providing the answer to the question of how industrial agglomerations are formed. Starrett (1978) established that, if the market is complete and production technology sustains constant returns to scale, at every point all goods are produced, and an ideal equilibrium will be achieved. This state is called "the spatial impossibility theorem," which means unless some sort of first nature exogenously causes a comparative advantage, it would be impossible for the geographical concentration of industries to form endogenously.[1] For this reason, it has been thought that industrial agglomeration arises when a comparative advantage is provided exogenously.

[1]For more on the spatial impossibility theorem, refer to Fujita and Thisse (2002).

According to classical theories of international trade, the source of comparative advantage is found in the region's climate, technology, and the differences in production factor endowment.[2]

It is assumed that the factors of production do not move between regions, products produced across all regions are the same, and economies of scale are not considered. In years past, when transportation infrastructures were undeveloped and technology had not matured to its current extent, industries that had a comparative advantage were competitive. Thus, it was thought that regions specializing in such industries had a competitive advantage. However, with the globalization of economic activity and rapid technological development in the background, current economists hold a common understanding that the traditional conceptions of comparative advantage cannot sufficiently explain the regional patterns of production specialization (Krugman 1991a; Armstrong and Tylor 2000). It is more plausible to think that strong trade ties are formed between countries or regions that have extremely similar industrial structures, since most of the global trades are conducted by industrialized countries that have similar primary factors of production. Above all, it is important that the condition that allows factors of production to move between regions easily goes against the premise of comparative advantage theories. According to established assumptions in international trade theory, the regional pattern of production specialization does not originate in the regional differences of climate, technology, or production factor endowment, but rather, it is understood as "specialization" based on increasing returns.[3]

Krugman (1991a), Fujita et al. (1999), and Fujita and Thisse (2002) used this insight in international trade theory to analyze the spatial agglomeration pattern within the framework of general equilibrium theory, and pioneered a new field called "spatial economics". In spatial economics, the source of comparative advantage is not found in the exogenous variables of a given location (i.e., weather, climate, and natural resources) but rather, it is found in the endogenous self-preoperational advantage called the "economies of agglomeration." The central mission of this theory is to discover how agglomerations are formed by using the micro-foundation of spatial agglomeration, which occurs endogenously from the interaction of economies of scale, transportation costs, and diversity.

---

[2]According to Ricardo's theory, division of labor between regions is explained through the difference in comparative production cost using labor as a measurement, and in the end, is determined by the unique climate of the region, or the regional differences in production technologies. Furthermore, according to the Heckscher-Ohlin theorem, even in cases where there are no differences in production technology between regions, the regional differences in early endowment of factors of production are used to explain the comparative advantage.

[3]In international trade theory, the "increasing returns" approach is understood as the ability for nations to conduct trade due to the advantage provided by specialization, even when endowment of production factors is similar. The reason this approach was not adopted for a long time is because it was difficult to determine whether the increasing returns were something exogenous or endogenous to firms (Krugman 1991a). That is, in the case of the former, the perfect competition model could be applied, but if it were the latter, an imperfect competition model would be necessary. Therefore, to adopt the latter approach, it was necessary to wait until industrial organizational theories advanced in the 1970s and the theory of imperfect competition model was formulated.

Table 2.1 Forces affecting geographical concentration

Centripetal forces	Market-size effects (linkages)	Market linkage effect
		Transaction cost savings
	Thick labor markets	Benefits obtained by a specialized labor market
	Pure external economy	Effect of technical knowledge spillovers
Centrifugal forces	Immobile factors	Immobile factors of production itself
		The rise of land value based on the rise of economic activity
	Scattered demand source	Geographically spread out demand source
	Pure external diseconomies	Congestion and environmental pollution

One of the key features of spatial economics is that "history" and "expectation" hold importance in relation to equilibrium selection. Once an agglomeration is formed, "cumulative causation," which is known as positive feedback, will "lock-in" the agglomeration, and its development will depend on its historical path (Fujita and Thisse 2002; Fujita et al. 1999).[4] In addition, the existence of expectation allows for the possibility of development in regions that were historically disadvantaged (Krugman 1991a). More specifically, it is the mechanism of "self-fulfilling expectations," which says that if an economic entity has an expectation that an ideal equilibrium will be the final equilibrium, and acts based on that expectation, the ideal equilibrium will be realized as a result.

According to spatial economics, the agglomeration of economic activity is endogenously determined by spatial "centripetal forces" that surpass spatial "centrifugal forces" (Krugman 1998) (See Table 2.1.) Centrifugal forces include the presence of external diseconomies brought on by overcrowding and congestion, the rise in land prices, and demands that are geographically scattered and dispersed. On the other hand, the centripetal forces are comprised of the three points Marshall (1890) argued regarding the benefits of agglomeration; that is, access to specialized suppliers in the agglomeration areas, a labor force that has specialized skills, and the spillover of technical knowledge.

[4]Kaldor (1970) attempted to formalize the model of cumulative causation, which was later refined by Dixon and Thirlwall (1975). According to Kaldor (1970), regions that experience faster growth than other regions will start to specialize in exportation due to its competitive advantage. As a result, the growth process of that area will take on a cumulative character. Dixon and Thirlwall (1975) considered the feedback effect of a region's growth against the increased competitiveness of the export departments to formulate the process of cumulative causation. "Verdoorn's law" plays a central role in determining the region's productivity growth rate. This law states that the rising output rate y improves the labor productivity rate q. This law is expressed in the following formula,

$$q = a + \lambda y_{-1} \quad (\lambda > 0)$$

where, a is the constant term representing autogenous growth of productivity, and λ is the Verdoorn coefficient.

First, access to specialized suppliers in an agglomeration area develops subsidiary industries which provide intermediate goods, and a vertical, inter-firm division of labor becomes more active. If there are economies of scale in the production of intermediate goods, then cheaper intermediate goods will be supplied in the area, which will benefit the producers of final goods. Having multiple related firms in the agglomeration area would also mean savings in corporate transaction costs by reducing information imperfections in inter-firm transactions. Second, the technically specialized labor force would benefit agglomerations because of the availability of diverse and experienced workers. If there are several workers with specialized skills, then firms do not need to train their workers themselves, and it would be easy to hire human resources based on need. The workers would more easily find opportunities for work when there are several firms that are in the same field, and that means even if they lose their job, they benefit by having a greater chance of shortening their period of unemployment. Finally, the spillover of technical knowledge is purely an external effect the firms get to enjoy. A strong geographical tie between firms is also a benefit as it heightens the effects of mutual interchange of information, ideas, and knowledge.

The economic benefit of industrial agglomeration manifests itself through the expansion of the firm's productive frontier. According to Glaeser et al. (1992), its effects can be divided into "static externalities" and "dynamic externalities."

Static externalities are high-productivity or high cost-efficiency, which are achieved through agglomeration. Since there is easy access to a variety of input resources, infrastructure, information, and various institutions in an agglomeration, firms can achieve high cost-efficiency in the sense that they are able to greatly reduce transportation and transaction costs. As mentioned earlier, Marshall (1890) discussed that, in addition to the possibility of inventions and improvements in machinery, the production process, and organizations, subsidiary industries will develop, which will increase opportunities for workers with special skills. Furthermore, Weber (1922) focused on the minimization of cost, such as the reduction in production and selling costs, as an effect of industrial agglomeration.

Dynamic externalities include the possibility of productivity growth and innovation that is achieved through agglomeration. For example, Porter (1990, 1998) has stated the following three points regarding the effects of industrial agglomeration. The first effect is the productivity growth of industries that comprise the agglomeration; the second is the strengthening of the capability to innovate and support industries, along with their productivity growth. The third effect is stimulation of innovation and the promotion of new business formation. Complementarity is necessary for innovation; for example, a cooperative relationship with associated businesses and institutions in an agglomeration area. The firm's research and development (R&D) activities not only generate technical knowledge, but they also accumulate over time. If other firms are active nearby, firms within the region will gain an advantage because it will be easier to absorb and utilize new techniques, operations, other technologies, and knowledge generated by other firms during their new product development.

Technical knowledge and information within a region is not only transmitted between firms through direct, face-to-face communication, but there are also cases where human capital facilitates their transfer. They can also be transmitted through the market in the form of intermediate input goods, giving regional firms an effect akin to path dependency (Henderson et al. 1995; Henderson 2003). As to the geographical boundary of the spillover effect, it may be confined to smaller regions such as within a city or a metropolitan area, or it may reach a whole nation or even to multiple neighboring nations. For example, in an area like Silicon Valley where similar businesses agglomerate, a certain industry's agglomeration transmits technical knowledge within the industry, and contributes to innovation and creation of new businesses. On the other hand, in larger metropolitan areas like Tokyo and New York, where a variety of industries agglomerate, spillover of technical knowledge occurs between various industries. If the stock of technical knowledge has strong, location-specific characteristics, then technical knowledge will not spread as fast to other areas. According to Henderson (2003), these are called "trade secrets" and are considered one of the competitive advantages that the location provides, as its nature does not allow easy access for those in other locations.[5] Since the firms located in innovative regions can benefit from external effects provided by nearby plants and R&D activities, they will have the potential to achieve higher productivity. For this reason, firms located in such a region will have no incentive to move to other regions.

Figure 2.1 is an illustration of the development path of a regional economy based on industrial agglomeration. Among the types of industrial agglomerations are large industrial regions, corporate towns, areas of production comprised of many businesses, and regions where universities and firms collaborate. It is to these industrial agglomerations that various firms, human resources, and research facilities agglomerate and create networks relating to one another. The existence of the various networks in agglomerations improves each firm's productivity and becomes the driving force behind the expansion of the regional industry's shipments and exports. When a firm's profitability improves, human resources and other enterprises will pour in from other regions, and the total market size of the region expands. As a result, expansion of the economic scale will be triggered and positive feedback will be realized as the firm's productivity is increased through economies of scale.

---

[5]In the field of business administration, this type of knowledge is called "tacit knowledge" and it is discussed in contrast to "codified knowledge."

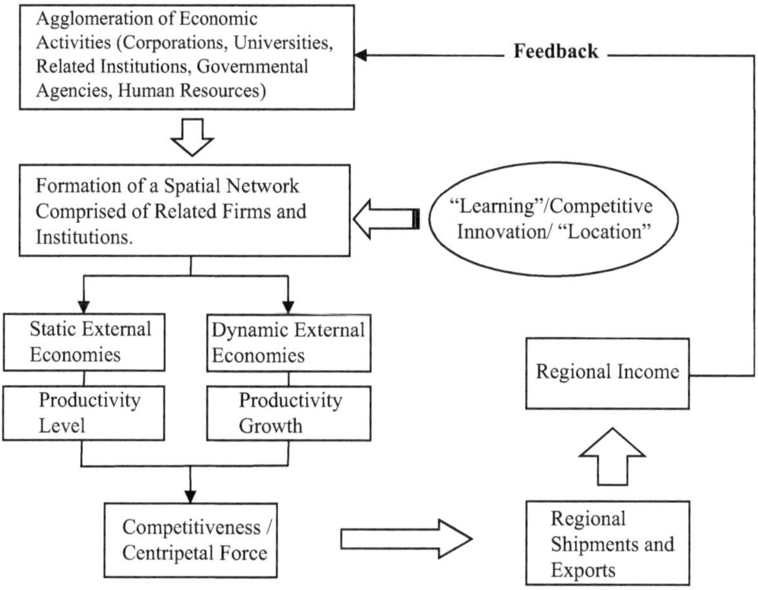

Fig. 2.1 Cumulative development of regional economies due to agglomeration

2.3 Empirical Approach

Industrial agglomeration effects are primarily organized based on two perspectives. The first perspective is to decide whether to look at the short-term or the long-term. Those who focus on the short-term will emphasize the point that industrial agglomeration can result in high productivity. On the other hand, those who focus on the long-term will emphasize the point that continuous productivity growth could be achieved by industrial agglomeration. The second perspective is to decide whether to focus on the demand side or the supply side. In other words, the question is whether to view agglomeration economies from the consumer side or the producer side. Traditionally, the focus has been from a short-term perspective, and many previous studies have focused on the static aspect of industrial agglomeration effects, or the static externalities. Industrial agglomeration effects have been evaluated by the region's economic scale, known as "scale effects," or by the density of economic activity, called "density effects." Scale effects refer to the phenomenon that occurs when the input scale is expanded, and the output scale increases more than the input scale. Another way of saying this is that compared to the output scale, cost has increased less. Density effects refer to the phenomenon that productivity increases as population density increases in a region, especially in regions where market density is high. This effect can be explained through the diversity of intermediate goods. In either case, as these effects are evaluated as influences on an industry's productivity, the analytical approach to industrial agglomeration effects is called "productivity analysis," which ties an industry's productivity factor to industrial agglomeration effects. In the next section, the scale effect, which is a traditional approach, will be explained and discussed first. After that, relatively recent insights gained on the density effect will be considered.

2.3.1 Traditional Approach

According to the traditional analytical approach, it is assumed that each firm is homogeneous and facing perfect competition. Under these assumptions, a region's aggregate production function is specified by the following equation:

$$Y_j = F(\mathbf{X}_j, Z_j), \tag{2.1}$$

where Y is the amount of a region's aggregate output and $\mathbf{X}$ is the region's aggregate production factor input vector, such as capital and labor, intermediate goods, and land. Z is an input element which has the characteristic of public goods, and represents a costless input. For example, if the technical knowledge that has accrued through the firm's R&D investment spreads to other firms, it becomes a part of the publicly available technical knowledge stock. In this case, Z is technical knowledge stock. Regarding Z, Chipman (1970) proved that even in cases where economies of scale acted upon individual production entities (firms) as an external effect, this does not contradict the premise of perfect competition. In that sense, Z is interpreted as a Marshallian external effect.

In a traditional analytical approach, the external effects relating to scale are represented as a Hicks-neutral production technology (Rosenthal and Strange 2004). Empirically, the external effects are considered as the shift term of the production function. Specifically, (2.1) can be rewristten as the following production function:

$$Y_j = g(Z_j)f(\mathbf{X}_j).$$

The size of $g(\cdot)$, which expresses the external effect, decreases as the distance widens. That is to say, $g'(Z_j) < 0$. Distance is made up of three dimensions: spatial distance, the distance of production activity (the similarities in the industrial field), and time (i.e. current, or a year or two ago).[6] For example, as firms are further away from the agglomerations area, the industrial agglomeration effects which the firms could enjoy would likely diminish. In addition, if there were an agglomeration of industries unrelated to one another, it would be difficult for an agglomeration to have any effect. Furthermore, it can also be expected that as more time passes, the effect of the spread of technical knowledge becomes weaker. This means that,

[6]Detail can be found in Rosenthal and Strange (2004).

whatever the dimension, distance can be understood as something that acts to diminish the effects of industrial agglomeration.

Many prior empirical studies have focused on the distance of industrial activities, and depending on the level of aggregation, have adopted a method to differentiate external effects. According to Weber (1922) and Hoover (1937), if Z is explained as a variable that represents the scale of a regional industry, the external economies are called "localization economies." Localization economies are the economic benefits firms enjoy in certain regions where many similar firms concentrate. The increasing returns that come from agglomeration act as an external economy to the individual firms but are internalized within the overall industry. That is, localization economies are realized as economies of scale at the industry level, and their size is measured as a function of the scale of an industry.

On the other hand, according to Jacobs (1969), when Z is explained as a variable that represents the scale of the entire region, or the diversity within a production environment, then such external economies are called "urbanization economies." Urbanization economies are the economic benefits firms in a region enjoy because of the expansion of the region's economic activities. The increasing returns that come from agglomeration are internalized to the entire region, and economies of scale are realized over the whole region. An urbanization economy is an external economy not only to the individual firms, but also to the industry, and its size is measured as the range of production activity or as a function of diversity.[7]

2.3.2 *Previous Studies*

In studies up to the 1980s, industrial agglomeration effects were evaluated based on labor productivity, which is expressed as a function of the population scale P of the region as in the following,

$$g(Z_j) = h(P_j),$$

where $h(\cdot)$ is a second order continuously differentiable convex function.

Various studies have attempted to identify the impact of industrial agglomeration on labor productivity from the viewpoint of urban size, demonstrating that a 100% increase in urban size is likely to increase labor productivity by three to 8% (Rosenthal and Strange 2004). Traditional works observe that labor productivity is generally higher in larger cities (Shefer 1973; Sveikauskas 1975; Segal 1976; Moomaw 1981; Moomaw 1983). Carlino (1979), on the other hand, reveals that population scale has a negative effect on productivity, causing diseconomies rather than economies of agglomeration.

[7]The size of the urban area is nothing but a proxy variable, assuming there is a high correlation between the range of economic activity and size of the urban area (Parr 2002).

Henderson (2003) and Graham (2009) examined the empirical impact of localization and urbanization on productivity. Henderson (2003), using plant-level data for the United States, found localization economies to be stronger. Graham (2009) estimates urbanization and localization economies for two-digit manufacturing and service industries. The analysis is based on estimation of a translog production inverse input demand system using data from British firms. He uses distance-based measures of localization to test for the spatial transmission of externalities, and identifies positive localization economies for 13 of the 27 sectors examined. The results indicate that where localization economies exist, they tend to weaken rapidly with distance.

Another way to specify the sources of industrial agglomeration effects is to use a labor demand function, which takes into consideration the degree to which urban employment is specialized. Glaeser et al. (1992) consider employment growth of industries in U. S. cities for the period 1956–1987 and find that diversity, and not regional specialization, encourages employment growth. They suggest that important knowledge spillovers might occur between, rather than within, industries. This view is consistent with the theories of Jacobs (1969). Henderson et al. (1995) consider employment growth for the period 1970–1987 and estimate it separately for two types of industries: those that are mature capital goods industries with stable technologies, and those that are rapidly evolving, new high-technology industries. They show that there is a positive effect of specialization, though not of diversity, for mature capital goods industries, while there is evidence of urbanization economies in new high-technology industries. Moreover, Henderson (1997) estimates agglomeration economies using data for five capital goods industries in the U.S., finding strong evidence of localization economies but little evidence of urbanization economies. Combes (2000) considers the effects of industrial agglomeration on local employment growth in France for the period 1984–1993, and finds that sharp differences exist between the results of agglomeration economies in the manufacturing and service industries. In the manufacturing industry, both specialization and diversity have a negative impact on growth in all but a few sectors. In the service industry, specialization continues to have a negative effect, although the effect of diversity becomes positive.

In the context of Japanese industries, Mano and Otsuka (2000) attempt to identify the factors that affected the changing patterns of industrial agglomeration during the period 1960–1995. Using prefectural data pertaining to the manufacturing industry, the analysis confirms a decline in the number of existing agglomeration economies. Moreover, they reveal that increasing competition with service sectors has had a pervasive impact on the geographical dispersion of manufacturing industrial sectors. Based on data pertaining to Japanese prefectures for the period 1975–1995, Dekle (2002) obtains the same findings as Mano and Otsuka. By estimating the labor demand functions for Japan at the one-digit level, he demonstrates that agglomeration economies are almost nonexistent in the manufacturing industry but do exist in the non-manufacturing industry, particularly in the finance, service, and wholesale and retail trade sectors. He thereby concludes that cross-fertilization of ideas is important, particularly for non-manufacturing industries, and that there is a tendency toward further geographical concentration in service sectors, such as the financial services sector.

The thinking behind these analytical approaches came about by explaining the effects of industrial agglomeration as just external effects that do not penetrate the market. The benefit of this method was that it was easier to create a model, and therefore easier to evaluate the effects of industrial agglomeration. However, when we consider the reality that large-scale metropolitan areas are comprised of a variety of economic agents, and that there are active transactions between businesses for goods and services, the premise of the traditional analytical approach is not realistic. For this reason, there are theoretical studies on the relationship between supply and demand of goods in the market. By assuming increasing returns in the production of intermediate goods, studies by Abdel-Rahman (1988), Fujita (1988), and Rivera-Batiz (1988) have made apparent the existence of industrial agglomeration effects, which arise from the diversity of intermediate goods.

Ciccone and Hall (1996) incorporated this theoretical model which assumed imperfect competition in the intermediate goods market and gave spatial density a clear function. They focused on spatial density as a determining element for industrial agglomeration effects, and point to the fact that the relationship between productivity and density can be explained by agglomeration and the influence of congestion, as well as through the diversity of intermediate goods.[8] Specifically, they assumed that regional employment density affects productivity, and analyzed labor productivity as a function of employment density. They found that when employment density doubles, labor productivity in the United States increases by 6%. This result indicates that for labor productivity to rise, close exchanges among workers are important.[9] For additional consideration, Ciccone (2002) applied Ciccone and Hall's (1996) analytical framework in five European countries. In terms of the estimated industrial agglomeration effects, there were no significant differences observed among the countries. In the analysis, it was found that when employment density doubles, labor productivity rises by approximately 5%, which is like the result of the study in the United States.

2.3.3 Open Issues of Previous Studies

Previous studies that took the traditional analytical approach have evaluated industrial agglomeration effects as an influence on the regional disparity in labor

[8]According to the micro-foundation by Ciccone and Hall (1996), with the density effect, in addition to the influence of agglomeration and congestion that final goods manufacturing firms would receive, intermediate goods supplying firms' markup ratio in relation to marginal cost is included.

[9]However, there may also be an aspect in which productivity growth may invite more workers to flood in, and as a result employment density may increase. The method of instrumental variables was employed in the estimation to consider this endogenous problem.

Table 2.2 The price markup of firms in the manufacturing industry in Japan

Industry name	Number of observations	Price mark-up
Food processing	1836	1.213
Textile	1515	1.133
Paper and pulp	617	1.259
Chemical products	2824	1.105
Pharmaceutical products	789	1.187
Petroleum products	208	1.566
Tire and rubber products	432	1.028
Glass, pottery, and cement	1220	1.055
Iron and steel	1174	1.204
Non-ferrous metals and metal products	1870	1.097
Industrial machinery	1619	1.048
Electronic machinery	1189	1.305
Ship building and repair	61	1.309
Automobile	462	1.102
Other transportation machinery	126	1.087
Precision machinery	254	1.094
Other manufacturing	535	1.082
Manufacturing industry Total	16,731	1.143

Source: Table 5 in Nishimura et al. (1999)

productivity. While it has succeeded in identifying the size and type of industrial agglomeration effects using cross-sectional analysis, it has also left us with other issues for further analysis.

The first is the issue of the micro-foundation of industrial agglomeration effects. According to the traditional analytical approach, industrial agglomeration effects are measured by economies of scale at the industrial level. It assumes that individual firms face perfect competition, and that they possess production capabilities that provide constant returns. In many previous studies, these two assumptions seem to have not been sufficiently empirically evaluated for their validity. Since manufacturing industries are expanding product differentiation, the premise of perfect competition likely lacks validity. For example, in Nishimura et al. (1999), the price markup of petroleum related firms was 1.57, and even firms that fit into electricity or shipbuilding categories reached a price markup of 1.30. All of this indicates there is no evidence that individual firms within the manufacturing industry face perfect competition (Table 2.2). Furthermore, it is also highly probable that the assumptions regarding constant returns to scale are restrictive. For example, Nakajima et al. (1998) examined the existence of economies of scale by industry, but their results did not support the hypothesis of constant returns to scale (Table 2.3).

The second issue relates to problems that arise with "endogeneity" and "omitted variables," which we would inevitably face when measuring industrial agglomeration effects. The endogeneity problem arises from the fact that production activity

Table 2.3 Economies of scale of firms in the manufacturing industry in Japan

Industry name	Economies of scale
Food/kindred products	1.080
Textiles	1.004
Apparels	1.019
Lumber/wood products	1.018
Furniture/fixture	1.047
Pulp/paper products	1.008
Chemicals	1.046
Petroleum/coal products	1.012
Rubber/plastic products	1.047
Leather/leather products	1.016
Pottery/glass products	1.073
Iron/steel	1.012
Non-ferrous metals	1.008
Metal products	1.030
General machinery	1.019
Electrical machinery	1.044
Transportation machinery	1.016
Precision	1.021
Manufacturing industry average	1.029

Source: Table 1 in Nakajima et al. (1998)

at a location is determined by the industry's demand and productivity (Hanson 2001). Industrial agglomeration effects are examined assuming that the individual firm's productivity depends on the scale of the economy. However, high productivity at the location is, by itself, an incentive for individual firms to establish their plants in that region, so that alone will expand the scale of the economy. That is, high productivity at a location does not allow us to distinguish whether it was an effect based on industrial agglomeration, or if highly productive firms happened to agglomerate. In econometrics, this is called the problem of "simultaneity," which means that the explanatory variable in a structural equation is endogenously decided within the system of simultaneous equations. Therefore, dealing with this problem requires an estimation method using instrumental variables, or a set of simultaneous equations (for examples, see Henderson 2003, and Combes and Gobillon 2015). However, estimating using a set of simultaneous equations that include instrumental variables means we need to select instrumental variables, and then there is a problem with identification. On top of that, the influence of instrumental variables is often weak, and thus it is difficult to obtain robust estimation results.

Next, omitted variables create measurement bias, which occurs when an explanatory variable, which should be in the estimation model, is excluded. The results are that, when verifying the effects of industrial agglomeration, if consideration is not given to regional characteristics that are not being measured, it is possible to measure the influence of regional characteristics as the effects of industrial agglomeration (Hanson 2001; Henderson 2005). For example, the existence of regional amenities such as the quality of the region's labor force, the regional infrastructure quality and so on, may manifest as the industrial agglomeration effect. However, there is one previous study which dealt with this problem by hypothesizing that the concerning variable is fixed chronologically; otherwise it is difficult to identify an omitted variable. For example, recent studies by Henderson et al. (2001) and Henderson (2003) have adopted panel analysis, so that the regional characteristics which are not observed are regarded as individual effects.[10] When individual effects are introduced, it is necessary to widen the scope of analysis and the observation period to avoid bias due to measurement error of the data. However, this raises another issue; using time series data to increase the number of observations means there is an increased probability that the error term will correlate with economic fluctuations.

2.4 Other Approaches

Many of the recent empirical studies have attempted to estimate industrial agglomeration effects from multiple perspectives.

The first example is a group of empirical studies that examine the relationship between industrial agglomeration and regional economic growth. If a competitive industry locates in a certain region, then that region is bound to grow rapidly. As mentioned earlier, the dynamic aspects of the effects of industrial agglomeration are called dynamic externalities. The kind of production environment needed to create a competitive industry is known to be expressed as a function of specialization, variety, and the degree of regional competition (Glaeser et al. 1992). There have been many recent empirical studies on this topic, such as Glaeser et al. (1992) and Henderson et al. (1995). According to their findings, emerging industries grow faster in regions where there is greater diversity, and mature industries grow faster when there is more specialization. Estimating the regional industry growth as a function of variables representing the initial production environment has been commonly adopted in empirical analysis.

[10]Particularly, Henderson (2003) conducted a panel analysis using the plant data to increase the number of observations. He analyzed the effect of industrial agglomeration at the plant level by considering the observable characteristics of the plant (i.e., the size and scale of the plant, its age, and organizational structure) in addition to regional characteristics.

In analyzing dynamic externalities, it is important to consider the connection between regional economic growth and supply and demand linkage for goods.[11] One of the paths through which industrial agglomeration helps grow an industry's productivity depends on whether the regional demand for goods is influencing the industry's productivity through the market size effect (Fujita 1988; Rivera-Batiz 1988; Krugman 1991b; Venables 1996).[12] Findings of empirical studies indicate that the regional supply and demand linkage for goods is brought about by industrial agglomeration. For example, Davis and Weinstein (1999) have discovered that regional production in Japanese prefectures increased in relation to regional demand at a ratio exceeding 1:1. This indicates the existence of specialization in regions where there is relatively high demand for specific goods. The point to note here is that firms that are located near a large consumption area enjoy economic benefits from having relatively lower transportation costs, and thus they have an incentive to pay their laborers a higher wage. Hanson (1996, 1997, 1998) analyzed the existence of regional demand linkage by examining the correlation between the indicators of market proximity and wages in Mexican states and in U.S. counties. In both cases, it was found that wages were higher at locations closer to larger consumption areas. These findings are consistent with the hypothesis that supply and demand linkage for goods in a region creates a location specific external economy.

The second example is a group of empirical studies on the relationship between industrial agglomeration and productive efficiency. Increased productivity can be achieved by shifting regional production frontiers to elevate output per unit of input (productivity effect), and by ascending to higher levels on an existing production frontier by making actual output closer to an existing production frontier per unit of input (productive efficiency effect). Industrial agglomeration should affect the success of both efforts. Agglomeration offers firms a larger, lower-cost labor pool, and proximity to suppliers of intermediate goods. Both advantages improve productivity of the firms. Furthermore, face-to-face communication of technical knowledge enhances productive efficiency through spillover effects.

---

[11]Originally, the supply and demand linkage effect for goods included not only the improvement of productivity but also an increase in consumers' real income. According to spatial economics, firms try to produce differentiated goods at a single location to satisfy both the consumer's desire for variety and economies of scale, but as they consider transportation cost to the market, they will try to build their plant near a large market to save on these costs. For this reason, firms will build in an area that has easy access to a large-scale market. At this point, there will be more specialized consumer goods suppliers moving into the area that start to supply a variety of consumer goods and the utility level for the consumers who prefer variety will increase. This increase in real income brings an influx of consumers from other areas, and because of expanding regional demand, the location of the firms in that area progresses. However, to the best of my knowledge, there have been few empirical studies that have attempted to find the influence of industrial agglomeration effects on a consumer market.

[12]Such an effect where production activity in a particular industry influences the production activity of other industries through the market is called the "market linkage effect". (Fujita et al. 1999; Fujita and Thisse 2002). Details will be covered in Chap. 5.

Traditional studies have focused on the idea that industrial agglomeration affects productivity of individual industries, while they have not fully considered the aspect that industrial agglomeration affects the industry's productive efficiency. A few recent studies investigate the productive efficiency effect (Beeson and Husted 1989; Mitra 1999, 2000; Driffield and Munday 2001; Tveteras and Battese 2006; Otsuka et al. 2010; Otsuka and Goto 2015; Otsuka 2017). To obtain sufficient knowledge about the productive efficiency effect of industrial agglomeration, we need to engage in many empirical studies to further understand and analyze the effect of industrial agglomeration from both the productivity and productive efficiency perspectives.

The third example is a group of empirical studies regarding industrial agglomeration and location selection. If firms choose their manufacturing location for profit maximization, then it follows that we can expect such plants will concentrate in the most productive region. Porter (1990, 1998) emphasized in his industrial clustering theory that new businesses will be supported in the agglomeration area. Generally, abundant information regarding market opportunities in the agglomeration area makes it easier to enter, and since the risk of entry and withdrawal is small even in terms of potential local customers and personal connections, new businesses are easily established. Additionally, information, infrastructure, and many raw material suppliers are available in the agglomeration area, all of which help turn the new business's ideas into a reality. That is, agglomeration also provides the benefit of ease of access to the personnel, skills, and resources needed by the business. Furthermore, there are financial institutions and investors seeking to invest in entrepreneurs, and since they already have greater trust in the agglomeration itself, it would be easier for new businesses to obtain capital in the agglomeration area.

The approach focused on new businesses has the advantage of not needing production data, and thus it is much easier to gather the data necessary for analysis. Rosenthal and Strange (2001) have discovered that, at the zip code level in the United States, the same-industry agglomeration makes it easier for new firms to be established. Using the data of Japanese prefectures, Otsuka (2008) analyzes the determinants of regional variations in new firm formation by industry, and reveals that industrial agglomeration contributes to stimulating new firm formation in the manufacturing industries.

2.5 Conclusion

This chapter organized the understanding of the role and economic effects of industrial agglomeration in regional economies, and reviewed empirical studies centered on static external economies. Traditional approaches primarily assumed perfect competition and constant returns to scale, and the influence of industrial agglomeration was measured as external economies of scale on individual firms.

This approach characteristically has treated the source of industrial agglomeration effects as a black box. In contrast, spatial economics finds the source of agglomeration economies in diversity, and the formation mechanism of agglomeration is clarified through the relationships among economies of scale, transportation costs, and diversity. Ciccone and Hall (1996) pointed out the importance of density in industrial agglomeration effects, and showed us that the influence of density on productivity is dependent on the degree of diversity of intermediate goods.

From the perspective of regional development, if localization economies are manifested, then specialization in an industry would be more desirable as firms in the same field concentrate in the same region. However, if urbanization economies are formed, it would be more desirable to have an agglomeration of multiple industries in a metropolitan area. The findings of empirical studies in developed countries show that localization economies created by an agglomeration of firms in the same industry will manifest more strongly than urbanization economies created by the agglomeration of firms from different industries. Therefore, this suggests it would be best to promote centralization of firms in the same industry, and create an industrial agglomeration for growing and developing a regional economy. However, considering the reality of urban agglomeration where multiple industries agglomerate, this statement is not an effective policy suggestion, and therefore, there has been recent criticism of empirical studies on industrial agglomeration (i.e., Henderson 2005).

We should pay attention to the fact that the role cost efficiency plays in the manufacturing industry has gradually weakened. According to Porter (1990, 1998), where globalization of economic activities is progressing, it is less necessary to be able to procure factors of production, trading goods, and services at the regional level. That is, since global industries can procure the factors of production from the cheapest region, their own region's scale of economy is not a relative advantage. In this situation, innovation, which improves productivity and brings sustained development to the regional economy, is the reason regional resources still carry importance. Porter pointed out that we should not focus so much on the static aspects of agglomeration, but rather on its dynamic aspects when considering competitiveness in a highly open industry, such as the manufacturing industry. There have not been many studies relating to industrial agglomeration that have focused on the spillover of innovation and technical knowledge. To achieve sustainable growth in a regional economy, it would be more useful to focus on the dynamic aspects of agglomeration, such as industrial development, rather than focusing on the advantage of cost efficiency.

References

Abdel-Rahman HM. Product differentiation, monopolistic competition and city size. Reg Sci Urban Econ. 1988;18(1):69–86.

Armstrong H, Taylor J. Regional economics and policy. 3rd ed. Malden: Blackwell; 2000.

Beeson PE, Husted S. Patterns and determinants of productive efficiency in state manufacturing. J Reg Sci. 1989;29(1):15–28.
Carlino GA. Increasing returns to scale in metropolitan manufacturing. J Reg Sci. 1979;19 (3):363–72.
Chipman JS. External economies of scale and competitive equilibrium. Q J Econ. 1970;84 (3):347–85.
Ciccone A. Agglomeration effects in Europe. Eur Econ Rev. 2002;46(2):213–27.
Ciccone A, Hall RE. Productivity and the density of economic activity. Am Econ Rev. 1996;86 (1):54–70.
Combes PP. Economic structure and local growth: France, 1984–1993. J Urban Econ. 2000;47 (3):329–55.
Combes PP, Gobillon L. The empirics of agglomeration economies. In: Duranton G, Henderson J, Strange W, editors. Handbook of regional and urban economics, volume 5A. Amsterdam: Elsevier; 2015. p. 247–348.
Davis DR, Weinstein DE. Economic geography and regional production structure: an empirical investigation. Eur Econ Rev. 1999;43(2):379–407.
Dekle R. Industrial concentration and regional growth: evidence from the prefectures. Rev Econ Stat. 2002;84(2):310–5.
Dixon RJ, Thirlwall AP. A model of regional growth-rate differences on kaldorian lines. Oxf Econ Pap. 1975;27(2):201–14.
Driffield N, Munday M. Foreign manufacturing, regional agglomeration and technical efficiency in UK industries: a stochastic production frontier approach. Reg Stud. 2001;35(5):391–9.
Fujita M. A monopolistic competition model of spatial agglomeration: differentiated product approach. Reg Sci Urban Econ. 1988;18(1):87–124.
Fujita M, Thisse J. Economics of agglomeration: cities, industrial location, and regional growth. Cambridge: Cambridge University Press; 2002.
Fujita M, Krugman P, Venables A. The spatial economy: cities, regions, and international trade. Cambridge: MIT Press; 1999.
Glaeser EL, Kallal HD, Scheinkman JA, Shleifer A. Growth in cities. J Polit Econ. 1992;100 (6):1126–52.
Graham DJ. Identifying urbanisation and localisation externalities in manufacturing and service industries. Pap Reg Sci. 2009;88(1):63–84.
Hanson GH. Localization economies, vertical organization, and trade. Am Econ Rev. 1996;86 (5):1266–78.
Hanson GH. Increasing returns, trade, and the regional structure of wages. Econ J. 1997;107 (440):113–33.
Hanson GH. Regional adjustment to trade liberalization. Reg Sci Urban Econ. 1998;28(4):419–44.
Hanson GH. Scale economies and the geographic concentration of industry. J Econ Geogr. 2001;1 (3):255–76.
Henderson JV. Externalities and industrial development. J Urban Econ. 1997;42(3):449–70.
Henderson JV. Marshall's scale economies. J Urban Econ. 2003;53(1):1–28.
Henderson JV. Urbanization and growth. In: Aghion P, Durlauf S, editors. Handbook of economic growth, volume 1B. Amsterdam: Elsevier; 2005. p. 1543–91.
Henderson JV, Kuncoro A, Turner M. Industrial development in cities. J Polit Econ. 1995;103 (5):1067–90.
Henderson JV, Lee T, Lee YJ. Scale externalities in Korea. J Urban Econ. 2001;49(3):479–504.
Hoover EM. Location theory and the shoe and leather industries. Cambridge, MA: Harvard University Press; 1937.
Jacobs J. The economy of cities. New York: Vintage Books; 1969.
Kaldor N. The case for region policies. Scott J Polit Econ. 1970;18:337–48.
Krugman P. Geography and trade. Cambridge, MA/London: MIT Press; 1991a.
Krugman P. Increasing returns and economic geography. J Polit Econ. 1991b;99(3):483–99.

Krugman P. What's new about the new economic geography? Oxf Rev Econ Policy. 1998;14 (2):7–17.
Mano Y, Otsuka K. Agglomeration economies and geographical concentration of industries: a case study of manufacturing sectors in postwar Japan. J Jpn Int Econ. 2000;14(3):189–203.
Marshall A. Principles of economics. London: Macmillan; 1890.
Mitra A. Agglomeration economies as manifested in technical efficiency at the firm level. J Urban Econ. 1999;45(3):490–500.
Mitra A. Total factor productivity growth and urbanization economies: a case of Indian industries. Rev Urban Reg Dev Stud. 2000;12(2):97–108.
Moomaw RL. Productivity and city size: a critique and evidence. Q J Econ. 1981;96(4):675–88.
Moomaw RL. Is population scale a worthless surrogate for business agglomeration economies? Reg Sci Urban Econ. 1983;13(4):525–45.
Nakajima T, Nakamura M, Yoshioka K. An index number method for estimating scale economies and technical progress using time-series of cross-section data: sources of total factor productivity growth for Japanese manufacturing, 1964–1988. Jpn Econ Rev. 1998;49(3):310–34.
Nishimura K, Ohkusa Y, Ariga K. Estimating the mark-up over marginal cost: a panel analysis of Japanese firms 1971–1994. Int J Ind Organ. 1999;17(8):1077–111.
Otsuka A. Determinants of new firm formation in Japan: a comparison of the manufacturing and service sectors. Econ Bull. 2008;18(4):1–7.
Otsuka A. Regional determinants of total factor productivity in Japan: stochastic frontier analysis. Ann Reg Sci. 2017;58(3):579–96.
Otsuka A, Goto M. Regional policy and the productive efficiency of Japanese industries. Reg Stud. 2015;49(4):518–31.
Otsuka A, Goto M, Sueyoshi T. Industrial agglomeration effects in Japan: productive efficiency, market access, and public fiscal transfer. Pap Reg Sci. 2010;89(4):819–39.
Parr JB. Missing elements in the analysis of agglomeration economies. Int Reg Sci Rev. 2002;25 (2):151–68.
Porter ME. The competitive advantage of nations. New York: Free Press; 1990.
Porter ME. On competition. Boston: Harvard Business School Press; 1998.
Rivera-Batiz FL. Increasing returns, monopolistic competition, and agglomeration economies in consumption and production. Reg Sci Urban Econ. 1988;18(1):125–53.
Rosenthal SS, Strange WC. The determinants of agglomeration. J Urban Econ. 2001;50 (2):191–229.
Rosenthal S, Strange W. Evidence on the nature and sources of agglomeration economies. In: Henderson JV, Thisse JF, editors. Handbook of regional and urban economics, volume 4. Amsterdam: Elsevier; 2004.
Segal D. Are there returns of scale in city size? Rev Econ Stat. 1976;58(3):339–50.
Shefer D. Localization economies in SMSAs: a production function analysis. J Reg Sci. 1973;13 (1):55–64.
Starrett D. Market allocations of location choice in a model with free mobility. J Econ Theory. 1978;17(1):21–37.
Sveikauskas L-A. The productivity of cities. Q J Econ. 1975;89(3):393–413.
Tveteras R, Battese GE. Agglomeration externalities, productivity, and technical inefficiency. J Reg Sci. 2006;46(4):605–25.
Venables AJ. Equilibrium locations of vertically linked industries. Int Econ Rev. 1996;37 (2):341–59.
Weber A. Über den Standort der Industrien, 2. Tubingen: Aufl; 1922.

Chapter 3
A Traditional Approach to Agglomeration Economies

Abstract This chapter sheds empirical light on the relationship between agglomeration economies and regional economic growth and the impact of that relationship on the convergence of regional disparities in productivity, using a traditional approach to agglomeration economies. Based on Japanese prefectural data, an empirical analysis indicates that agglomeration economies have significant effects on regional economic growth. Furthermore, agglomeration economies contribute to economic convergence in the manufacturing industry, while they contribute to increasing disparities across regions in the non-manufacturing industry. These results suggest that an increase in the proportion of non-manufacturing industries has the potential to create regional disparities.

Keywords Industrial agglomeration • Regional economic growth • Agglomeration economies • Economic convergence

3.1 Introduction

The importance of industrial agglomeration for achievement of regional economic growth has been discussed in the field of regional science. As described in Chap. 2, the effects of industrial agglomeration are defined as product efficiency derived from spatial and industrial interdependency, and these effects are usually considered to be external to firms' decision-making processes. The nature and sources of industrial agglomeration effects are summarized in Rosenthal and Strange (2004) and Combes and Gobillon (2015), which discuss this important concept in an organized manner. Numerous empirical studies have investigated whether industrial agglomeration effects are related to the concentration of an industry and/or to

---

This chapter is based on Otsuka and Yamano (2008) "Industrial agglomeration effects on regional economic growth: A case of Japanese regions" Discussion Papers 08-T-2, Regional Economics Applications Laboratory, University of Illinois, IL and Otsuka (2008) "Industrial agglomeration and economic convergence: the case of Japanese regions," published in The Economic Analysis (The Keizai Bunseki) (No. 180, pp. 1–19, in Japanese).

A. Otsuka, *A New Perspective on Agglomeration Economies in Japan*,
New Frontiers in Regional Science: Asian Perspectives 20,
DOI 10.1007/978-981-10-6490-6_3

city size, and have attempted to identify the impact of industrial agglomeration on labor productivity from the viewpoint of city size. It is reported that firms in population agglomerated areas benefit from industrial agglomeration and that agglomeration effects vary by industry. Most studies demonstrate that for manufacturing industries, localization economies are more advantageous for production than urbanization economies, while for non-manufacturing industries, urbanization economies tend to have a stronger influence. The study in this chapter reexamines whether these trends apply to Japanese regional industries.

There are two primary results obtained from this study.

First, this study shows the application of the traditional approach to clarify the influence of agglomeration economies on regional economic growth. Agglomeration economies have been regarded as an influence on the level of labor productivity, but little attention has been paid to their influence on dynamic change. Base on a traditional production function, this study provides sufficient clarification of how agglomeration accelerates economic growth in regions. This study also considers the existence of market access effects, which is the other side of agglomeration economies. The recent classification of agglomeration economies incorporates linkage externalities, as well as localization and urbanization economies (Parr 2002). Agglomeration theory has clarified that the best location for firms should be determined based on market demand and transportation costs, and that market access affects economic performance through backward and forward linkages (Fujita 1988; Rivera-Batiz 1988; Krugman 1991; Venables 1996). Davis and Weinstein (1999) reveal that the extent of geographic concentration depends on the size of market demand in the region of interest. Nevertheless, this effect has not necessarily been included in the traditional approach to agglomeration economies because of the limitations of available data, particularly the lack of data on the economic distance between regions.

Second, this study uses a traditional approach to clarify the contribution of industrial agglomeration to the convergence of regional disparities in labor productivity. In Japan, "balanced development of the nation" has been regarded as a target strategy for realizing economic growth, and several policies have been implemented that aim to decrease regional disparities. To promote local decentralization of high-productivity industrial sectors, the government has developed transportation facilities, industrial sites, and other infrastructure, and has provided support measures such as assisting with technological development. To evaluate these policies, it is first necessary to assess the extent to which industrial agglomeration contributes to growth in the process of economic convergence. The wide-ranging interest in regional income disparities has recently gained a renewed emphasis. Numerous empirical studies have investigated growth rate differentials in the last few decades across countries and regions, focusing on the evolution of economic disparities and the process of convergence among regions (Magrini 2004; Benos and Karagiannis 2008). To the best of my knowledge, there are very few studies that consider population agglomeration as a factor of regional economic disparity (Kilicaslan and Ozatagan 2007; Bosker 2007). This study proposes a novel method to analyze the influence of industrial agglomeration on economic convergence, and verifies whether the improved productivity of regional industries that results from industrial agglomeration influences interregional disparities.

This chapter is organized as follows. Section 2 describes a traditional approach for analyzing agglomeration economies. Section 3 builds an estimation model and considers the impacts of industrial agglomeration on Japanese regions. Section 4 concludes the study.

3.2 Traditional Framework for the Analysis

In a traditional setting, the production function for estimating industrial agglomeration effects is based on two assumptions. The first assumption is that agglomeration economies are external factors in firms' production functions. The second is that each firm in the same industry uses identical technology. Based on these assumptions, estimations of industrial level production functions are obtained by aggregating the production functions of all firms.

The value-added production function at the firm level is defined as follows:

$$y = g(Z)f(k, l),$$

where y is value-added, k denotes the capital input, and l denotes the labor input. Note that $g(Z)$ represents the external economies to a firm and shifts the production function $f(k, l)$. It is assumed that firms are competitive and have a homogeneous production function. Therefore, firms in different regions have identical production technology.

Agglomeration economies are categorized as localization and urbanization economies (McCann 2001). The scale of industrial production $Y\ (\equiv \sum y)$ is adopted as a proxy variable for localization economies. The population density *DENS*, which is the total population of a region divided by the residential area, is used as a proxy variable for urbanization economies.

In this study, market access is also defined by the following index, which enables us to measure the spillover effects:

$$ACC_j \equiv \sum\nolimits_{k \neq j} \left[\left(d_{jk}^{-1} / \sum\nolimits_{k \neq j} d_{jk}^{-1} \right) \cdot Q_k \right],$$

where d_{jk} represents the economic distance between regions j and k. The gross output Q_k is used to capture the local market demand. The leading characteristic of this index is that the extent of market access is evaluated not only by market size but also by the economic costs incurred to access the market.

The agglomeration economies $g(Z)$ are specialized as

$$g(Z) = \alpha_0 e^{\alpha_T t} \left[DENS^{\alpha_D} Y^{\alpha_S} ACC^{\alpha_A} \right],$$

where α_0, α_T, α_D, α_S, and α_A are parameters. Table 3.1 summarizes the forms of agglomeration economies. In this specification, the effect of market demand on

Table 3.1 Classification of agglomeration economies

Agglomeration Economies	Variable	Description
Localization Economies	Y	The scale of industrial production
Urbanization Economies	DENS	Population density
Market Access Effects	ACC	Market access index

labor productivity can be captured independently in terms of the influences of home and outside markets. In other words, the influence of the home market is measured as the agglomeration effect, while the influence of the outside market is measured as the market access effect.

Major studies estimate agglomeration economies using the translog production function (e.g., Henderson 2003; Graham and Kim 2008; Graham 2009). It is preferable to adopt this function form because it is more flexible than the Cobb–Douglas production function and other types of function forms. This study specifies the following translog functional form to estimate the equations:

$$\begin{aligned}\ln y = \alpha_0 + \alpha_T t + \alpha_D \ln DENS + \alpha_S \ln Y + \alpha_A \ln ACC + \alpha_K \ln k + \alpha_L \ln l \\ + \frac{1}{2}\beta_{KK}(\ln k)^2 + \frac{1}{2}\beta_{LL}(\ln l)^2 + \beta_{KL}(\ln k)(\ln l),\end{aligned} \tag{3.1}$$

where the α's and β's are parameters to be estimated. If the parameters α_D, α_S, and α_A are positive, the implication is that the respective factor has a positive influence on productivity, while if these parameters are negative, the implication is that agglomeration economies and market access have a negative influence on productivity.

If inputs are rented in competitive markets, the first-order conditions from the output maximization subject to an expenditure constraint are

$$\frac{\partial y}{\partial k} = \lambda r, \tag{3.2}$$

$$\frac{\partial y}{\partial l} = \lambda w, \tag{3.3}$$

where r and w are the capital cost and wage rate, respectively. λ is a Lagrange multiplier. The expenditure constraint is given by

$$rk + wl = c, \tag{3.4}$$

where c is total cost. From (3.2), (3.3) and (3.4),

$$\lambda = \frac{(dy/dk)k + (dy/dl)l}{c}. \tag{3.5}$$

And substituting (3.5) back into (3.2) and (3.3) after rearrangement yields the inverse input demand equations,

$$\frac{r}{c} = \frac{dy/dk}{(dy/dk)k + (dy/dl)l}, \tag{3.6}$$

$$\frac{w}{c} = \frac{dy/dl}{(dy/dk)k + (dy/dl)l}. \tag{3.7}$$

The input demand Eqs. (3.6) and (3.7) can be written in input share equations as

$$\frac{rk}{c} = \frac{d\ln y/d\ln k}{(d\ln y/d\ln k) + (d\ln y/d\ln l)}, \tag{3.8}$$

$$\frac{wl}{c} = \frac{d\ln y/d\ln l}{(d\ln y/d\ln k) + (d\ln y/d\ln l)}. \tag{3.9}$$

Given Eqs. (3.8) and (3.9), differentiation of Eq. (3.1) yields the cost share equations:

$$\frac{rk}{c} = \frac{\alpha_K + \beta_{KK}\ln k + \beta_{KL}\ln l}{\alpha_K + \alpha_L + (\beta_{KK} + \beta_{KL})\ln k + (\beta_{LL} + \beta_{KL})\ln l},$$

$$\frac{wl}{c} = \frac{\alpha_L + \beta_{KL}\ln k + \beta_{LL}\ln l}{\alpha_K + \alpha_L + (\beta_{KK} + \beta_{KL})\ln k + (\beta_{LL} + \beta_{KL})\ln l}.$$

In a traditional setting, the homogeneity restriction is given as $\beta_{KK}+\beta_{KL}=\beta_{LL}+\beta_{KL}=0$, and the symmetric restriction is also given by $\beta_{KL}=\beta_{LK}$. Furthermore, constant returns to scale is given by $\alpha_K+\alpha_L=1$. Therefore,

$$\frac{rk}{c} = \alpha_K + \beta_{KK}\ln\frac{k}{l},$$

$$\frac{wl}{c} = \alpha_L + \beta_{KL}\ln\frac{k}{l}.$$

The agglomeration economies of both types, i.e., localization and urbanization economies, are external economies at the firm-level. However, at the industrial-level, localization economies are internalized and the two types of agglomeration economies are separated, while market access effects are determined by the external economies (Chipman 1970; Nakamura 1985).[1]

[1]Chipman (1970) first formulated internalization of external economies of scale in the production function framework. His formulation shows that the industrial-level production is increasing returns to scale by internalization, while the firm-level production is constant returns to scale. Nakamura (1985) has set out to distinguish the productivity effects of urbanization and localization based on Chipman's work.

Based on the assumption of identical and constant returns to scale technologies, the production function at the industrial level can be obtained by aggregating the production functions of all firm as follows:

$$\begin{aligned}(1-\alpha_S)\ln Y &= \alpha_0 + \alpha_T t + \alpha_D \ln DENS + \alpha_A \ln ACC + \alpha_K \ln K + \alpha_L \ln L \\ &\quad + \frac{1}{2}\beta_{KK}(\ln K)^2 + \frac{1}{2}\beta_{LL}(\ln L)^2 + \beta_{KL}(\ln K)(\ln L).\end{aligned}$$

The next equation is obtained by dividing both sides of the above equation by $1-\alpha_S$, subtracting ln$L$, and using the homogeneity restriction, the symmetric restriction, and constant–returns–to–scale:

$$\begin{aligned}\ln\frac{Y}{L} &= \frac{\alpha_0}{1-\alpha_S} + \frac{\alpha_T}{1-\alpha_S}t + \frac{\alpha_D}{1-\alpha_S}\ln DENS + \frac{\alpha_A}{1-\alpha_S}\ln ACC \\ &\quad + \frac{\alpha_K}{1-\alpha_S}\ln\frac{K}{L} + \frac{\alpha_S}{1-\alpha_S}\ln L + \frac{1}{2}\frac{\beta_{KK}}{1-\alpha_S}\left(\ln\frac{K}{L}\right)^2,\end{aligned} \tag{3.10}$$

where $K(\equiv\sum k)$ and $L(\equiv\sum l)$ are the capital and labor inputs, respectively, at the industrial level.

The traditional setting yields the following input share equations:

$$\frac{\sum r\cdot k}{Y} = \alpha_K + \beta_{KK}\ln\frac{K}{L}$$

and

$$\frac{\sum w\cdot l}{Y} = \alpha_L + \beta_{KL}\ln\frac{K}{L}. \tag{3.11}$$

This translog production function approach has evolved as a way to relax constraints on production functions. A translog production-inverse input demand system, which was proposed by Kim (1992), alleviates the homogeneity restriction and the symmetric restriction, and the condition of constant returns to scale. This revised approach makes it possible to widen the range of interpretation; thus, recent major empirical studies on agglomeration economies generally adopt this method (see Graham and Kim 2008). However, we must recognize that it is difficult to obtain stable estimation results using this approach because of the number of parameters that need to be estimated.

3.3 Empirical Method and Results

3.3.1 Data

The data set is comprised of Japanese prefectural data pertaining to the manufacturing and non-manufacturing industries for the period 1980–2002. Although there are many related regional statistics, it is necessary to compile data from various sources to obtain an appropriate set of estimates. The data for this study is gathered primarily from the *Annual Report on Prefectural Accounts*, which is compiled by the Economic and Social Research Institute, Cabinet Office.

Industrial value-added is measured as the real value-added deflated by the value-added deflator reported in the *System of National Accounts* (SNA). This study retroactively estimates the data before 1990 because official statistics only include data after 1990. Labor input is represented by man-hours. Capital input comprises the fixed capital stock adjusted by its rate of utilization. Fixed capital stock is obtained from the Central Research Institute of the Electric Power Industry's regional economics database, where stock is estimated based on gross investment using the benchmarking year method. The available data is limited to data pertaining to manufacturing and non-manufacturing industries. The utilization rate—which is the production capacity of a unit of fixed assets—for the manufacturing industry is derived from a set of indices published by the Ministry of Economy, Trade and Industry (METI) that describe the operating ratios. Regarding the non-manufacturing industry, the inverse of the capital coefficient is used to calculate the utilization rate.[2] Labor cost is the total compensation provided to employees, comprising salaries and wages in cash or kind, other employee benefits, and compensation required by law. Capital cost is given by $p_K(r+d)/(1-\tau)$, where p_K is an investment deflator; r, an interest rate; d, an industry- and year-specific depreciation rate; and τ, a corporate tax rate. Economic distance is adopted as the distance weight. The data on economic distance is based on highway travel time. According to "Net Freight Flow Census (census logistics) 2000," vehicular transportation accounts for 81.7% of Japan's shipment share. On the other hand, the shares of marine, air, and rail transportation are a mere 13%, 4.2%, and 1.2%, respectively. These findings imply that the cost of using vehicular transportation is

[2]It is expected that variations in the logarithm of the inverse of the capital coefficient, $\ln\left(\frac{Y}{K}\right)$, have a constant slope over time under a production system employing capital-intense technology over the long term. However, the value fluctuates every year in an observed data set. Hence, this study assumes the fluctuations in $\ln\left(\frac{Y}{K}\right)$ can be attributed to a change in capital utilization as well as a time trend. Based on that assumption, a proxy of the capital utilization rate can be measured with a residual error term (ε) in the regression $\ln(Y/K)=\alpha+\beta T+\varepsilon$, where T is a time trend and β is a time-invariant slope of $\ln\left(\frac{Y}{K}\right)$.

the most appropriate data with which to determine economic distance. Gross output is measured as the real gross output deflated by the gross output deflator.

3.3.2 Method

Adding the regional and time-specific dummies to the production function in (3.10), the panel estimation model can be written as:

$$\begin{aligned}\ln\frac{Y_{jt}}{L_{jt}} = & \frac{\alpha_0}{1-\alpha_S} + \frac{\alpha_D}{1-\alpha_S}\ln DENS_{jt} + \frac{\alpha_A}{1-\alpha_S}\ln ACC_{jt} \\ & + \frac{\alpha_K}{1-\alpha_S}\ln\frac{K_{jt}}{L_{jt}} + \frac{\alpha_S}{1-\alpha_S}\ln L_{jt} + \frac{1}{2}\frac{\beta_{KK}}{1-\alpha_S}\left(\ln\frac{K_{jt}}{L_{jt}}\right)^2 \\ & + \sum_{p=1}^{n}\frac{\alpha_{T,p}}{1-\alpha_S}\cdot regdum_j^p\cdot t + \sum_{p=2}^{n}\alpha_P\cdot regdum_j^p \\ & + \sum_{\tau=2}^{T-1}\alpha_\tau\cdot timedum_t^\tau + \varepsilon_{jt},\end{aligned} \tag{3.12}$$

where $t = 0, \ldots, T$ and $j = 1, \ldots, n$. In addition, n is the number of regions. It is assumed that technological progress differs across prefectures due to differences in regional industrial policies. Thus, the prefectural dummy variable *regdum*, multiplied by the time trend t, is included as an independent variable in (3.12). The value of *regdum* takes one for $p = j$ and zero for $p \neq j$. *Timedum* is a time dummy used to control for business-cycle effects. This variable takes one for $\tau = t$ and zero for $\tau \neq t$.

Klette and Griliches (1996) and Klette (1999) explain that the fact that the production factor is endogenous in the estimation of the production function causes a bias in the ordinary least squares (OLS) estimator. They highlight the following two specific points. First, demand—the influencing element of productivity shock—introduces an upper bias to the OLS estimator. Second, the measurement error of data introduces a lower bias to the OLS estimator. To address the problem of endogeneity of the production factor, of all the possible estimation methods, this study uses the iterative three-stage least squares (3SLS) method. The estimation of the translog production function in (3.12) and the labor cost share function in (3.11) is conducted using the 3SLS method with instrumental variables.

The estimation results are summarized in Table 3.2. To test whether the findings are sensitive to different estimation techniques, Table 3.2 presents the OLS estimation results as an alternative estimation method. For each parameter, the upper row contains the estimated value, while the lower row contains the t value (enclosed in parentheses). This study employed F-statistics to test whether fixed and time effects exist—the null hypothesis that the two effects do not exist is rejected for both the manufacturing and non-manufacturing industries. In addition, the

Table 3.2 Estimation results

	All Industries				Manufacturing Industry				Non-manufacturing Industry			
	3SLS		OLS		3SLS		OLS		3SLS		OLS	
α_0	0.4305		0.4085		0.3186		0.2619		0.4687		0.4500	
	(37.79)	**	(64.96)	**	(13.86)	**	(29.33)	**	(39.92)	**	(61.04)	**
α_S	0.0786		0.0786		0.0678		0.0564		0.0803		0.0792	
	(21.84)	**	(18.65)	**	(10.81)	**	(7.92)	**	(21.07)	**	(17.52)	**
α_D	0.0156		0.0154		0.0422		0.0393		0.0268		0.0262	
	(5.63)	**	(4.75)	**	(7.51)	**	(6.22)	**	(9.22)	**	(7.65)	**
α_A	0.1997		0.1919		0.2865		0.2735		0.2344		0.2332	
	(20.08)	**	(16.91)	**	(14.14)	**	(12.24)	**	(22.60)	**	(19.48)	**
α_K	0.4208		0.4456		0.4987		0.5715		0.4151		0.4523	
	(29.41)	**	(36.85)	**	(20.03)	**	(48.29)	**	(25.96)	**	(30.33)	**
β_{KK}	−0.0326		−0.0375		−0.0186		−0.0286		−0.0374		−0.0407	
	(−13.73)	**	(−72.08)	**	(−4.65)	**	(−34.79)	**	(−14.46)	**	(−51.65)	**
F-statistic	22.3259				11.4533				19.9496			
	[0.00]				[0.00]				[0.00]			
LM-e	0.7240				0.1761				1.3486			
	[0.40]				[0.68]				[0.25]			
$\bar{R}^2$	0.9679		0.9602		0.9559		0.9469		0.9679		0.9447	

Notes:
Due to space constraints, the estimation results of the time-trend and time-effect terms have been omitted
The constant and lag of dependent variables are used as the instrumental variables
The *t*-statistics are enclosed in parentheses and the *p*- statistics are enclosed in brackets
LM-e is a test based on the principle of Lagrange multipliers (Burridge 1980)
Number of observations: 1034
** Significance at the 1% level; * significance at the 5% level

Lagrange multiplier (LM) test was conducted to examine whether the influence of a spatial error exists, and the null hypothesis that a spatial error does not exist is not rejected.

The parameter for localization economies (α_S) is significant and has a positive sign for both industries. The positive value of α_S for the manufacturing industry is 0.0678; for the non-manufacturing industry, it is 0.0803. These findings imply that labor productivity increases by approximately 7–8% when the industrial scale doubles. These parameters are greater than the parameter for urbanization economies (α_D). The positive value of α_D for the manufacturing industry is 0.0442; for the non-manufacturing industry, it is 0.0268. These positive parameters for agglomeration effects demonstrate that industrial agglomeration positively affects labor productivity. The parameters imply that the agglomeration benefits that arise from specialization are more significant than those that arise from diversity. The parameter for market access (α_A) also shows a positive sign for both industries, and it is greater than the values of both localization and urbanization economies. These findings imply that linkages with other markets are an important factor in both industries.[3]

3.3.3 Regional Growth

The impact of industrial agglomeration on regional economic growth is obtained by using these estimated coefficients. The growth rates of a regional economy are generally divided according to the contributions of capital, labor, and total factor productivity (TFP) (Solow 1957). Agglomeration economies are contained in TFP, which represents productivity growth or product efficiency. The difference between the initial and final period terms in the production function in (3.12) yields the following equation:

$$\begin{aligned}\frac{1}{T}\ln\left(\frac{Y_{jT}}{Y_{j0}}\right) &= \frac{\theta_{K,j}}{T}\ln\left(\frac{K_{jT}}{K_{j0}}\right)+\frac{\theta_{L,j}}{T}\ln\left(\frac{L_{jT}}{L_{j0}}\right)\\ &+\left[\alpha_{T,j}+\frac{\alpha_S}{T}\ln\left(\frac{Y_{jT}}{Y_{j0}}\right)+\frac{\alpha_D}{T}\ln\left(\frac{DENS_{jT}}{DENS_{j0}}\right)+\frac{\alpha_A}{T}\ln\left(\frac{ACC_{jT}}{ACC_{j0}}\right)+\frac{1-\alpha_S}{T}\left(\varepsilon_{jT}-\varepsilon_{j0}\right)\right],\end{aligned}$$

where $\theta_{K,j}$ and $\theta_{L,j}$ represent the factor of elasticity of production. The terms on the right-hand side of the equation correspond to the degree of contribution to value-added growth in capital and labor inputs, technological progress, economies of scale, population density changes, and market access changes, respectively. The Solow residual is the summation of the terms in brackets. The last term is the error

[3]According to Harrington and Warf (1995), local demand could be an important driver for the service sector because this sector is, to a large extent, reliant on face-to-face contact, which leads to high transport costs for service delivery.

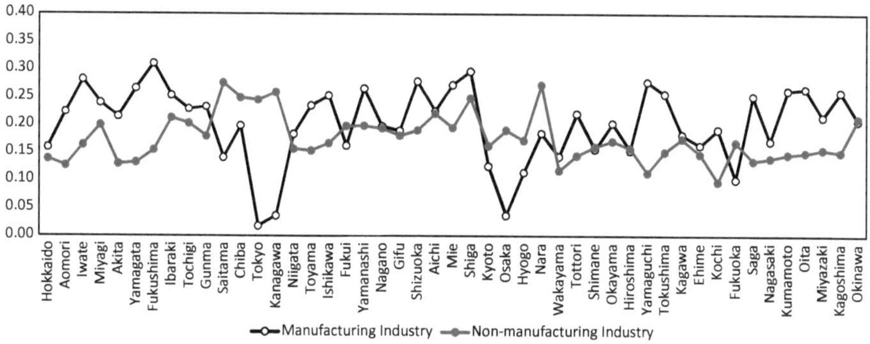

Fig. 3.1 Growth contribution of localization economies (in %, annual rate, 1980–2002)

component. From the translog production function, the output elasticities of the production factors are obtained as follows:

$$\theta_{K,j} = \alpha_K + \frac{\beta_{KK}}{2}\left(\ln K_{jT} + \ln K_{j0}\right) + \frac{\beta_{KL}}{2}\left(\ln L_{jT} + \ln L_{j0}\right),$$
$$\theta_{L,j} = \alpha_L + \frac{\beta_{KL}}{2}\left(\ln K_{jT} + \ln K_{j0}\right) + \frac{\beta_{LL}}{2}\left(\ln L_{jT} + \ln L_{j0}\right).$$

The growth contribution of localization economies is relatively high in the areas that specialize in the manufacturing industry, such as Aichi, Shizuoka, and Mie prefectures (Fig. 3.1).[4] In Japan, there have been secular changes in the location of manufacturing firms; in other words, they have shifted away from large metropolitan areas. Further, the geographical dispersion of manufacturing firms continued both domestically and internationally between the 1980s and 1990s. Therefore, this evidence implies that the geographical dispersion to non-metropolitan areas enforced the production scale in those areas. In the prefectures with large metropolitan areas, such as Tokyo, Kanagawa, and Osaka prefectures, the effects of localization economies on growth are small with respect to the manufacturing industry, while the non-manufacturing industry receives considerable benefits from localization economies. The average growth contribution of localization economies in the Greater Tokyo Area—including Saitama, Chiba, Tokyo, and Kanagawa prefectures—is 0.26% per year. This evidence implies that non-manufacturing firms located in regions with a high share of gross value-added receive benefits from the economies of scale. On the other hand, the growth contribution of urbanization economies to the manufacturing industry is 0.01 on average, while that of localization economies has fallen below 0.20%. Similarly, the average growth contribution of urbanization economies to the non-manufacturing industry is 0.00, while that of localization economies has fallen below 0.18%. These findings indicate that the growth contribution of urbanization

[4]See Appendix for detailed decomposition results.

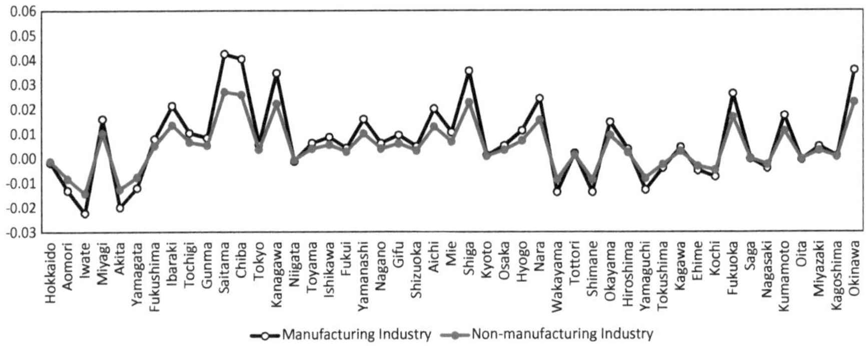

Fig. 3.2 Growth contribution of urbanization economies (in %, annual rate, 1980–2002)

economies is weak as compared to that of localization economies; therefore, urbanization economies could not be a driving force in regional economic growth (Fig. 3.2). This result implies that the geographical concentration of an industry is more important for growth than the diversity of the industrial structure.

The implication is consistent with numerous previous studies, particularly with respect to the manufacturing industry. On the other hand, the result is inconsistent with some previous studies such as Mano and Otsuka (2000) and Dekle (2002), which demonstrated that urbanization economies tend to have a stronger influence on industrial growth than do localization economies. Further, in both industries, the market access effect is a more important factor in industrial growth than are agglomeration economies (Fig. 3.3). Note that the growth contribution of market access is greater not only in areas where plants are concentrated but also in large metropolitan areas, such as Tokyo, Osaka, and Kanagawa, and it exceeds the effect of localization economies in almost all prefectures. This result indicates that road transportation infrastructure strengthens market linkages across regions and contributes to the growth of regional industries.

3.3.4 Economic Convergence

According to Fujita and Tabuchi (1997), economic disparities across Japanese regions converged during the postwar period. The contribution of industrial agglomeration to the convergence of regional productivity disparities will be evaluated in this section. Convergence is typically verified by cross-sectional regressions known as "Barro regressions" (Barro and Sala-i-Martin, 1995). Defining labor productivity as $v \equiv Y/L$, the beta coefficient over period $(0, T)$ is given by

$$(1/T)\ln\left[v_{jT}/v_{j0}\right] = \alpha + \beta \ln v_{j0} + \varepsilon_j.$$

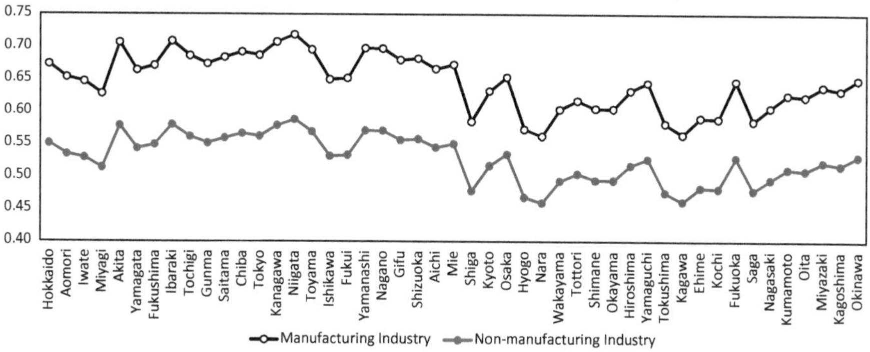

Fig. 3.3 Growth contribution of market access (in %, annual rate, 1980–2002)

Defining the variable on the left-hand side as $\dot{v}_j \equiv (1/T)\ln\left[v_{jT}/v_{j0}\right]$, the beta coefficient is represented by

$$\beta = \frac{\sum_j \left(\ln v_{j0} - \overline{\ln v_0}\right) \cdot \left(\dot{v}_j - \overline{\dot{v}}\right)}{\sum_j \left(\ln v_{j0} - \overline{\ln v_0}\right)^2}.$$

If this coefficient shows a negative sign, it is interpreted as evidence of convergence in labor productivity.

Subtraction of the growth rate of labor inputs from both sides of the translog production function in (3.12) yields the following equation:

$$\dot{v}_j = \alpha_{T,j} + \frac{\theta_{K,j}}{T}\ln\left(\frac{K_{jT}}{K_{j0}}\right) + \frac{\theta_{L,j} - 1}{T}\ln\left(\frac{L_{jT}}{L_{j0}}\right) + \frac{\alpha_S}{T}\ln\left(\frac{Y_{jT}}{Y_{j0}}\right)$$
$$+\frac{\alpha_D}{T}\ln\left(\frac{DENS_{jT}}{DENS_{j0}}\right) + \frac{\alpha_A}{T}\ln\left(\frac{ACC_{jT}}{ACC_{j0}}\right) + \frac{1-\alpha_S}{T}\left(\varepsilon_{jT} - \varepsilon_{j0}\right).$$

For convenience, each term on the right-hand side is replaced with $\dot{v}_j(\cdot)$ as follows:

$$\dot{v}_j = \dot{v}_j(T) + \dot{v}_j(K) + \dot{v}_j(L) + \dot{v}_j(S) + \dot{v}_j(DENS) + \dot{v}_j(ACC) + \dot{v}_j(RES).$$

From the above definition, the covariance of v_{j0} and $\dot{v}_j$ is obtained as follows:

$$\mathrm{cov}\left(v_{j0}, \dot{v}_j\right) = \frac{1}{N}\sum_j \left(\ln v_{j0} - \overline{\ln v_0}\right)\left(\dot{v}_j - \overline{\dot{v}}\right)$$
$$= \mathrm{cov}\left(v_{j0}, \dot{v}_j(T)\right) + \mathrm{cov}\left(v_{j0}, \dot{v}_j(K)\right) + \mathrm{cov}\left(v_{j0}, \dot{v}_j(L)\right) + \mathrm{cov}\left(v_{j0}, \dot{v}_j(S)\right)$$
$$+\mathrm{cov}\left(v_{j0}, \dot{v}_j(DENS)\right) + \mathrm{cov}\left(v_{j0}, \dot{v}_j(ACC)\right) + \mathrm{cov}\left(v_{j0}, \dot{v}_j(res)\right).$$

As a result, the covariance of v_{j0} and $\dot{v}_j$ becomes equal to the total covariance of v_{j0} and each element of $\dot{v}_j$. The division of both sides by the variance in the logarithm of v_{j0} yields the following:

$$\frac{\sum_j \left(\ln v_{j0} - \overline{\ln v_0}\right)\left(\dot{v}_j - \overline{\dot{v}}\right)}{\sum_j \left(\ln v_{j0} - \overline{\ln v_0}\right)^2} = \frac{\sum_j \left(\ln v_{j0} - \overline{\ln v_0}\right)\left(\dot{v}_j(T) - \overline{\dot{v}(T)}\right)}{\sum_j \left(\ln v_{j0} - \overline{\ln v_0}\right)^2}$$
$$+\frac{\sum_j \left(\ln v_{j0} - \overline{\ln v_0}\right)\left(\dot{v}_j(K) - \overline{\dot{v}(K)}\right)}{\sum_j \left(\ln v_{j0} - \overline{\ln v_0}\right)^2}$$
$$+\frac{\sum_j \left(\ln v_{j0} - \overline{\ln v_0}\right)\left(\dot{v}_j(L) - \overline{\dot{v}(L)}\right)}{\sum_j \left(\ln v_{j0} - \overline{\ln v_0}\right)^2}$$
$$+\frac{\sum_j \left(\ln v_{j0} - \overline{\ln v_0}\right)\left(\dot{v}_j(S) - \overline{\dot{v}(S)}\right)}{\sum_j \left(\ln v_{j0} - \overline{\ln v_0}\right)^2}$$
$$+\frac{\sum_j \left(\ln v_{j0} - \overline{\ln v_0}\right)\left(\dot{v}_j(DENS) - \overline{\dot{v}(DENS)}\right)}{\sum_j \left(\ln v_{j0} - \overline{\ln v_0}\right)^2}$$
$$+\frac{\sum_j \left(\ln v_{j0} - \overline{\ln v_0}\right)\left(\dot{v}_j(ACC) - \overline{\dot{v}(ACC)}\right)}{\sum_j \left(\ln v_{j0} - \overline{\ln v_0}\right)^2}$$
$$+\frac{\sum_j \left(\ln v_{j0} - \overline{\ln v_0}\right)\left(\dot{v}_j(res) - \overline{\dot{v}(res)}\right)}{\sum_j \left(\ln v_{j0} - \overline{\ln v_0}\right)^2}$$

or

$$\beta = \beta_T + \beta_K + \beta_L + \beta_S + \beta_{DENS} + \beta_{ACC} + \beta_{RES},$$

Table 3.3 Decomposition results of the β coefficient (1980–2002)

	All Industries		Manufacturing Industry		Non-manufacturing Industry	
Convergence Coefficient	−0.0069		−0.0085		−0.0070	
	(−2.61)	*	(−2.45)	*	(−3.22)	**
Capital	−0.0027		−0.0104		0.0044	
	(−1.16)		(−4.06)	**	(1.85)	
Labor	−0.0062		0.0013		−0.0090	
	(−5.10)	**	(0.72)		(−7.39)	**
Localization Economies	0.0008		−0.0008		0.0016	
	(2.69)	**	(−2.22)	*	(5.24)	**
Urbanization Economies	0.0002		0.0003		0.0003	
	(4.72)	**	(3.39)	**	(4.36)	**
Market Access	0.0003		0.0001		0.0005	
	(1.23)		(0.34)		(1.56)	
Technological Progress	0.0109		0.0083		0.0090	
	(3.25)	**	(1.91)		(2.55)	*
Others	−0.0102		−0.0073		−0.0139	
	(−3.06)	**	(−2.19)	*	(−4.11)	**

Notes:
The *t*-values are enclosed in parentheses
** Significance at the 1% level; * significance at the 5% level

where

$$\beta_x = \frac{\sum_j \left(\ln v_{j0} - \overline{\ln v_0}\right)\left(\dot{v}_j(x) - \overline{\dot{v}(x)}\right)}{\sum_j \left(\ln v_{j0} - \overline{\ln v_0}\right)^2} \qquad (x = T, K, L, S, DENS, ACC, RES).$$

Each item on the right-hand side of the equation is the regression coefficient of labor productivity in the initial period to the growth contribution components (Fukao and Yue 2000).[5] The equation implies that the beta coefficient can be decomposed into the following seven components: the contributions of technological progress β_T toward convergence, capital input β_K, labor input β_L, localization economies β_S, urbanization economies β_{DENS}, market access to other regions β_{ACC}, and the error term β_{RES}. A positive value for β implies that input growth contributes to an increase in labor productivity disparities. On the other hand, if β is negative, then input growth contributes to a reduction in labor productivity disparities.

Table 3.3 summarizes the decomposition results. The beta coefficient has a negative value for both industries, and it is also significantly greater than zero at the 5% significance level. This result indicates the existence of economic convergence over the sample periods.

[5]Using this method, Fukao and Yue (2000) have clarified the contribution of social overhead capital toward labor productivity disparities for Japanese prefectures.

However, the factors that contribute to convergence vary by industry. In the manufacturing industry, capital input, localization economies, and other factors contribute to economic convergence. One of the reasons for this is that plant locations in prefectures with large metropolitan areas, such as Tokyo, Kanagawa, and Osaka prefectures, were restricted by the prevailing industrial policy. Specifically, between the 1980s and 1990s, the government implemented a policy that promoted local decentralization of plant locations. As a result, plant locations in large metropolitan areas were remarkably limited. In addition, fiscal incentives were provided to manufacturing firms to relocate to or open branches in non-metropolitan areas. It is evident that these policies encouraged capital transfer from large metropolitan areas to non-metropolitan areas, and improved the scale of production in non-metropolitan areas. Consequently, the contribution of capital input and localization economies toward decreasing the productivity disparity has been strengthened. In contrast, localization economies contribute to the increase in productivity disparity in the non-manufacturing industry. This result appears to be related to the types of service sectors present in each area. In other words, high-productivity sectors, such as information, technology, and mobile information sectors, are concentrated in the Greater Tokyo Area, while labor-intensive, low-productivity sectors such as the medical sector are concentrated in local areas. This suggests that the continued development of service sectors has the potential to increase regional disparities. Urbanization economies also contribute to expanding regional disparities in both industries, although their influence on the beta coefficient is smaller than that of localization economies. This suggests the possibility that urbanization economies lead to a concentration of the population in large metropolitan areas, thus expanding the regional disparities in productivity for both industries.

3.4 Conclusion

This chapter investigated the effects of industrial agglomeration on regional economic growth, with particular emphasis on economic convergence. The traditional analysis, which was based on Japanese prefectural data, indicated that localization economies had greater effects on regional growth than did urbanization economies. In particular, localization economies in the manufacturing industry were concentrated locally, while those in the non-manufacturing industry were concentrated in the Greater Tokyo Area. This empirical evidence suggests that the expansion of industrial scale is preferable to diversity for both the manufacturing and non-manufacturing industries. Furthermore, for both industries, the empirical analysis indicated that the growth contribution of the market access effect exceeded that of agglomeration economies, and that the effects had a remarkable influence on productivity growth. This implies that it is very important to develop a road transportation system to promote interregional access because the economic gains obtained from efficient transport networks to the metropolitan areas are more beneficial than the availability of plentiful labor.

This study also examined the impact of agglomeration economies, including market access effects, on economic convergence. The results revealed that regional convergence progressed during the sample period of 1980–2002, and that localization economies contributed to economic convergence in the manufacturing industry. This suggests that the development policy promoting local decentralization in high-productivity sectors was effective in achieving convergence of regional disparities. In contrast, these effects continued to increase the regional disparities in the non-manufacturing industry. Particularly, the result related to urbanization economies suggests that the concentration of population in large metropolitan areas increased productivity in these areas, contributing to the widening of disparities in regional productivity. Therefore, it appears reasonable to conclude that the expansion of the non-manufacturing industry can potentially create regional economic disparities.

This evidence is significant because it suggests that the changing sectoral composition of industries requires a revision of the existing policy. Thus, it is necessary to conduct an industrial analysis that employs sectoral data in further detail to identify policy implications. In particular, the data construction corresponding to different sectors will be important in investigating whether the growth of service sectors has the potential to increase regional disparities. This extension will be a subject for future research.

Appendix: Growth accounts (in %, annual growth rate, 1980–2002)

	Product Growth	Capital Growth	Labor Growth	TFP Localization Economies	Urbanization Economies	Market Access	Technological Progress	Other
(a) Manufacturing industry								
Hokkaido	2.340	1.108	−0.810	0.159	−0.002	0.673	1.356	−0.144
Aomori	3.288	2.571	0.063	0.223	−0.013	0.653	−0.415	0.206
Iwate	4.147	2.408	−0.006	0.281	−0.022	0.646	0.821	0.018
Miyagi	3.533	2.232	−0.255	0.240	0.016	0.628	1.425	−0.752
Akita	3.165	2.159	−0.383	0.215	−0.020	0.706	0.455	0.033
Yamagata	3.916	2.582	−0.270	0.266	−0.012	0.664	0.431	0.256
Fukushima	4.573	2.557	−0.437	0.310	0.008	0.671	1.279	0.184
Ibaraki	3.727	2.283	−0.175	0.253	0.021	0.708	1.048	−0.412
Tochigi	3.362	2.416	−0.327	0.228	0.010	0.686	1.661	−1.312
Gunma	3.422	2.391	−0.264	0.232	0.008	0.674	1.353	−0.971
Saitama	2.072	1.994	−0.496	0.141	0.042	0.683	−0.267	−0.026
Chiba	2.917	1.239	−0.535	0.198	0.040	0.692	0.571	0.712
Tokyo	0.258	1.096	−1.636	0.018	0.006	0.687	1.122	−1.033
Kanagawa	0.530	1.243	−1.125	0.036	0.035	0.707	0.285	−0.651

(continued)

	Product Growth	Capital Growth	Labor Growth	TFP Localization Economies	Urbanization Economies	Market Access	Technological Progress	Other
Niigata	2.693	1.867	−0.672	0.183	−0.001	0.719	−0.108	0.706
Toyama	3.450	1.830	−0.547	0.234	0.006	0.696	1.596	−0.365
Ishikawa	3.725	2.192	−0.745	0.253	0.009	0.650	1.702	−0.334
Fukui	2.388	2.017	−0.860	0.162	0.004	0.652	0.332	0.082
Yamanashi	3.915	3.260	−0.131	0.266	0.016	0.698	0.955	−1.148
Nagano	2.904	2.524	−0.586	0.197	0.006	0.697	0.621	−0.554
Gifu	2.792	2.180	−0.676	0.189	0.009	0.680	−0.113	0.523
Shizuoka	4.108	2.123	−0.258	0.279	0.005	0.682	0.881	0.396
Aichi	3.310	2.018	−0.397	0.225	0.020	0.666	0.855	−0.078
Mie	4.011	1.963	−0.212	0.272	0.010	0.673	0.887	0.419
Shiga	4.370	2.403	0.224	0.297	0.035	0.585	2.885	−2.058
Kyoto	1.850	1.579	−1.202	0.126	0.001	0.632	1.674	−0.959
Osaka	0.545	1.176	−1.287	0.037	0.005	0.653	0.290	−0.330
Hyogo	1.685	1.433	−0.901	0.114	0.011	0.573	0.999	−0.544
Nara	2.723	2.251	−0.442	0.185	0.024	0.562	1.866	−1.724
Wakayama	2.107	1.129	−1.387	0.143	−0.014	0.603	1.645	−0.012
Tottori	3.243	1.900	−0.804	0.220	0.002	0.617	1.957	−0.648
Shimane	2.296	2.123	−0.978	0.156	−0.014	0.605	0.396	0.009
Okayama	2.988	1.243	−0.807	0.203	0.015	0.604	1.625	0.106
Hiroshima	2.266	1.241	−0.908	0.154	0.004	0.632	0.920	0.224
Yamaguchi	4.087	1.375	−0.667	0.277	−0.013	0.645	2.371	0.099
Tokushima	3.764	1.924	−1.084	0.255	−0.004	0.582	2.377	−0.285
Kagawa	2.684	1.348	−0.896	0.182	0.004	0.565	1.839	−0.359
Ehime	2.406	1.359	−0.864	0.163	−0.005	0.590	1.319	−0.156
Kochi	2.824	1.897	−1.062	0.192	−0.008	0.589	1.844	−0.628
Fukuoka	1.502	1.057	−0.882	0.102	0.026	0.647	1.336	−0.784
Saga	3.713	2.470	−0.456	0.252	0.000	0.585	1.983	−1.122
Nagasaki	2.518	1.701	−0.867	0.171	−0.004	0.606	1.112	−0.201
Kumamoto	3.862	2.266	−0.174	0.262	0.017	0.626	1.546	−0.680
Oita	3.904	1.328	−0.443	0.265	−0.001	0.623	3.521	−1.388
Miyazaki	3.157	1.704	−0.387	0.214	0.005	0.638	0.789	0.194
Kagoshima	3.819	2.576	−0.809	0.259	0.001	0.633	1.399	−0.240
Okinawa	3.058	2.002	−0.766	0.208	0.036	0.649	0.783	0.146
(b) Non-manufacturing industry								
Hokkaido	1.718	1.433	−0.505	0.138	−0.001	0.551	0.487	−0.384
Aomori	1.567	2.080	−0.415	0.126	−0.008	0.534	−0.015	−0.736
Iwate	2.032	1.616	−0.463	0.163	−0.014	0.529	0.127	0.074
Miyagi	2.478	1.932	0.079	0.199	0.010	0.513	0.381	−0.637
Akita	1.606	1.606	−0.759	0.129	−0.013	0.578	0.164	−0.099
Yamagata	1.640	1.634	−0.659	0.132	−0.008	0.543	0.032	−0.033
Fukushima	1.919	1.717	−0.350	0.154	0.005	0.549	−0.035	−0.121
Ibaraki	2.640	1.609	−0.043	0.212	0.013	0.579	0.348	−0.079
Tochigi	2.518	1.603	0.083	0.202	0.007	0.561	0.146	−0.084
Gunma	2.225	1.558	0.038	0.179	0.005	0.551	−0.085	−0.020
Saitama	3.428	2.073	0.733	0.275	0.027	0.559	0.010	−0.249

(continued)

	Product Growth	Capital Growth	Labor Growth	TFP Localization Economies	Urbanization Economies	Market Access	Technological Progress	Other
Chiba	3.103	2.058	0.558	0.249	0.026	0.566	−0.021	−0.334
Tokyo	3.047	2.338	0.239	0.245	0.004	0.562	0.771	−1.111
Kanagawa	3.221	2.172	0.816	0.259	0.022	0.579	−0.157	−0.469
Niigata	1.943	1.826	−0.483	0.156	−0.001	0.588	0.139	−0.282
Toyama	1.905	1.287	−0.266	0.153	0.004	0.569	1.107	−0.949
Ishikawa	2.070	1.697	−0.089	0.166	0.005	0.532	0.775	−1.016
Fukui	2.456	1.402	−0.206	0.197	0.003	0.533	0.938	−0.410
Yamanashi	2.466	1.934	−0.174	0.198	0.010	0.571	0.010	−0.083
Nagano	2.407	1.819	−0.159	0.193	0.004	0.571	−0.291	0.271
Gifu	2.243	1.892	0.026	0.180	0.006	0.556	0.276	−0.693
Shizuoka	2.367	1.966	0.018	0.190	0.003	0.558	−0.414	0.046
Aichi	2.741	1.872	0.257	0.220	0.013	0.545	0.219	−0.385
Mie	2.424	1.999	−0.231	0.195	0.007	0.550	0.529	−0.625
Shiga	3.087	1.444	0.507	0.248	0.023	0.478	1.494	−1.107
Kyoto	2.017	1.938	−0.173	0.162	0.001	0.517	0.678	−1.105
Osaka	2.370	1.862	0.093	0.190	0.003	0.535	0.690	−1.002
Hyogo	2.138	2.002	−0.065	0.172	0.007	0.469	0.308	−0.754
Nara	3.389	1.990	0.415	0.272	0.015	0.460	1.363	−1.126
Wakayama	1.467	1.396	−0.487	0.118	−0.009	0.494	−0.206	0.162
Tottori	1.800	2.523	−0.474	0.145	0.001	0.505	0.239	−1.138
Shimane	1.996	2.099	−0.656	0.160	−0.009	0.495	0.133	−0.226
Okayama	2.125	1.506	−0.146	0.171	0.009	0.494	0.563	−0.473
Hiroshima	1.964	2.171	−0.009	0.158	0.002	0.517	0.730	−1.605
Yamaguchi	1.412	1.655	−0.582	0.113	−0.008	0.527	0.366	−0.660
Tokushima	1.883	1.795	−0.565	0.151	−0.003	0.476	0.418	−0.389
Kagawa	2.177	1.764	−0.326	0.175	0.003	0.462	0.768	−0.669
Ehime	1.836	1.676	−0.310	0.147	−0.003	0.483	0.242	−0.399
Kochi	1.215	1.857	−0.620	0.098	−0.005	0.482	0.187	−0.783
Fukuoka	2.098	1.798	0.069	0.168	0.017	0.529	0.372	−0.855
Saga	1.685	1.622	−0.319	0.135	0.000	0.479	0.366	−0.599
Nagasaki	1.745	1.910	−0.537	0.140	−0.003	0.496	−0.027	−0.235
Kumamoto	1.831	1.818	−0.590	0.147	0.011	0.512	0.038	−0.105
Oita	1.871	1.694	−0.622	0.150	−0.001	0.510	0.341	−0.201
Miyazaki	1.940	1.702	−0.475	0.156	0.003	0.522	0.035	−0.003
Kagoshima	1.877	1.903	−0.569	0.151	0.000	0.518	−0.035	−0.090
Okinawa	2.640	2.443	0.392	0.212	0.023	0.531	−0.117	−0.845

References

Barro RJ, Sala-i-Martin X. Economic growth. New York: McGraw-Hill, Inc; 1995.

Benos N, Karagiannis S. Convergence and economic performance in Greece: evidence at regional and prefecture level. Rev Urban Reg Dev Stud. 2008;20(1):52–69.

Bosker M. Growth, agglomeration and convergence: a space-time analysis for European regions. Spat Econ Anal. 2007;2(1):91–108.

Burridge P. On the Cliff-Ord test for spatial correlation. J R Stat Soc Ser B (Methodological) 1980; 107–108.
Chipman JS. External economies of scale and competitive equilibrium. Q J Econ. 1970;84 (3):347–85.
Combes P, Gobillon L. The empirics of agglomeration economies. In: Duranton G, Henderson J, Strange W, editors. Handbook of regional and urban economics, volume 5A. Amsterdam: Elsevier; 2015.
Davis DR, Weinstein DE. Economic geography and regional production structure: an empirical investigation. Eur Econ Rev. 1999;43(2):379–407.
Dekle R. Industrial concentration and regional growth: evidence from the prefectures. Rev Econ Stat. 2002;84(2):310–5.
Fujita M. A monopolistic competition model of spatial agglomeration: differentiated product approach. Reg Sci Urban Econ. 1988;18(1):87–124.
Fujita M, Tabuchi T. Regional growth in postwar Japan. Reg Sci Urban Econ. 1997;27(6):643–70.
Fukao K, Yue X. Regional factor inputs and convergence in Japan. The Economic Review (The Keizai Kenkyuu) 2000;51(2):136–51. (in Japanese)
Graham DJ. Identifying urbanisation and localisation externalities in manufacturing and service industries. Pap Reg Sci. 2009;88(1):63–84.
Graham DJ, Kim H. An empirical analytical framework for agglomeration economies. Ann Reg Sci. 2008;42(2):267–89.
Harrington JW, Warf B. Industrial location: principles, practice, and policy. London: Routledge; 1995.
Henderson JV. Marshall's scale economies. J Urban Econ. 2003;53(1):1–28.
Kilicaslan Y, Ozatagan G. Impact of relative population change on regional income convergence: evidence from Turkey. Rev Urban Reg Dev Stud. 2007;19(3):210–23.
Kim HY. The translog production function and variable returns to scale. Rev Econ Stat. 1992;74:46–552.
Klette TJ. Market power, scale economies and productivity: estimates from a panel of establishment data. J Ind Econ. 1999;47(4):451–76.
Klette TJ, Griliches Z. The inconsistency of common scale estimators when output prices are unobserved and endogenous. J Appl Econ. 1996;11(4):343–61.
Krugman P. Geography and trade. Cambridge, MA/London: MIT Press; 1991.
Magrini S. Regional (di) convergence. Handbook of urban and regional economics. 2004;4
Mano Y, Otsuka K. Agglomeration economies and geographical concentration of industries: a case study of manufacturing sectors in postwar Japan. J Jpn Int Econ. 2000;14(3):189–203.
McCann P. Urban and regional economics. Oxford/New York: Oxford University Press; 2001.
Nakamura R. Agglomeration economies in urban manufacturing industries: a case of Japanese cities. J Urban Econ. 1985;17(1):108–24.
Otsuka A. Industrial agglomeration and economic convergence: the case of Japanese regions. The Economic Analysis (The Keizai Bunseki) 2008;180:1–19. (in Japanese)
Otsuka A, Yamano N. Industrial agglomeration effects on regional economic growth: a case of Japanese regions, Discussion Papers 08-T-2, Regional Economics Applications Laboratory, University of Illinois, IL; 2008
Parr JB. Missing elements in the analysis of agglomeration economies. Int Reg Sci Rev. 2002;25 (2):151–68.
Rivera-Batiz FL. Increasing returns, monopolistic competition, and agglomeration economies in consumption and production. Reg Sci Urban Econ. 1988;18(1):125–53.
Rosenthal SS, Strange WC. Evidence on the nature and sources of agglomeration economies. In: Henderson JV, Thisse JF, editors. Handbook of regional and urban economics, vol. 4. Amsterdam: Elsevier; 2004.
Solow RM. Technical change and the aggregate production function. Rev Econ Stat. 1957;39 (3):312–20.
Venables AJ. Equilibrium locations of vertically linked industries. Int Econ Rev. 1996;37 (2):341–59.

Chapter 4
A New Approach to Agglomeration Economies

Abstract This chapter proposes a new approach to measure agglomeration economies in Japan. Specifically, this study employs the Solow residual to confirm whether agglomeration economies exist in both manufacturing and non-manufacturing industries. This study also shows that social overhead capital has a positive effect on agglomeration economies. Currently, such economies are robust only in large metropolitan areas; however, they are present throughout Japan because of the disproportionate allocation of social overhead capital within the country.

Keywords Agglomeration economies • Solow residual • Social overhead capital

4.1 Introduction

Rosenthal and Strange (2004) and Combes and Gobillon (2015) provide comprehensive reviews of empirical studies on agglomeration economies.[1] Most of these studies focus on explaining agglomeration economies in production, and tend to adopt analytical approaches that involve production functions.[2] These studies make several assumptions and verify them using different types of production functions, such as Cobb–Douglas, the constant elasticity of substitution (CES), and translog. Furthermore, many researchers assume Hicks-neutral technological progress, and attempt to ascertain agglomeration economies as a component of the total factor

This chapter is based on Otsuka and Goto (2015) "Agglomeration economies in Japanese industries: the Solow residual approach," published in The Annals of Regional Science (Vol. 54, No. 2, pp. 401–416).

[1]Rosenthal and Strange (2004) conclude that labor productivity for a firm increases from 3 to 8% when the size of a city doubles.

[2]Glaeser et al. (2001) indicate that agglomeration economies exist for consumption, although most studies focus on explaining agglomeration economies in production. In addition, some previous studies demonstrate that agglomeration economies play an important role in improving the productive efficiency of local firms and industry (Beeson and Husted 1989; Mitra 1999, 2000; Driffield and Munday 2001; Tveteras and Battese 2006; Otsuka et al. 2010, 2014; Otsuka and Goto 2013; Otsuka 2017).

A. Otsuka, *A New Perspective on Agglomeration Economies in Japan*,
New Frontiers in Regional Science: Asian Perspectives 20,
DOI 10.1007/978-981-10-6490-6_4

productivity. However, these approaches have a disadvantage because they must assume a specific type or form of production function to identify agglomeration economies, and the result may differ depending on the specific formulation of the function. In more concrete terms, if one study determines the influence of agglomeration economies through a Cobb–Douglas function, that influence may not be detected in a study that uses a CES or translog function. In other words, the agglomeration effect depends on the type of production function, which is arbitrarily selected by the researcher. Since previous findings are mixed, it is difficult to identify the type of function that results in agglomeration, or the specific element that increases the benefits from agglomeration.

To overcome these problems, this study measures total factor productivity through the Solow residual. This approach enables us to determine the robustness of agglomeration economies as a component of total factor productivity and to investigate the relationship between industry clustering and social overhead capital using a direct connection between total factor productivity and agglomeration economies.

This chapter is organized as follows. Section 4.2 outlines the theoretical background forming the basis for the empirical analysis. Section 4.3 describes the new method using the Solow residual to measure total factor productivity. The results of the investigation are presented in Sect. 4.4. Section 4.5 concludes the study.

4.2 Theoretical Background

Economies of agglomeration, or agglomeration economies, are often expressed as economies of scale at the urban and regional level. Kanemoto et al. (1996) describe the theoretical relationship between agglomeration economies and economies of scale. According to them, a region's production function is expressed as $Y = F(K, L, A)$, where Y is a region's gross product, A is its production technology, K is the capital input, and L is the labor input in the region. Agglomeration economies are measured by the economies of scale in the region's production function based on the setting of firms' production behavior.

Assuming technological externalities created through inter-firm, off-market transactions, or the spillover of technical knowledge,[3] the production function of firms benefiting from agglomeration economies is expressed as $f(k, l, L, A)$, where k is the capital input and l is the labor input. All firms are homogeneous,

[3]The existence of agglomeration economies, as discussed in spatial economics, is explained through pecuniary external economies while considering the heterogeneity of intermediate goods. Therefore, this theoretical model is limited in that it only considers such technological external economies (see Fujita and Thisse 2002).

and because of the free entry and exit of individual firms, it is assumed they possess a production technology that generates constant returns to scale under conditions of perfect competition. That is to say, $f(k, l, L, A)$ is constant with respect to k and l, and when m is the total number of firms in the region, the region's production function is written as $Y = m \cdot f(K/m, L/m, L, A)$. From this, it becomes possible to express the number of firms as a function of three variables, $m = m^*(K, L, A)$. The region's production function can be expressed as a function of K, L, and A using the following equation:

$$F(K,L,A) = m^*(K,L,A) \times f\left(\frac{K}{m^*(K,L,A)}, \frac{L}{m^*(K,L,A)}, L, A\right).$$

By taking the first derivative with respect to L, we obtain:

$$F_L(K,L,A) = m\left[\frac{1}{m}f_l + f_L\right] + m_L^*[f - kf_k - lf_l].$$

Because the firms' production functions exhibit constant returns to scale, the second square bracket in this equation becomes zero. That is,

$$F_L(K,L,A) = f_l(k,l,L,A) + mf_L(k,l,L,A).$$

Therefore, the second term, mf_L, expresses the marginal net benefit from agglomeration economies.

4.3 Empirical Method

4.3.1 The Solow Residual Approach

If the agglomeration economy is internalized in the aggregation process at the regional level, then it is measured through economies of scale in regional production functions. Based on this theoretical background, this study assumes that economies of scale for a region are agglomeration economies.

Various technology assumptions can be made about production in a region. For this study, a Hicks-neutral production technology is assumed,

$$Y_t = A_t f(K_t, L_t).$$

When both sides are differentiated with respect to time t and divided by Y, the following expression is obtained:

$$\frac{1}{Y}\frac{dY}{dt} = \frac{1}{A}\frac{dA}{dt} + \frac{A}{Y}\frac{\partial f}{\partial K}\frac{dK}{dt} + \frac{A}{Y}\frac{\partial f}{\partial L}\frac{dL}{dt}. \tag{4.1}$$

Let the price of a product be P, the capital-input price be P_K, and the labor-input price be P_L. Then, the first-order condition to maximize profits becomes

$$A\frac{\partial f}{\partial K} = \frac{P_K}{P}, \; A\frac{\partial f}{\partial L} = \frac{P_L}{P}.$$

The following equation representing the returns to scale of production is established:

$$\frac{\partial Y}{\partial K}\frac{K}{Y} + \frac{\partial Y}{\partial L}\frac{L}{Y} = A\frac{\partial f}{\partial K}\frac{K}{Y} + A\frac{\partial f}{\partial L}\frac{L}{Y} = \gamma.$$

Under this condition, Eq. (4.1) can be rewritten as

$$\frac{d\ln Y}{dt} = \frac{d\ln A}{dt} + (1 - s_L)\frac{\partial \ln K}{\partial t} + s_L\frac{\partial \ln L}{\partial t} + (\gamma - 1)\frac{d\ln K}{dt},$$

where $s_L = P_L L/PY$. Here, the Solow residual SR can be defined as

$$SR \equiv \frac{d\ln Y}{dt} - (1 - s_L)\frac{\partial \ln K}{\partial t} - s_L\frac{\partial \ln L}{\partial t},$$

and the following equation is derived:

$$SR = \frac{d\ln A}{dt} + (\gamma - 1)\frac{d\ln K}{dt}. \tag{4.2}$$

Here, γ indicates the agglomeration effect expressing economies of scale in production.

4.3.2 Data

The empirical analysis was conducted using annual data of Japanese prefectures over the period 1980 to 2009. All industry groups, consisting of both manufacturing and non-manufacturing industries, are analyzed. Although various geographic levels including city, region, administrative division, and regional block were available, the prefectures were selected to facilitate analyzing the effect of appropriately targeted and aligned Japanese regional industrial policies. We expect that agglomerations are evident in large-scale industrial areas, company towns, industrial areas with several small-sized companies, and regions where universities and industry cooperate. All types of agglomerations are included at the prefecture level for this study.

The data for this study is gathered primarily from the *Annual Report on Prefectural Accounts*. Industrial value-added (Y) is measured as the real value-added deflated by the value-added deflator reported in the *System of National Accounts* (SNA). Labor input (L) is represented by man-hours. Capital input (K) is the fixed capital stock adjusted by its rate of utilization. Fixed capital stock is obtained from the Central Research Institute of the Electric Power Industry's regional economics database, where stock is estimated based on gross investment using the benchmarking year method. The utilization rate for manufacturing industries is derived from a set of indices published by the Ministry of Economy, Trade, and Industry (METI) that describe the operating ratios. Because there are no publicly available data on the utilization rate for non-manufacturing industries, a deviation calculated from the inverse of the capital coefficient[4] is used as a proxy. Moreover, total prefectural production and employer remuneration allow the computation of the relative labor share (S_L).

The advantage of using an approach based on the Solow residual is that it is possible to specify the agglomeration economy with economies of scale in production. In this setting, various elements, including the scale and concentration of the population, explain agglomeration economies, as well as the concentration of businesses. This study investigates whether developments in social overhead capital increase the effect of agglomeration to provide policy suggestions for social infrastructure development. Indeed, the development of social infrastructure is expected to improve the accessibility of a region, leading to easier procurement of intermediate goods, and thus the ability to produce goods at a lower cost. Otsuka et al. (2010) and Otsuka and Goto (2013) identified the enhancement effect for Japanese industries of agglomeration economies resulting from a region's market access. These studies demonstrate that a region endowed with good market access attracts businesses and boosts the effect of agglomeration economies. Based on these results, this study assumes that social overhead capital enhances market access and strengthens economies of agglomeration.

Social overhead capital stock (G) data are from the regional economic database at the Central Research Institute of the Electric Power Industry. Social overhead capital stock value combines data related to agriculture, forestry and fisheries facilities, roads, harbors, airports, communications, parks, water supply and sewer systems, social insurance and welfare facilities, schools, hospitals, and soil, water control and conservation facilities.

Table 4.1 shows the descriptive statistics and the average annual growth rate for different measurement periods. The average annual growth rate of the value-added

[4]It is expected that variations in the logarithm of the inverse of the capital coefficient, $\ln\left(\frac{Y}{K}\right)$, have a constant slope over time under a production system that employs capital-using technology over the long term. However, the value fluctuates every year in the observed dataset. Hence, we assume that the fluctuations in $\ln\left(\frac{Y}{K}\right)$ can be attributed to a change in capital utilization, as well as a time trend. Based on this assumption, a proxy of the capital utilization rate can be measured using the residual error term (ε) in the regression $\ln(Y/K)=\alpha+\beta T+\varepsilon$, where T is a time trend and β is the time-invariant slope.

Table 4.1 Descriptive statistics

		Value-added (million yen)			Labor (people)			Capital stock (million yen)			Social overhead capital (million yen)
		All industries	Manufacturing	Non-manufacturing	All industries	Manufacturing	Non-manufacturing	All industries	Manufacturing	Non-manufacturing	
1980	Mean	6,506,742	1,484,249	5,022,494	1,143,063	281,833	861,230	7,770,225	3,097,096	4,673,129	7,012,692
	Max	50,819,621	9,804,571	41,015,050	7,040,813	1,711,959	5,328,854	41,007,593	13,227,422	32,297,752	38,549,405
	Min	1,325,040	101,876	1,124,369	311,395	31,293	251,677	1,058,307	232,709	689,821	2,237,826
1990	Mean	9,857,259	2,291,870	7,565,389	1,261,658	311,546	950,111	14,838,714	5,209,024	9,629,690	11,506,329
	Max	83,413,308	11,539,058	71,874,250	8,274,800	1,718,244	6,556,556	97,284,770	24,487,829	84,458,419	54,177,887
	Min	1,839,861	162,983	1,469,345	309,843	31,964	240,828	2,566,210	450,013	1,907,170	3,714,267
	Annual growth rate (%, 1980–1990)	4.24	4.44	4.18	0.99	1.01	0.99	6.68	5.34	7.50	5.08
2000	Mean	10,910,478	2,376,725	8,533,753	1,278,406	260,164	1,018,242	21,904,323	7,172,980	14,731,343	16,687,046
	Max	92,738,081	10,633,550	82,104,531	8,055,188	1,267,828	6,787,360	152,732,726	34,897,185	137,093,393	69,668,958
	Min	2,034,119	207,609	1,612,244	305,096	29,268	247,471	3,933,096	685,060	2,941,218	5,606,332
	Annual growth rate (%, 1990–2000)	1.02	0.36	1.21	0.13	−1.79	0.69	3.97	3.25	4.34	3.79
2009	Mean	11,219,023	2,541,274	8,677,749	1,167,389	210,988	956,401	25,251,063	8,469,297	16,781,766	18,070,794
	Max	93,598,435	12,480,468	83,411,942	7,206,859	938,693	6,287,304	187,711,453	43,976,067	172,161,493	70,721,332
	Min	1,912,928	204,858	1,522,368	262,418	29,095	221,992	4,406,332	828,810	3,268,722	6,316,431
	Annual growth rate (%, 2000–2009)	0.31	0.75	0.19	−1.00	−2.30	−0.69	1.59	1.86	1.46	0.89

1980–2009	Mean	9,782,316	2,193,289	7,589,026	1,239,886	273,510	966,377	17,536,021	5,935,442	11,600,579	13,559,909
	Max	103,252,534	16,637,807	91,557,541	8,410,857	1,741,519	6,930,154	187,819,901	43,976,067	172,357,066	71,183,506
	Min	1,325,040	101,876	1,124,369	262,418	28,496	221,992	1,058,307	232,709	689,821	2,237,826
	Annual growth rate (%, 1980–2009)	1.42	1.36	1.43	0.28	–0.10	0.40	2.85	2.27	3.18	2.30

in each industry increased in the 1980s, with the overall industry growth rate at 4.24%, manufacturing industries at 4.44%, and non-manufacturing industries at 4.18%. However, the growth rate fell to 1.02% for all industries in the 1990s, with both manufacturing and non-manufacturing industry growth rates falling to 0.36% and 1.21%, respectively. In the 2000s, manufacturing growth increased slightly to 0.75%, but non-manufacturing growth fell further to 0.19%. The average annual growth rate for all industries across all measurement periods was 1.42%, with the growth rate for manufacturing and non-manufacturing industries at 1.36% and 1.43%, respectively. The trend in the growth rate represented by these figures reflects the overall path of growth of the Japanese economy, namely a move from higher growth in the 1980s to a prolonged slowdown throughout the 1990s and the 2000s.

Furthermore, the employment growth rate was negative from 2000 to 2009 in all industries, with a very low average annual value across all periods: the employment growth rate for all industries was 0.28%, with the growth rates for manufacturing industries at −0.1% and non-manufacturing industries at 0.4%. In contrast, capital stock maintained a relatively high growth rate in both manufacturing and non-manufacturing industries from the 1980s through the 2000s. Across all measurement periods, the average annual growth rate of capital stock was 2.85% for all industries, 2.27% for manufacturing industries, and 3.18% for non-manufacturing industries. These observed trends in employment and capital stock indicate a change in the industrial structure over the measurement periods, from a labor-intensive structure toward a capital-intensive one. The average annual growth rate of social overhead capital was high in the 1980s (5.08%) and in the 1990s (3.79%). However, owing to a reduction in public spending that is partly attributed to government efforts to increase its fiscal health, the rate fell sharply in the 2000s (0.89%).

4.3.3 Concerns About Agglomeration Economies Estimation

In the traditional analysis of agglomeration economies, it is necessary to use a production function with a specific functional form. Two potential concerns are raised when a production function is estimated (Graham 2009, Combes and Gobillon 2015), which can be avoided by employing the Solow residual.

4.3.3.1 Endogeneity

The first potential problem raised by estimating a specific production function is the endogeneity of the agglomeration effect. When estimating the agglomeration effect from a production function, it is generally assumed that the error term is distributed independently from the regression variables. The presence of endogeneity could violate this assumption, because it implies that the element increasing the agglomeration effect is associated with productivity, and may thus be an endogenous variable. For example, hoping to succeed in business, corporate management seeks the region that will increase productivity the most. As a result, locations that increase productivity are expected to become agglomeration areas with a high concentration of employment (population) and businesses, because businesses move to such areas. If this process holds true, high productivity could breed high agglomeration as those elements move into productive areas. The determinants of the direction of this causal connection are not well developed in agglomeration theory. Nonetheless, agglomeration may be determined from productivity.

The endogeneity problem of agglomeration has recently been studied by Ciccone and Hall (1996), Ciccone (2002), Henderson (2003), and Rosenthal and Strange (2005). Henderson (2003) estimates agglomeration economies using firm level panel data, with the possibility of using the generalized method of moments (GMM) estimates. Other studies respond to the endogeneity problem by adopting a two-stage least squares regression method and employing instrumental variables. Ciccone and Hall (1996) use the long-term lag of population density as an instrumental variable. Their argument is that the density we observe today is determined by the influence of past population density patterns that are not correlated with the current productivity level. The problem with this approach is that it requires detailed spatial information relating to density that spans past decades, and these data are especially hard to retrieve for small spatial areas. Ciccone (2002) considers the total land area of the EU as an instrumental variable, while Rosenthal and Strange (2005) use data on the geographic features that do not correlate with productivity.

Nonetheless, the potential endogeneity bias in the agglomeration estimates in previous studies appears to be small. Specifically, Ciccone and Hall (1996) and Ciccone (2002) note that the estimated value of agglomeration economies using instrumental variables differs only slightly from the least-squares estimate. Rosenthal and Strange (2005) also conclude that the influence of the endogenous regression coefficient is limited. Henderson (2003) also reports that the correlation between the endogenous regression coefficient and the error terms is not important. Thus, it can be concluded that recent studies have not found strong evidence of an endogeneity bias. Meanwhile, this problem can be avoided in determining the degree of agglomeration by using the Solow residual measurements rather than a production function with specific factors that represent externalities.

4.3.3.2 Input/Output Element Measuring Errors

The second potential problem when estimating agglomeration economies relates to measurement errors of the input and output variables. Production is often used as a proxy variable for output, which includes output price and volume. Input variables tend to reflect only two elements, namely labor and capital, and there is no precise information about the range of "quality" or "frequency of use" of these elements. Ideally, one should break inputs down into land, raw materials, and energy, but the related data are usually not easy to access. In addition, capital is measured in monetary values, expressed in Japanese yen, not in physical values like labor input, which could cause another measurement problem. In practice, it is possible that the price of capital inputs, especially the price of land and buildings, has a positive correlation with the city or the regional scale.

Since the ideal proxy variables for inputs are difficult to obtain empirically, this study alleviates these potential problems by considering utilization rates of labor and capital, namely working hours for labor and capital utilization for capital. Because of data constraints, we do not consider any variable relating to input quality, which is hard to concisely express.

4.4 Results

Table 4.2 shows the fundamental statistics for the Solow residual measurements. The table indicates that the mean value for all industries in 1980 is 0.4499, with a maximum value of 0.9877 for Tokyo, and a minimum value of 0.1758 for Fukui. The mean values remained stable during the 1980s and 1990s, but increased after 2000 and then fell significantly in 2009. Tokyo consistently presented the maximum value throughout the observation period. Moreover, this value gradually increased over time, expanding the regional disparities of the Solow residual. Table 4.2 also shows a different trend for manufacturing industries when compared with all industries. That is, for manufacturing industries, the Solow residual increased throughout the observation period. In 1980, the mean value was 0.2605, but by 2009 it had increased significantly to 0.7285. The Solow residual for Tokyo (the maximum value) also increased substantially. The minimum value also increased, but the maximum value grew more, indicating an increasing difference between the two values.

It should be noted that the trends observed in non-manufacturing and manufacturing industries differ over the period. The mean value of the Solow residual for non-manufacturing industries remained practically unchanged during the 1980s and 1990s, and then fell substantially in 2000 because of a decline in technological progress in those industries. Even the maximum value declined from 0.9569 to 0.8405. Non-manufacturing industries experienced declining production efficiency over the same period because of the slow pace of change in those industrial structures. Therefore, gains from productivity decreased in non-manufacturing industries. On the other hand, manufacturing industries strengthened their international competitiveness through aggressive R&D investments in tandem with globalization.

The size of agglomeration economies, measured as economies of scale in this study, are estimated using the Solow residual measurements. Specifically, assuming a constant rate of regional technical progress, Eq. (4.2) can be reformulated as follows:

Table 4.2 Fundamental statistics for the Solow residual

	All industries				Manufacturing industries				Non-manufacturing industries			
	1980	1990	2000	2009	1980	1990	2000	2009	1980	1990	2000	2009
Mean	0.4499	0.4364	0.4776	0.4044	0.2605	0.3333	0.4946	0.7285	0.5436	0.5094	0.5158	0.4013
Standard deviation	0.1512	0.1515	0.1453	0.1659	0.2120	0.2330	0.2984	0.3763	0.1517	0.1600	0.1401	0.1685
Max	0.9877	1.0530	0.9566	0.9925	1.0150	1.3627	1.6796	2.1562	0.9569	0.9835	0.8453	0.8405
Min	0.1758	0.1970	0.2287	0.0679	–0.2510	–0.1562	–0.1347	0.1143	0.2027	0.1844	0.2258	0.0085

Table 4.3 Estimation results – Eq. (4.3)

	All industries	Manufacturing industries	Non-manufacturing industries
α_0	–0.0061	0.0138	–0.0062
	(0.0014)**	(0.0031)**	(0.0013)**
γ	1.1135	1.0601	1.0313
	(0.0301)**	(0.0638)**	(0.0264)**
$\bar{R}^2$	0.0104	0.0007	0.0010

Note: The standard error is listed within parentheses
** Significance at the 1% level; * significance at the 5% level

$$SR_{jt} = \alpha_0 + (\gamma - 1)\Delta K_{jt} + \varepsilon_{jt}. \tag{4.3}$$

Table 4.3 shows the results from the estimation of Eq. (4.3) obtained through the pooling least-squares method (Plain OLS).

All regression coefficients are statistically significant at the 1% level. The strength of agglomeration economies, γ, measuring economies of scale, is 1.1135 for all industries. Because γ is greater than one, it is possible to say that economies of scale exist in our sample. A comparison between manufacturing and non-manufacturing industries shows that agglomeration economies are marginally higher for the former: the regression coefficients are 1.0601 and 1.0313, respectively.

Next, we examine the impact of social overhead capital on economies of agglomeration. Kanemoto et al. (1996) estimate a specific production function to examine the effect of social overhead capital, which they consider to be an element that enhances economies of agglomeration. We compare our results with theirs.

When we assume $\gamma = g(G)$, the productivity effect of social overhead capital can be measured as follows:

$$SR_{jt} = \alpha_0 + \left(\delta G_{jt} - 1\right)\Delta K_{jt} + \varepsilon_{jt}. \tag{4.4}$$

Table 4.4 shows the estimation results from the pooling least-squares method (Plain OLS) for Eq. (4.4).

For all industries, the coefficient of social overhead capital, δ, is 0.0708, with statistical significance at the 1% level. Kanemoto et al. (1996) found a lower coefficient (0.026), and thus smaller economies of scale for large metropolitan areas. The results of this study exhibit a relatively large influence of social overhead capital on productivity when compared with Kanemoto et al. (1996), mainly because we adopt the Solow residual approach and use prefecture level data. The differences suggest that availability of social overhead capital has a major influence on production activity at the prefecture level but not at the metropolitan level. Social overhead capital has a slightly higher impact on manufacturing industries (0.0681) than on non-manufacturing industries (0.0649). This suggests that providing social overhead capital has a larger marginal impact on total factor productivity

Table 4.4 Estimation results – Eq. (4.4)

	All industries	Manufacturing industries	Non-manufacturing industries
α_0	–0.0069	0.0127	–0.0065
	(0.0014)**	(0.0031)**	(0.0014)**
δ	0.0708	0.0681	0.0649
	(0.0019)**	(0.0040)**	(0.0017)**
$\bar{R}^2$	0.0172	0.0077	0.0018

Note: The standard error is listed within parentheses
** Significance at the 1% level; * significance at the 5% level

for manufacturing industries. The difference between manufacturing and non-manufacturing industries can be attributed to the unique characteristics of manufacturing industries. Specifically, they exchange more intermediate goods with other regions during the production process than non-manufacturing industries do. Thus, it is expected that the level of social infrastructure development in a region (e.g., roads) is positively correlated with the impact of social overhead capital on manufacturing industries' productivity. For example, industrial manufacturing areas are often located near highway interchanges, because these industries depend on highway infrastructure for their businesses. In contrast, non-manufacturing industries, particularly service industries, usually complete production of goods within the region. The exchange of intermediate goods with other regions is extremely low when compared with manufacturing industries, which suggests that social overhead capital is unlikely to have the same impact on production activity for non-manufacturing industries as for manufacturing industries.

Table 4.5 evaluates the degree of agglomeration across 11 regions. The evaluation is based on social overhead capital data at the prefecture level. The results of agglomeration are greater than one for all industries in all regions; therefore, we conclude that economies of scale exist. In 2009, the Greater Tokyo Area presents the highest value (1.3393); Kansai has the second highest value (1.3171); and Chubu the third highest (1.3097), indicating that large metropolitan areas show higher values. In other regions, values are comparatively low, particularly in Okinawa, which has the lowest value of 1.1499. However, agglomeration economies increased in those regions between 1980 and 2009. This trend was strongest in Okinawa, followed by Hokuriku and Shikoku, indicating that agglomeration economies strengthened in rural areas more than in large metropolitan areas. The results show that investments in social overhead capital during the observation period were distributed more favorably toward rural areas than large metropolitan areas. Indeed, rural areas received excessive investment in social overhead capital under the government's regional policy. This investment, which aimed to strengthen regional economic activity, resulted in stronger economies of agglomeration. Agglomeration economies were greater for manufacturing industries than for non-manufacturing industries in all regions. Thus, it is evident that social overhead

Table 4.5 Economies of scale considering social overhead capital effects

	All industries		Manufacturing industries		Non-manufacturing industries	
	2009	$\Delta\delta G$	2009	$\Delta\delta G$	2009	$\Delta\delta G$
Hokkaido	1.2763	0.0708	1.2273	0.0681	1.1685	0.0648
Tohoku	1.3092	0.0714	1.2589	0.0687	1.1987	0.0654
Kita-Kanto	1.2564	0.0732	1.2081	0.0704	1.1503	0.0670
Greater Tokyo Area	1.3393	0.0552	1.2878	0.0531	1.2262	0.0505
Chubu	1.3097	0.0677	1.2594	0.0651	1.1991	0.0620
Hokuriku	1.2202	0.0749	1.1733	0.0720	1.1172	0.0686
Kansai	1.3171	0.0639	1.2665	0.0614	1.2059	0.0585
Chugoku	1.2717	0.0696	1.2228	0.0670	1.1643	0.0637
Shikoku	1.2289	0.0742	1.1817	0.0713	1.1251	0.0679
Kyushu	1.3047	0.0719	1.2546	0.0691	1.1946	0.0658
Okinawa	1.1499	0.1085	1.1058	0.1043	1.0528	0.0993

Note: Hokkaido: Hokkaido
Tohoku: Aomori, Iwate, Miyagi, Akita, Yamagata, Fukushima, and Niigata
Kita-Kanto: Ibaraki, Tochigi, Gunma, and Yamanashi
Greater Tokyo Area: Saitama, Chiba, Tokyo, and Kanagawa
Chubu: Nagano, Gifu, Shizuoka, Aichi, and Mie
Hokuriku: Toyama, Ishikawa, and Fukui
Kansai: Shiga, Kyoto, Osaka, Hyogo, Nara, and Wakayama
Chugoku: Tottori, Shimane, Okayama, Hiroshima, and Yamaguchi
Shikoku: Tokushima, Kagawa, Ehime, and Koch
Kyushu: Fukuoka, Saga, Nagasaki, Kumamoto, Oita, Miyazaki, and Kagoshima
Okinawa: Okinawa

capital investment played an important role in improving the productivity of manufacturing industries and thus enhancing regional economic growth.

4.5 Conclusion

This chapter examined the influence of agglomeration economies on regional economic growth. Specifically, this study attempted to determine the degree of agglomeration economies in Japanese prefectures using Solow residual measurements to construct economies of scale, rather than using a production function that can be accompanied by specification error bias. The findings indicate that economies of scale exist in Japanese prefectures in the industrial sector overall, and in both manufacturing and non-manufacturing industries.

Furthermore, this study investigated the effects of social overhead capital on acceleration of agglomeration economies. The results show that social overhead capital had a significantly positive effect on productivity growth, which was greater for manufacturing industries than for non-manufacturing industries. Moreover, this study examines the varying degrees of agglomeration across Japanese regions using social overhead capital data. The results indicate that agglomeration economies were strongest in large metropolitan areas in Japan, particularly in the Greater Tokyo Area, followed by Kansai and Chubu. However, from the review of the annual changes in the robustness of agglomeration economies, it emerges that the rural areas, as compared to large metropolitan areas, had stronger growth in agglomeration over time, especially Okinawa, Hokuriku, and Shikoku. These larger changes could be attributed to the disproportionate investment in social overhead capital in rural areas.

In conclusion, economies of agglomeration play a significant role in regional growth and development. Investment in social overhead capital is particularly critical for increasing the degree of agglomeration. Past Japanese national land plans have diverted a significant amount of public spending to rural areas with low agglomeration. As a result, disparities in the level of economic activity among regions have been corrected by social overhead capital investments. However, many superfluous, ineffectively utilized roads, harbors, and airports have been built in rural areas. To increase economic efficiency with limited resources, targeted investments are increasingly important, which implies that Japan should increase its allocation of social overhead capital investments to large cities with robust agglomeration economies.

In the future, further investigation on how agglomeration economies affect inter-regional trade will be necessary, because both inter-regional collaboration and more open regional economies are essential for increased regional development. Specifically, a method for quantitatively examining the extent to which agglomerations in large metropolitan areas affect local and other regions (i.e., inter-regional trade) will be required.

References

Beeson PE, Husted S. Patterns and determinants of productive efficiency in state manufacturing. J Reg Sci. 1989;29(1):15–28.

Ciccone A. Agglomeration effects in Europe. Eur Econ Rev. 2002;46(2):213–27.

Ciccone A, Hall R. Productivity and the density of economic activity. Am Econ Rev. 1996;86(1):54–70.

Combes PP, Gobillon L. The empirics of agglomeration economies. In: Duranton G, Henderson JV, Strange W, editors. Handbook of regional and urban economics, volume 5A. Amsterdam: Elsevier; 2015. p. 247–348.

Driffield N, Munday M. Foreign manufacturing, regional agglomeration and technical efficiency in UK industries: a stochastic production frontier approach. Reg Stud. 2001;35(5):391–9.

Fujita M, Thisse J. Economics of agglomeration. Cambridge: Cambridge University Press; 2002.

Glaeser EL, Kolko J, Saiz A. Consumer city. J Econ Geogr. 2001;1(1):27–50.

Graham DJ. Identifying urbanization and localization externalities in manufacturing and service industries. Pap Reg Sci. 2009;88(1):63–84.

Henderson JV. Marshall's scale economies. J Urban Econ. 2003;53(1):1–28.

Kanemoto Y, Ohkawara T, Suzuki T. Agglomeration economies and a test for optimal city sizes in Japan. J Jpn Int Econ. 1996;10(4):379–98.

Mitra A. Agglomeration economies as manifested in technical efficiency at the firm level. J Urban Econ. 1999;45(3):490–500.
Mitra A. Total factor productivity growth and urbanization economies: a case of Indian industries. Rev Urban Reg Dev Stud. 2000;12(2):97–108.
Otsuka A. Regional determinants of total factor productivity in Japan: stochastic frontier analysis. Ann Reg Sci. 2017;58(3):579–96.
Otsuka A, Goto M. Regional policy and the productive efficiency of Japanese industries. Reg Stud. 2013;49(4):518–31.
Otsuka A, Goto M. Agglomeration economies in Japanese industries: the Solow residual approach. Ann Reg Sci. 2015;54(2):401–16.
Otsuka A, Goto M, Sueyoshi T. Industrial agglomeration effects in Japan: productive efficiency, market access, and public fiscal transfer. Pap Reg Sci. 2010;89(4):819–40.
Otsuka A, Goto M, Sueyoshi T. Cost-efficiency of Japanese local governments: effects of decentralization and regional integration. Reg Stud Reg Sci. 2014;1(1):207–20.
Rosenthal S, Strange W. Evidence on the nature and sources of agglomeration economies. In: Henderson JV, Thisse JF, editors. Handbook of regional and urban economics, volume 4. Amsterdam: Elsevier; 2004.
Rosenthal S, Strange W. The attenuation of human capital spillovers: a Manhattan skyline approach. Working Paper, Syracuse University; 2005.
Tveteras R, Battese GE. Agglomeration externalities, productivity, and technical inefficiency. J Reg Sci. 2006;46(4):605–25.

Chapter 5
Dynamic Externalities: Theory and Empirical Analysis

Abstract This chapter focuses on dynamic externalities that are a source of competitive advantages, and reviews the related empirical studies. Research on technical-knowledge spillover, the core of dynamic externalities, is being widely conducted, mainly in the field of industrial organization theory. However, there are few empirical studies that have considered technical-knowledge spillover from the viewpoint of industrial agglomeration. Some studies estimate the extent and type of dynamic externalities, and find evidence consistent with dynamic externalities. Despite the different data sources used, methodologies are similar. This chapter reviews the main methodologies of dynamic externalities, and discusses empirical analysis issues of previous studies.

Keywords Dynamic externalities • Agglomeration economies • Solow residual • Total factor productivity

5.1 Introduction

The role of innovation and technical knowledge spillover in economic growth has been discussed as a central issue within endogenous growth theory. It has been argued that technical-knowledge spillover is indispensable for sustainable economic growth, and that the accumulation of technical knowledge is the source of economic growth. Arrow (1962) and Romer (1986) argued for the importance of technical knowledge from R&D investment and learning, experience effects, and human capital, while Lucas (1988) pointed to their importance in urban areas. In addition, Jacobs (1969) noted as important the fact that the agglomeration of diverse economic agents in urban areas creates contact benefits, while conversely, Porter (1990, 1998, 2000) argued that competition and cooperation between economic agents promotes the creation of innovation and technical-knowledge spillover.

Each of these studies indicates that, in addition to the resources accumulated within firms, productivity growth also relies on the resources accumulated at

This chapter is based on Otsuka (2004) "Dynamic externalities of industrial agglomeration: A survey," published in Okayama Economic Review (Vol. 35, No. 4, pp. 27–50, in Japanese).

A. Otsuka, *A New Perspective on Agglomeration Economies in Japan*,
New Frontiers in Regional Science: Asian Perspectives 20,
DOI 10.1007/978-981-10-6490-6_5

their locations. In other words, the accumulation of substitutable material and human resources enables producers to easily secure those resources when they need them, which contributes to productivity growth. Also, the formation of inter-firm networks affects the productivity of producers through inter-firm cooperation. Because the region's historical production environment contributes to an accumulation of technical knowledge not easily accessed from other areas, a formed locational competitive advantage has sustainability. The view of Porter (1990, 1998, 2000) is that a competitive advantage formed by a region's production environment is defined as one created by a location.

This chapter focuses on the dynamic externalities that are a source of competitive advantages, and reviews related empirical studies. Study on technical-knowledge spillover is being widely conducted, although mainly in the field of industrial organization theory. There have also been several recent empirical studies aiming to verify the effects of technical-knowledge spillover that accompanies R&D activities. Conversely, there is little empirical study that has considered technical-knowledge spillover from the viewpoint of industrial agglomeration. Since it was discussed in Glaeser et al. (1992), only a few studies are noted in reviews by McDonald (1997) and Carlino and Kerr (2015). To supplement this, this chapter reviews the principal empirical studies, and discusses the issues with the empirical analyses in previous studies.

Section 5.2 introduces the theories on dynamic externalities. Section 5.3 reviews previous studies, and uses the analytical approaches to arrange the points of discussions. Section 5.4 describes the issues with the empirical analyses in previous studies. The final section summarizes this chapter.

5.2 Theoretical Background

Dynamic externalities are the various conditions that continuously affect producers in a production environment accompanying the formation of an urban area. Specifically, they indicate that region-specific material resources, human resources, and technical knowledge accumulate over time, and that they have pathway-dependent effects on the producers in that region. What is important here is the creation and use of technical knowledge because technical-knowledge spillover plays an important role in realizing sustainable growth in urban areas (Glaeser et al. 1992).

A theoretical basis for dynamic externalities can be derived from endogenous growth theory. Endogenous growth theory is a theory that searches for the endogenous determinants of the steady-state growth rate that is discussed in neoclassical growth theory. It is assumed that technological progress is determined endogenously, and the existence of human capital is considered as one of its factors. Barro (1991), Lucas (1988), and Romer (1986) showed that when the marginal productivity of human capital does not decrease, it becomes a source of long-term economic growth. Also, Romer (1990) and Grossman and Helpman (1991) proved that technological progress is not determined exogenously, but through firms' profit-maximizing behavior.

Duranton and Puga (2004) attempted to provide a micro-foundation for dynamic externalities based on the argument of Lucas (1988). As a result, they clarified that the steady-state production growth rate in a region is determined by the historical factors of that region. The creation and accumulation of technical knowledge not only makes high levels of productivity possible, it also allows for sustainable growth of productivity through technical-knowledge spillover. The primary researchers in this field, such as Romer and Lucas, also pointed out that, in addition to productivity level, the external effects from technical-knowledge spillover are important in realizing productivity growth in urban areas.[1]

Since technical-knowledge spillover is an extremely vague concept, it is difficult to model. According to Glaeser et al. (1992), the theory of dynamic externalities is in fact composed of three theories – "Marshall-Arrow-Romer's theory (MAR's theory), "Jacobs' theory," and "Porter's theory," – and they are classified as different from each other in the following two dimensions. The first dimension is whether technical-knowledge spillover occurs between firms in the same industry or firms in different industries. The second is the question of whether the market structure that affects technical-knowledge spillover is competitive or monopolistic. In other words, the question is whether technological progress is promoted by a "monopoly" or an "oligopoly" because the funds allocated to R&D investment are supplemented, or that the ceaseless pressure to competition promotes technological progress.

The first dimension pertains to where technical knowledge spillover occurs, and MAR's theory focuses on the role of technical-knowledge spillover that occurs between firms within the same industry. This spillover was first pointed to as an external effect by Marshall (1890), and Arrow (1962) subsequently attempted to formulate it. It then became the focus of attention following Romer's thesis (1986). In this theory, agglomeration of firms is important for a specific industry to develop new products, improve existing products, and to promote improvements to production systems. Productivity is also improved by the presence of highly trained workers who share the same problems and tasks. The technical knowledge accumulated by one firm spills over, without any form of recompense, to other firms through patent disclosure, transfer of intellectual workers between firms, business conferences, meetings, vocational training, imitation, or reverse engineering. The transmission of technical knowledge can be expected to further accelerate if firms are close to each other. Therefore, it has been suggested that industries that are specialized in a region, receiving the many benefits from the transfer of knowledge within the industry achieve rapid growth, and the urban areas where these industries are located also grow rapidly.

---

[1]However, Krugman (1991) is an exception. Although he recognized the importance of technical-knowledge spillover, he argued that the effects of the labor market and the intermediate goods market are linked to the dynamic aspect of agglomeration economies.

Conversely, Jacobs' theory considers that the geographical proximity of various industries promotes innovation, rather than geographical proximity of firms in the same industry. It considers diversity rather than uniformity of the industrial structure to be more important for the creation of new products, and that a geographical agglomeration of various industries stimulates the creation of new ideas. It particularly emphasizes the effects of the mutual exchange of ideas among firms conducting different work, and it considers that the agglomeration of people with different skills strengthens the transmission of ideas.[2]

Porter's theory focuses on so-called industrial clusters.[3] There are customers with high levels of demand in industrial clusters, and the presence of this type of customer encourages innovation, like ideas for new products and improvements to existing products. Also, the agglomeration of and close cooperation among related industries, supporting industries, specialized organizations, and various other types of organizations not only provides the complementarities that are necessary for innovation, it also makes it easier to incorporate and utilize the technical knowledge from other industries for aspects such as new technologies, operations, and new-product development.

The second dimension pertains to the market environment that promotes technical-knowledge spillover. Jacobs' theory and Porter's theory emphasize the point that competition strengthens innovation. Jacobs (1969) argues that competition speeds up the adoption of technologies, but that, in contrast, a monopoly restricts alternative methods and production. In addition, Porter (1990) stresses that competition pressure becomes an incentive for innovation. He argues that the ceaseless competition between firms promotes the adoption, imitation and improvement of innovations made by others, which becomes the driving force behind productivity growth.

Conversely, MAR's theory considers that a monopolistic market is preferable to a competitive market (Romer 1986) for promotion of technical-knowledge spillover. A regional monopoly restricts the flow of ideas to the outside and makes it possible for innovators to internalize externalities. The theory particularly emphasizes the possibility that the pace of innovation will be delayed when patent rights have not been secured. In other words, if the patent rights have not been secured, innovators are aware that their ideas may be imitated by these around them without any form of compensation, and the incentive to invest in activities that create externalities, such as investment in R&D, is lost. Therefore, if innovators have exclusive rights to their own ideas, or at a minimum only a few agents will soon imitate their ideas, it is expected that the pace of innovation will accelerate.

---

[2]Even as the shift to IT has progressed, it is known that face-to-face communication remains important (Gaspar and Glaeser 1998).

[3]An industrial cluster has been defined as "geographic concentrations of interconnected companies, specialized suppliers, service providers, firms in related industries, and associated institutions (e.g., universities, standards agencies, trade associations) in a particular field that compete but also cooperate." (Porter 1990).

Table 5.1 Theories of dynamic externalities

		Market structure	
		Strong competition	Weak competition
Occurrence of technical-knowledge spillover	Within industries (specialization)	Porter-type external effects Porter (1990, 1998, 2000)	MAR-type external effects Marshall (1890), Arrow (1962), and Romer (1986)
	Between industries (diversity)	Jacobs-type external effects Jacobs (1969)	–

Schumpeter had already noted the importance of a monopoly or oligopoly to innovation (Schumpeter 1934). He expected that those with an entrepreneurial spirit would acquire the monopoly profits from new ideas. In other words, the desire to secure a monopoly position becomes the driving force behind innovation. Furthermore, in the sense of increasing the certainty of innovation, he noted that many modern innovations occur within those major firms that can endure a monopolistic competition environment. The thought is that innovation would not occur unless an organizational cohesive force that transcends the abilities of individuals is introduced into R&D activities. However, given the existence of venture capital, it is not realistic to say that only major firms are responsible for innovation, and the debate over whether a monopoly or oligopoly environment is necessary for innovation has still not been resolved.

Table 5.1 summarizes the differences between these three main theories of dynamic externalities. MAR's and Porter's theories emphasize that external effects occur between firms within the same industry, and that these external effects are internalized within the industry as whole.[4] Jacobs' theory focuses on external effects occurring between firms in different industries, which are then internalized within the entire relevant urban area. In either case, the productivity of producers grows sustainably due to the internalization of external effects. Porter's and Jacobs' theories stress the role played by competition in this productivity growth, but in contrast, MAR's theory emphasizes the role of a regional monopoly environment.

[4]It is important to note that the spatial clustering explained by Porter's theory cannot be uniformly defined. In many cases, the industrial clusters do not have a uniform definition in terms of scope and are made up of industries that belong to different standard industry classifications. Strictly speaking, the definition of a cluster is determined by the strength of the linkage between industries, and it is considered that these are rarely consistent with the standard industry classifications. In the conventional classifications relating to manufacturing industries and service industries, the classifications are extremely vague when considering the linkages between industries, so it is difficult to accurately ascertain the linkages between them. Also, even if discussing only one industry, the linkages that exist between industries cannot be seen, so it is considered that the effects that clusters have on competition will not be considered (Porter 1990, 1998, 2000).

5.3 Features and Issues in Previous Studies

5.3.1 *Analytical Approach*

The previous research on dynamic externalities is broadly categorized into two approaches based on the differences in their analytical methods. The "employment growth approach" adopts the neoclassical growth model for employment growth. This was the approach used by Glaeser et al. (1992), in which dynamic externalities are measured as external effects to employment growth. The "total factor productivity approach" second uses total factor productivity. This is an analytical approach typified by Beeson (1987, 1990), and it has been adopted by researchers such as Dekle (2002) and Henderson (2003). Highly aggregated data is applied to the aggregated industry sectors of regions in both approaches, but Henderson (1997, 2003) recently used microdata to conduct an empirical analysis at the plant level.

5.3.1.1 The Employment Growth Approach

The employment growth approach was introduced by Glaeser et al. (1992). In this approach, firms located in a certain region are assumed to have a value-added production function (5.1).

$$V_t = A_t f(L_t), \tag{5.1}$$

where V_t is the firm's value added in period t, and L_t is the labor input in period t. A_t is the level of technology in period t. The assumptions are that firm face perfect competition and possess production technologies for constant returns to scale. Therefore, it is considered that each firm, with output price P_t and labor price P_{Lt} as given, maximizes (5.2).

$$P_t A_t f(L_t) - P_{Lt} L_t. \tag{5.2}$$

Alongside the standardization of P_t as 1, from the first-order condition for profit maximization, the following formula is established.

$$A_t f'(L_t) = P_{Lt}. \tag{5.3}$$

With regards to (5.3), taking the logarithmic difference to represent the growth rate term, the formula becomes as follows.

$$\ln\left(\frac{A_t}{A_{t-1}}\right) = \ln\left(\frac{P_{Lt}}{P_{Lt-1}}\right) - \ln\left(\frac{f'(L_t)}{f'(L_{t-1})}\right). \tag{5.4}$$

Here, the level of technology A_t is comprised of two parts – the nationwide, universal element $A_{national,t}$, and the local element $A_{local,t}$ – and it is assumed that each independently affects the firm's technological level (Glaeser et al. 1992). Therefore, A_t is formulated as follows.

$$A_t = A_{local,t} A_{national,t}.$$

The rate of technological progress, as the sum of nationwide and local technological growth, is expressed as follows.

$$\ln\left(\frac{A_t}{A_{t-1}}\right) = \ln\left(\frac{A_{local,t}}{A_{local,t-1}}\right) + \ln\left(\frac{A_{national,t}}{A_{national,t-1}}\right). \tag{5.5}$$

Local technological growth, which depends on the local production environment from its nature of being local-area specific, is expressed as follows.

$$\ln\left(\frac{A_{local,t}}{A_{local,t-1}}\right) = h(\mathbf{Z}_{t-1}) + e_t. \tag{5.6}$$

$h(\cdot)$ is the function expressing the local area's historical production environment and $\mathbf{Z}$ is the characteristic vector expressing the local area's production environment.[5] Also, e_t is the error term that includes other elements.

Variables expressing "specialization," "diversity," "market conditions," and "initial conditions" are used as the characteristic vector. MAR's theory and Porter's theory interpret industrial specialization as bringing about productivity growth, but in contrast, Jacobs' theory interprets the diversity of production activities as promoting technical-knowledge spillover. In addition, the hypothesis that the greater the competition in the market environment, the more innovation is accelerated, is supported by both Jacobs' theory and Porter's theory, but not by MAR's theory.

Next, on specifying the function $f(L_t)$ as $f(L_t) = L_t^{1-\alpha}$ $(0 < \alpha < 1)$, the following formula is obtained by combining (5.4), (5.5), and (5.6).

$$\alpha \ln\left(\frac{L_t}{L_{t-1}}\right) = -\ln\left(\frac{P_{Lt}}{P_{Lt-1}}\right) + \ln\left(\frac{A_{national,t}}{A_{national,t-1}}\right) + h(\mathbf{Z}_{t-1}) + e_t. \tag{5.7}$$

The empirical analysis using the employment growth approach uses mainly (5.7). (5.7) relates a firm's employment growth rate to the scale of technical knowledge. In the estimations, technical-knowledge spillover is often regarded as being constant over time.

[5]It is known that local areas' historical production environment has important effects on industries' locations (Rauch 1993b).

Table 5.2 Effects on the employment growth rates of urban industries (1956 to 1987)

Dependent variable	Estimated value	Standard errors
Constant	−0.513	(0.149)
Log (U.S. employment in 1987/U.S. employment in 1956) in the industry outside the city	1.148	(0.056)
Wage in the city-industry in 1956	0.027	(0.104)
Employment in the city-industry in 1956 (in millions)	−4.080	(1.073)
Dummy variable indicating presence in the south	0.378	(0.055)
(specialization) City-industry's share of city employment relative to industry's share of U.S. employment in 1956	−0.00799	(0.003)
(state of competition) Establishments per employee in the city-industry relative to establishments per employee in the U.S. industry in 1956	0.561	(0.057)
(diversity) City's other top five industries' share of total city employment in 1956	−0.913	(0.245)
Adjusted R^2	0.450	
Number of observations	1016	

Source: Table 3 in Glaeser et al. (1992)

Glaeser et al. (1992) analyzed urban industries in the United States from 1956 to 1987 (Table 5.2). They clarified that diversity of the industrial structure tends to have an important effect on employment growth. From their analysis, when diversity progresses by 1 point, employment growth of 0.913 of a point is realized. In addition, the degree of regional competition affects employment growth, and if competition increases by 1 point, this causes employment growth to rise by 0.561 of a point. However, the scale of regional specialization was not found to have a positive effect on employment growth and no result was obtained indicating that specialization contributes to growth. In conclusion, external effects based on MAR's theory, which predicts that technical-knowledge spillover within an industry leads to sustainable growth in a region, were not verified.

In the empirical study by Glaeser et al. (1992), because it is estimated that external effects are constant between sample industries, their interpretation was restricted by the fact that they could not consider the industrial product cycle hypothesis that external effects are only important when new products are introduced. Henderson et al. (1995) focused on this point, and conducted a complementary analysis for the urban manufacturing industries in the United States from 1970 to 1987. The objective of their analysis was to divide the industries into mature industries (capital-assets industries) and emerging industries (high-tech industries) and verify the industrial product cycle hypothesis. They took an overview of the locational distribution of the mature industries, noted that a constant specialization pattern could be observed, and explained this geographical adhesion using the

MAR externalities.[6] The analysis clarified that diverse production environments in urban areas contribute to employment growth in emerging industries, and that regional specialization contributes to employment growth in mature industries. In other words, they concluded that new goods are created in diversified urban areas. On the other hand, the production of mature goods tends to be conducted in specialized urban areas.

Other previous studies that adopted the employment growth approach include empirical studies on urban manufacturing industries in Mexico and Spain (Hanson 1998; Lucio et al. 2002). Both studies obtained the result that specialization exerts important effects on employment growth in urban manufacturing industries, but found no cases where the effects of diversity were realized. Studies on urban areas in Japan include Mano and Otsuka (2000), who clarified that external effects from regional specialization were weak over the analysis period. They observed dispersion of the distribution of industries over the period, indicating that the effects of congestion and intensification of locational competition with the service sector acted as a dispersing force for locations of manufacturing industries.

There has been a tendency to adopt this approach mainly in empirical analyses of cities and other urban areas, as capital input data is often not available. However, not considering capital input causes this excluded variable to introduce bias in the estimations of the dynamic externalities (Dekle 2002). In other words, if it is true that capital input growth significantly affects employment growth, not considering it creates the omitted-variable bias (OVB) in the estimation parameters for the dynamic externalities.[7] To begin with, employment growth tends to be strongly influenced by demand side factors related to the business cycle; thus, it is difficult to ascertain the supply-side effects. In this sense, it cannot be said that an employment growth approach is an appropriate one when ascertaining technical-knowledge spillover effects as a supply-side effect. In addition, if only labor input, is considered only labor-saving technological innovations can be ascertained and it becomes impossible to consider innovation from the accumulation of physical capital.[8] As stated by Glaeser et al. (1992) and Lucio et al. (2002), it is necessary to use the total factor productivity approach to consider the different types of technological progress.

[6]There are many studies that have verified the role played by technical-knowledge spillover in the locations of emerging industries (high-tech industries). For example, Jaffe et al. (1993) showed that in many cases, new patents will be created based on the existing patents in the surrounding area. Also, it is known that wages tend to be high in regions where human capital is accumulating (Rauch 1993a).

[7]Refer to Greene (2017) for the problems in estimate values that are caused by omitting important variables.

[8]Innovation includes "product innovation," such as the development of products, and "process innovation," such as improvements to manufacturing processes.

5.3.1.2 The Total Factor Productivity Approach

Originally, total factor productivity growth or the "Solow residual" represents the magnitude of technological progress in economic growth, and is defined as the residual obtained by deducting the growth rate of total input from the output growth rate (Solow 1957). The official production statistics do not reflect the quality of the labor force, the performance of capital equipment, the improvement of standards and quality of raw materials and intermediate input goods, the expansion of new goods and services, and so on as external effects. Therefore, in terms of the production function, the indirect and supplementary benefits from introducing new technologies must be measured as a rise in total factor productivity.

In empirical studies on total factor productivity, there have been attempts to explicitly incorporate these external effects into the production function. Caballero and Lyons (1990, 1992) developed a model that divided internal economies and external economies based on the value-added production function. Using data on manufacturing industries in the United States and four European countries, they clarified the existence of external effects on industrial production activities. Basu and Fernald (1995) pointed out that external effects are overestimated in Caballero and Lyons' model, which does not consider intermediate input goods, and attempted to formulize them based on the gross output production function. Burnside (1996), Oulton (1996), and Benarroch (1997) extended the model and provided various considerations on external effects. Each of these studies focused on external effects arising in the entire country, so each had the constraint of no difference in external effects among industries.

Beeson (1987, 1990) is the representative study for empirical studies that used total factor productivity at the urban and regional areas. Beeson (1987) targeted manufacturing industries at the state level in the United States and considered the relationship between industrial agglomerations and productivity growth, while Beeson (1990) provided additional considerations, using total factor productivity to explain the cause of long-term stagnation in manufacturing industries in metropolitan areas.

Deckle (2002) applied dynamic externalities to the discussion of total factor productivity in Beeson (1987, 1990). He developed an analytical approach where total factor productivity growth is measured as the Solow residual, and dynamic externalities are understood to be an element included in the Solow residual. First, a firm's value-added production function is obtained as follows.

$$V_t = A_t K_t^{\alpha} L_t^{1-\alpha}, \ 0 < \alpha < 1, \tag{5.8}$$

where V_t, K_t and L_t respectively express a firm's value added, capital input, and labor input in the period t. A_t is the production function's shift factor and represents the technological level in period t. It is also assumed that firms face perfect competition and have production technologies that provide constant returns to scale. Therefore, it is considered that each firm maximizes (5.9), with output price P_t, capital price P_{Kt}, and labor price P_{Lt} as given.

$$P_tV_t - P_{Kt}K_t - P_{Lt}L_t. \tag{5.9}$$

From the first-order condition for profit maximization,

$$\alpha = s^v_{Kt}, 1 - \alpha = s^v_{Lt},$$

where $s^v_{Kt} \equiv \frac{P_{Kt}K_t}{P_tV_t}, s^v_{Lt} \equiv \frac{P_{Lt}L_t}{P_tV_t}$, is established.

On taking the total differential of the value-added production function (5.8) and the logarithmic difference, it becomes as follows.

$$\begin{aligned} \ln\left(\frac{V_t}{V_{t-1}}\right) &= \ln\left(\frac{A_t}{A_{t-1}}\right) + \alpha \ln\left(\frac{K_t}{K_{t-1}}\right) + (1-\alpha)\ln\left(\frac{L_t}{L_{t-1}}\right) \\ &= \ln\left(\frac{A_t}{A_{t-1}}\right) + \left[s^v_{Kt}\ln\left(\frac{K_t}{K_{t-1}}\right) + s^v_{Lt}\ln\left(\frac{L_t}{L_{t-1}}\right)\right]. \end{aligned} \tag{5.10}$$

Here, using the definition of the Solow residual SR^v evaluated by value added, from (5.10),

$$\begin{aligned} \ln\left(\frac{SR^v_t}{SR^v_{t-1}}\right) &\equiv \ln\left(\frac{V_t}{V_{t-1}}\right) - \left[(1 - s^v_{Lt})\ln\left(\frac{K_t}{K_{t-1}}\right) + s^v_{Lt}\ln\left(\frac{L_t}{L_{t-1}}\right)\right] \\ &= \ln\left(\frac{A_t}{A_{t-1}}\right), \end{aligned} \tag{5.11}$$

is obtained. (5.11) shows that the Solow residual is consistent with the rate of technological progress.[9]

It is assumed that dynamic externalities are reflected in this Solow residual, and as the result, (5.11) is expressed as follows.

$$\ln\left(\frac{SR^v_t}{SR^v_{t-1}}\right) = h(\mathbf{Z}_{t-1}) + e_t. \tag{5.12}$$

Dekle (2002) applied this analytical approach to data on Japanese prefectures and conducted an empirical analysis (Table 5.3). According to the estimation results of (5.12), no result was obtained indicating that dynamic externalities were being actualized in the manufacturing industry. Productivity growth from specialization occurs in the financial industry, the service industry, and wholesale

[9]Strictly speaking, total factor productivity is not the same as the Solow residual (Hall 1990). Total factor productivity is the aggregate output divided by the aggregate input, and it does not assume either constant returns to scale from production technologies, producers' profit maximization, or a perfectly competitive market. Therefore, growth in total factor productivity is not necessarily consistent with the rate of technological progress.

Table 5.3 Effects on growth in total-factor productivity in local industry (1975–1995)

	Financial industry				Manufacturing industry				Service industry				Wholesale and retail industries			
Dependent variable	(1)	(2)	(3)	(4)	(1)	(2)	(3)	(4)	(1)	(2)	(3)	(4)	(1)	(2)	(3)	(4)
(Specialization) GDP per square kilometer	0.089	0.089		0.089	0.0022	0.0053		0.0049	0.04	0.04		0.05	0.041	0.041		0.022
	(3.3)	(3.5)		(2.6)	(0.2)	(0.5)		(0.5)	(2.4)	(2.4)		(1.88)	(5.4)	(5.3)		(0.37)
(Diversity) Herfindahl-Hirschman Index		–0.89				–0.58				–0.86				–0.17		
		(–1.5)				(–0.7)				(–1.19)				(–0.3)		
(State of Competition) GDP per establishment in the region-industry relative to GDP per establishment in Japan			0.14	–0.19			0.027	0.044			0.29	–0.33			0.45	0.27
			(1.4)	(–1.3)			(0.5)	(0.7)			(1.82)	(–1.53)			(4.2)	(1.7)

Source: Table 2 in Dekle (2002)
Note: The t-statistics are enclosed in parentheses

and retail industries, with the greatest effect in the financial industry. When specialization in the financial industry is increased by 1 point, total factor productivity goes up by 0.089 of a point. In the wholesale and retail industries, when local competition conditions are increased by 1 point, total factor productivity is raised by 0.45 of a point, and therefore the results indicate that local competition contributes to improved productivity. In conclusion, he argued that the industries that benefit from proximity are mainly non-manufacturing industries, and therefore industries such as the financial industry tend to become even more geographically concentrated. He emphasized that manufacturing industries, which hardly benefit from the effects of dynamic externalities, should continue to be geographically dispersed not only nationally, but internationally. This is the same conclusion as Mano and Otsuka (2000), who also argued for the geographical dispersion of the manufacturing industries.

5.3.2 Features of Previous Research

The previous studies on dynamic externalities have been primarily cross-sectional analyses using aggregated data of urban and regional areas with the goal of elucidating the characteristics of dynamic externalities. In any of the approaches, the dynamic externalities' analytical framework can be understood to be a simple application of an empirical-analysis framework for economic growth theory. An original version is obtained from the cross-country estimation formula shown below, which is called the Barro regression (1991).

$$x_{jt} - x_{j0} = \beta_0 + \beta_1 x_{j0} + \mathbf{Z}_{j0}\boldsymbol{\beta}_2.$$

x_{jt} represents the logarithmic value of the arbitrary variable X_{jt} in period t, that is, the employment level or total factor productivity β's are parameters to be estimated. $\mathbf{Z}_{j0}$ is the attributes vector that represents the local production environment. In the dynamic externalities' analytical framework, $\mathbf{Z}_{j0}$ is used as the indicator representing specialization and diversity, and local competition. With the effects of convergence controlled, the effect of local characteristics $\mathbf{Z}_{j0}$ on employment growth or total-factor productivity growth is estimated. However, in previous studies, the effects of convergence were strongly realized; for example, in the estimation results of Glaeser et al. (1992), the estimated value of the initial conditions was comparatively large.

There are various indices for specialization, diversity, and local competition contained in $\mathbf{Z}_{j0}$ but there is no unified consensus on them. The main ones are the location quotient (LQ) and the Hirschman-Herfindahl index (HHI).[10] LQ is an

[10]There are various indices beside the ones introduced here. This section introduces mainly indices which are used in typical empirical studies such as Glaeser et al. (1992).

index that represents the concentration and specialization of an industry, and the location quotient LQ_{ij} of industry i in region j is defined as follows,

$$LQ_{ij} = \frac{L_{ij}/\sum_i L_{ij}}{\sum_j L_{ij}/\sum_i \sum_j L_{ij}}.$$

L_{ij} is the number of employment in industry i in region j. Therefore, the numerator shows the employment share of industry i in region j, and the denominator expresses the employment share of industry i nationwide. If this value exceeds 1, this signifies that the employment share of industry i in that region is high compared to the nationwide share.

The Hirschman-Herfindahl index is often used as an index for diversity. The Hirschman-Herfindahl index HHI_j of region j is defined as follows,

$$HHI_j = \sum_i \left[\frac{L_{ij}}{\sum_i L_{ij}}\right]^2.$$

The interpretation is that diversity decreases the closer that HHI_j gets to 1, and conversely, diversity increases the closer HHI_j gets to 0. This index may be defined as follows, in a form where users do not include the share from their own industry (for example, Henderson 2003).

$$HHI_{kj} = \sum_{k \notin i} \left[\frac{L_{ij}}{\sum_i L_{ij}}\right]^2.$$

This operation is performed not to ascertain diversity from the viewpoint of the entire region, but to ascertain it from the viewpoint of the industry located in that region.

The relative number of establishments is often used as a scale that expresses whether a market is competitive or monopolistic. The CMP scale, introduced by Glaeser et al. (1992), which expresses the strength of local competition with the region as j and the industry as i, is defined as follows.

$$CMP_{ij} = \frac{N_{ij}/L_{ij}}{\sum_j N_{ij}/\sum_j L_{ij}}.$$

N_{ij} is the number of establishments in industry i in region j. When this index is above 1, the ratio of the number of establishments on a regional scale, which is evaluated by the number of employment, is relatively high compared to the average nationwide level. In other words, it signifies that the market is competitive.

5.3.3 Issues with Previous Studies

In terms of the analytical issues relating to previous studies, some of the issues relating to the employment growth approach were described above. At the risk of being repetitive, the two main points are as follows.

The first point relates to the micro foundations of the analytical approach. In previous studies, when measuring dynamic externalities, it was assumed that individual producers face perfect competition, have technologies that produce constant returns to scale, and maximize profits. However, for a Solow residual based on value-added SR^v that is measured assuming perfect competition and constant returns for production, as shown below, price markup μ and economies of scale γ correlate with the Solow residual, which they should not (Hall 1990).[11]

$$\begin{aligned} SR^v &\equiv dv - \left[\left(1 - s_L^v\right)dk + s_L^v dl\right] \\ &= da + s_L^v(\mu - 1)(dl - dk) + (\gamma - 1)dk, \end{aligned} \tag{5.13}$$

In this formula, the lower-case variables represent the growth rate (log difference). dv is value-added growth, and dk, dl, and da are capital input growth, labor input growth, and technological progress, respectively. In the event of imperfect competition and economies of scale, as $\mu > 1$ and $\gamma > 1$, (5.13) shows that the Solow residual overestimates technological progress.

Furthermore, as previous studies only considered capital and labor as inputs, systematic bias occurs by not considering intermediate input goods when using the Solow residual, (Basu and Fernald 1995).[12] The following relationship is established between the gross output based Solow residual SR and the value-added based Solow residual SR^v.[13]

$$SR^v = \frac{SR}{1 - s_M}, \tag{5.14}$$

where s_M is the intermediate input goods' factor distribution ratio; the intermediate input share. Equation 5.14 shows that the value-added based Solow residual tends to exceed the gross-output based Solow residual. Further, (5.14) shows that the gross-output based Solow residual and the value-added based Solow residual move differently according to the intermediate share.

Figure 5.1 and Table 5.4 show the trends in s_M in all manufacturing industries and the manufacturing industry two-digit classifications. In all manufacturing industries, as s_M declines over time, the value-added based Solow residual is highly

[11] Refer to the appendix for the derivation.

[12] In addition, a point to be aware of with regards to the data is the measurement of inputs. There are various ways of measuring them, including those that take into consideration the quality of capital, the capital utilization rate, the quality of labor, and working hours.

[13] Refer to the appendix for the derivation.

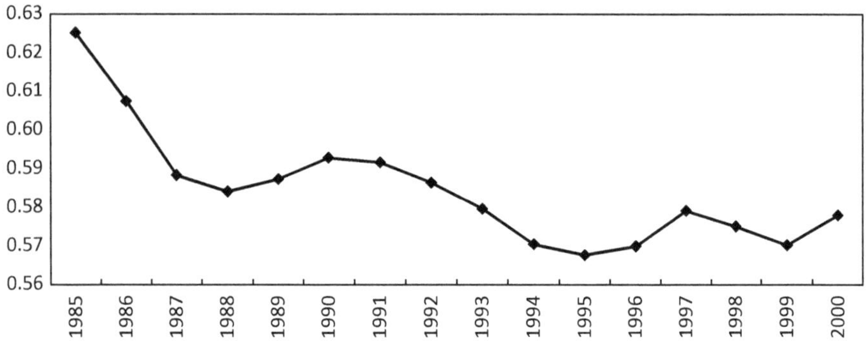

Fig. 5.1 Intermediate input share in the manufacturing industry
Source: METI's *Census of Manufacture*, Statistics for Establishments with 30 Employees or More
Note: The intermediate input share is calculated as the ratio of the intermediate inputs in the production

likely to move differently than the gross-output based Solow residual. The bias is especially evident in industries in which s_M decreased significantly over the observation period, such as petroleum and coal products and chemical and allied industries. However, as there are industries in which s_M hardly changes at all, such as transportation equipment and electrical machinery, equipment, and supplies, it is also inferred that, alongside the variations in s_M, systematic bias is different among the industries.

Second, from an econometrics viewpoint, we face the problems associated with endogenous and excluded variables when we measure dynamic externalities. All the variables relating to specialization, diversity, and local competition are understood to be not only causes of dynamic externalities, but also results. It is necessary to select proxy variables with exogeneity, or use instrumental variables to deal with the problem of endogeneity. In addition, because it is highly likely that the variables related to initial conditions and specialization will correlate with each other, it is very possible that the result obtained will be that neither is significant when they are simultaneously used. In consideration of this problem, there are also studies that use initial conditions as an index of specialization (Henderson et al. 1995; Mano and Otsuka 2000).

Further, in most of the previous studies, region-specific shocks to growth were not considered in the estimations. Therefore, variables not included in $\mathbf{Z}_{j0}$ or variables that cannot be observed might potentially affect industry growth. It is also expected that the local time invariant factors, such as the status of local natural endowments and the existence of local institutions, will affect industrial growth. Therefore, it can be argued that when measuring dynamic externalities, it is appropriate to consider individual effects (Dekle 2002; Henderson 2003).

Table 5.4 Intermediate input share in the manufacturing industry (%)

2-digit classifications	1985	1990	1995	2000	Changes from 1985 to 2000
Food	66.22	64.77	62.78	62.23	−3.99
Beverages, tobacco & feed	45.95	42.94	40.60	39.14	−6.81
Textile mill products	63.61	62.33	59.89	59.61	−4.00
Apparel & other finished products made from fabrics & similar materials	53.87	52.87	53.39	52.10	−1.77
Lumber & wood products	68.27	64.27	63.30	65.19	−3.09
Furniture & fixtures	58.98	58.02	57.64	56.48	−2.50
Pulp, paper & paper products	67.23	63.59	61.35	60.72	−6.51
Publishing, printing & allied industries	48.27	47.93	48.25	48.08	−0.19
Chemical & allied products	56.91	50.12	46.78	45.68	−11.23
Petroleum & coal products	82.36	72.83	63.00	61.46	−20.89
Plastic products	62.52	61.36	59.97	60.07	−2.45
Rubber products	57.00	54.82	51.12	51.64	−5.36
Leather tanning, leather products & fur skins	63.84	62.50	61.35	60.87	−2.96
Ceramic, stone & clay products	49.73	47.92	44.31	43.45	−6.28
Iron & steel	65.77	64.78	60.69	57.85	−7.91
Non-ferrous metals & products	73.10	69.71	67.67	68.54	−4.56
Fabricated metal products	58.11	58.02	56.73	56.38	−1.73
General machinery	58.69	58.94	59.22	59.23	0.54
Electrical machinery, equipment & supplies	60.10	60.37	59.95	59.94	−0.15
Transportation equipment	68.62	70.64	68.84	68.68	0.06
Precision instruments & machinery	57.17	55.73	57.72	57.37	0.20
Miscellaneous manufacturing industries	57.64	57.68	55.54	57.94	0.29
Manufacturing total	62.52	60.74	58.83	58.41	−4.11

Source: METI's *Census of Manufacture*, Statistics for Establishments with 30 employees or More
Note: The intermediate input share is calculated as the ratio of the intermediate inputs in the production

5.4 Developing the Analytical Approach

5.4.1 Research on the Timing of Dynamic Externalities

In many previous studies, structural changes were not taken into consideration for dynamic externalities, as the past was considered to have influence up to the present time. Henderson (1997, 2003) conducted an analysis focusing on the timing of dynamic externalities by introducing lag effects into the estimations. This study is characterized by separating the spillover effect of technical knowledge into static and dynamic aspects. "Static spillover" means the spillover from repeated experiences ascertaining market trends in urban areas and determining the choices for suppliers and sellers. In other words, the selection of suppliers and sellers and the responses to regulatory authorities at a plant immediately affect decision-making at other plants. On the other hand, "dynamic spillover" means spillover relating to decision-making that takes years to achieve. As the results of decision-making only diffuse slowly and locally, the effects appear with a lag. In other words, because of the problems of time and distance, or the opportunities for contact, a time lag occurs in the diffusion of information. Also, the process of the cumulative build-up of technical knowledge in an urban area depends not only on current economic activity at the location, but also the past, so it is considered that spillover effects occur with a lag.

In the analytical model of Henderson (2003), the following equation, which is a first-order approximation of the general production function from the Taylor expansion, is used.

$$\ln Y_t = \alpha \ln X_t + \sum_{s=0}^{2} \beta_s \ln Z_{t-s} + \ln T_t, \tag{5.15}$$

where Y_t represents the gross output in period t, while X_t is the aggregated production factor input in period t. T_t is the variable representing the production technology level in period t. The second term on the right side of (5.15) represents the external effects from technical-knowledge spillover, and it is assumed that these effects are composed of the current production environment condition Z_t and its lag term. α and β_s are parameters.

Then, total factor productivity (TFP) become as follows.

$$\begin{aligned} \ln TFP_t &\equiv \ln Y_t - \ln X_t \\ &= (\alpha - 1) \ln X_t + \sum_{s=0}^{2} \beta_s \ln Z_{t-s} + \ln T_t. \end{aligned}$$

Therefore, taking the logarithmic difference to convert to a growth-rate basis,

$$\ln \frac{TFP_t}{TFP_{t-1}} = (\alpha - 1) \ln \frac{X_t}{X_{t-1}} + \sum_{s=0}^{2} \beta_s \ln \frac{Z_{t-s}}{Z_{t-s-1}} + \ln \frac{T_t}{T_{t-1}},$$

is obtained. According to Henderson, the effects of the production environment on total factor productivity at the current point in time (β_0) are understood to be static spillover effects, but the effects of the production environment in the past (lag term) on total factor productivity (β_1 and β_2) are understood to be dynamic spillover effects.

When estimating these spillover effects, there is a possibility of multi-collinearity because of a correlation with the attribute variables that represent the production environment of the urban area. The local production environment depends in the long-term on economic trends and the industrial structure, and so may change. However, the location of the plant itself is not as mobile as the production factors of capital and labor because of relatively high moving costs. In other words, in the short term, it is inferred that the local production environment will not change much. Originally, due to the path-dependent nature of growth with regard to dynamic externalities, it is inferred that initial conditions are a dominant factor in determining growth. Therefore, it is highly likely that the production environment lag variable will be explained as a function of the attribute variable at the initial point in time.

Henderson's analytical approach offers prospects for empirical research in the future; despite concerns for the estimations, it questions how an economic paradigm shift or structural changes should be considered. In the past, the analytical framework of dynamic externalities, with regards to the pathways affecting productivity growth, treated the historical production environment as a black box. Henderson considered the timing of the occurrence of externalities using lag effects, and discussed dynamic externalities in terms of decision-making. Lag effects mean that production activities at the current point in time are affected by historical conditions. To consider this from the opposite viewpoint, it means that decision-making at the current point in time affects future production activities through the accumulation and diffusion of technical knowledge. In other words, it is possible to consider that the pace of the accumulation of technical knowledge is determined by producers' expectations for the contribution of the production environment condition on their production activities. For example, it is possible that developing a social infrastructure that will contribute to investment in local physical and human capital will stimulate firms' willingness to invest in R&D, activate local R&D activities, and as a result, lead to the creation and accumulation of local intellectual capital. In addition, it is necessary to consider what will be appropriate as a policy to reduce investment risk, because risks and uncertainties are associated with the outcomes of investment in both physical capital and human capital. Whatever the case, to clarify the mechanism that forms dynamic externalities, it is necessary to develop a model that incorporates the effects of expectations. Thus, it is hoped that this will be reflected in empirical research in the future.

5.4.2 Research on Dynamic Externalities' Pathways

The previous studies did not explicitly discuss technical-knowledge spillover transmission pathways as a source of growth. According to Griliches (1992), the pathways to transmit technical knowledge can be divided into cases of direct and indirect transmission. "The direct transmission of technical knowledge" signifies that technical knowledge created by the activities of one firm, such as from R&D, is transmitted to other firms in the form of patents and published information. This way, if technical knowledge is public property at the local level, there is no payment for its use, and it will be useful for production activities of other firms in the same region. Conversely, "the indirect transmission of technical knowledge" means that technical knowledge is transmitted to other firms after being embodied in a good. That is, the results of a firm's

R&D become embodied in a good, and this contributes to improving the productivity of firms that use that good as an intermediate good because of quality improvements or lower prices.

Both Marshall's argument and endogenous growth theory emphasize the direct spillover aspect of technical knowledge. In the discussion on dynamic externalities, it has also been emphasized that local production environments directly generate growth for the entire region, such as through the promotion of R&D, creating competitive advantages resulting from location. The role of the indirect spillover of technical knowledge has not been explicitly discussed so far, with related discussions being limited to Fujita et al. (1999) and Fujita and Thisse (2002), who discussed external effects accompanying the linkage of supply and demand for local goods as "market linkages." Market linkages are the effects that production activities in a specific industry have on the production activities of other industries through the market, and in the definition of Hirschman (1958) are divided into "forward linkages" and "backward linkages." Forward linkages signify that the growth of an industry lowers the output price of the industry, and induces production of other industries that use the output as a raw material. Backward linkages induce the production of industries that manufacture intermediate goods by expanding the industrial scale as the industry grows. The results obtained in empirical studies suggest that industrial agglomerations are created by linkages of supply and demand for local goods (for example, Davis and Weinstein 1999).

Empirical studies that focused on the indirect transmission of technical knowledge alongside linkages of supply and demand for goods include Bartelsman et al. (1994).[14] They attempted a quantitative analysis of market linkages from both demand side and supply side aspects. Specifically, they used the U.S. industrial input-output tables and, targeting three-digit manufacturing industry classifications, defined an index expressing forward linkages and backward linkages and evaluated the sizes of the linkages. In their measurement of market linkages, they used the transaction tables of the industrial input-output tables. The rows and columns of the industrial input-output tables represent market structure and cost structure respectively.

In Bartelsman et al.'s (1994) model, the following formula is used for the logarithmic total differential of the general production function that includes externalities.

[14]There is also the empirical study of Knarvik and Steen (1999). They measured the size of "pecuniary externalities" in a form that distinguished them from "technological externalities" to clarify the external effects between individual industries forming a marine industrial cluster in Norway. However, the analytical model they used lacked a theoretical basis, and measurement bias may have occurred in their measurements of external effects from the impact of the intermediate input goods' factor distribution ratio.

$$dy_i = \gamma dx_i + de_i + dt_i, \tag{5.16}$$

where dy_i is gross output growth in industry i, and dx_i is input growth in industry i. This input growth is defined as the weighted average of the growth rates of capital, labor, and intermediate goods input, and the cost shares of each production factor are used for the weight. de_i is the variable expressing external effects, while dt_i is the variable representing technological progress. γ is the parameter representing economies of scale.

Then, external effects are resolved as follows.

$$de_i = \beta^{OW} dx_i^{OW} + \beta^{IW} dx_i^{IW}, \tag{5.17}$$

dx_i^{OW} is the index representing forward linkages in industry i, and the weighted input growth of industry i is defined by the following formula:

$$dx_i^{OW} \equiv \sum_{j \neq i} \frac{\alpha_{ij}}{\sum_{j \neq i} \alpha_{ij}} dx_j,$$

α_{ij} is the matrix ij factor. The weight applied to the activities in industry j is the factor of the number ij divided by the sum of row j in the matrix. This index indicates the aspect of the sales of goods by i industry from demand of other industries. Conversely, dx_i^{IW} is an index representing the backward linkages in the industry and dx_i^{IW}, as the weighted input growth of the supply of goods in industry i, is defined by the following formula.

$$dx_i^{IW} \equiv \sum_{j \neq i} \frac{\alpha_{ji}}{\sum_{j \neq i} \alpha_{ji}} dx_j$$

The weight applied to the activities of industry j is the factor of number ji divided by the sum of column j in the matrix. This index represents the ratio of purchases of other industries' goods as intermediate input goods alongside the growth in the industry. From (5.17), (5.16) becomes as follows.

$$dy_i = \gamma dx_i + \beta^{OW} dx_i^{OW} + \beta^{IW} dx_i^{IW} + dt_i \tag{5.18}$$

If the parameters of β^{OW} and β^{IW} are significantly positive, this can be interpreted as indicating market linkages exist.

As seen in (5.18), the features of this analysis are that it attempts to directly estimate the effects of market linkages on output growth, and quantitatively ascertains the effects from forward and backward linkages. On the other hand, as data with a high degree of aggregation is used in this analysis, it does not consider differences in market linkages among individual industries. Therefore, a problem for the analysis is that it is impossible to quantitatively ascertain the linkages between specific industries. This is a topic that will be researched in the future.

5.5 Conclusion

This chapter reviewed the analytical approaches to dynamic externalities, presented the characteristics of the previous studies, and issues with their analyses. According to the results of the empirical analyses in the United States, technical-knowledge spillover tended to occur between industries, rather than within an industry. In addition to this, from the study that focused on the industrial product cycle, the results showed that emerging industries tend to benefit from ideas obtained from various industries, but mature industries tend to benefit from proximity to similar firms to efficiently carry out standardized mass production. Conversely, in the empirical study on Japanese manufacturing industries, practically no effects were observed from dynamic externalities. Much of the empirical study adopted an employment growth approach, but even if MAR-type external effects are actualized, the strength of their effects becomes smaller over the years as the local distribution becomes dispersed. The effects of dynamic externalities are mainly observed in non-manufacturing industries, and these industries tend to benefit from local diversity.

Within the extant studies on dynamic externalities, there have been studies that indicate a new direction for empirical research in the future. But in every case, the theoretical grounds for the analytical approaches appear weak and the correspondence with static externalities is ambiguous. As discussed in Henderson et al. (1995), dynamic externalities and static externalities can be understood as a pair. Following the conventional discussion in urban economics, MAR-type externalities signify localization economies and are external effects that are internalized at the industry level, while Jacobs-type externalities signify urbanization economies and are external effects that are internalized at the urban-area level. This relationship was not explicitly included in the model in any of the previous studies, and it cannot be said that consistent interpretations were derived from their empirical analyses.

In the studies that focused on lag effects in relation to technical-knowledge spillover, past conditions were assumed to affect productivity growth, but the conditions that bring about increasing returns in urban areas were not explicitly included in their models. Further, in the empirical study on dynamic externalities in Japan, the industrial product cycle aspect was not sufficiently considered, and it will be necessary to conduct empirical research using more detailed industry classifications, such as three-digit and four-digit levels, to provide suggestions for policies. Therefore, to research the formation and development potential of dynamic externalities, it seems necessary to develop an empirical study with stronger theoretical foundations.

Appendix: Solow Residual Measurement Bias

Two points are described in this appendix, as problems related to the measurement of the Solow residual discussed in this chapter: (1) the presence of measurement bias that occurs when assuming perfect competition and constant returns to scale, and (2) differences using value-added versus gross output as the output element.

1. The basic model

For simplicity, the Hicks neutral-type production function shall be assumed.

$$V = AF(K, L), \tag{A.1}$$

where, V is the value added as the output element, and K and L are the capital input and the labor input. A represents the production technologies, and technological progress can be ascertained through the production function shift term.

Conducting a logarithmic total differential on (A.1), and dividing both sides by V, the formula becomes as follows.

$$\frac{dV}{V} = \frac{dA}{A} + A\frac{\partial F}{\partial K}\frac{K}{V}\frac{dK}{K} + A\frac{\partial F}{\partial L}\frac{L}{V}\frac{dL}{L}. \tag{A.2}$$

Here, when taking $x = \log X$ for the arbitrary variable X, (A.2) can be rewritten as follows.

$$dv = da + A\frac{\partial F}{\partial K}\frac{K}{V}dk + A\frac{\partial F}{\partial L}\frac{L}{V}dl. \tag{A.3}$$

Assuming perfect competition, (A.4) is established from the first-order condition for profit maximization.

$$A\frac{\partial F}{\partial K} = \frac{P_K}{P}, \; A\frac{\partial F}{\partial L} = \frac{P_L}{P}, \tag{A.4}$$

where P is the output price, while P_K and P_L represent the capital and labor prices, respectively.

Further, assuming the condition of constant returns to scale, the following formula is established from Euler's theorem.

$$A\frac{\partial F}{\partial K}\frac{K}{V} + A\frac{\partial F}{\partial L}\frac{L}{V} = 1. \tag{A.5}$$

From this relation between (A.4) and (A.5),

$$PQ = P_K K + P_L L \tag{A.6}$$

is established as "exhaustion of the total product theorem." Therefore, when rewriting (A.3) from (A.4) and (A.5), the following formula is established.

$$dv = da + \left(1 - s_L^v\right)dk + s_L^v dl \tag{A.7}$$

where, s_L^v is labor share.

$$s_L^v \equiv \frac{P_L L}{PV}.$$

Therefore, the value-added base Solow residual (SR^v) becomes as follows,

$$SR^v \equiv dv - \left[\left(1 - s_L^v\right)dk + s_L^v dl\right] = da. \tag{A.8}$$

The Solow residual is consistent with the rate of technological progress.

2. Markup and economies of scale

Next, it is assumed that producers have "monopoly power" and do not set price equal to marginal cost. Then, from the first-order condition for profit maximization by producers with monopoly power, the formula becomes as follows.

$$A\frac{\partial F}{\partial K} = \frac{P_K}{P}\mu,\ A\frac{\partial F}{\partial L} = \frac{P_L}{P}\mu, \tag{A.9}$$

where, μ is the price markup and is defined as the ratio of price P and the marginal cost MC.

$$\mu \equiv \frac{P}{MC} = \frac{\eta - 1}{\eta}.$$

η is the price elasticity of demand.

Further, assuming increasing returns to scale,

$$A\frac{\partial F}{\partial K}\frac{K}{V} + A\frac{\partial F}{\partial L}\frac{L}{V} = \gamma \tag{A.10}$$

is established. γ is the parameter indicating homogeneity.

From this relation between (A.9) and (A.10), the formula becomes as follows.

$$PQ = \frac{\mu}{\gamma}\left[P_K K + P_L L\right]. \tag{A.11}$$

Therefore, if $\mu = \gamma$ is not established, exhaustion of the total product theorem is also not established.

On rewriting (A.3) from (A.9) and (A.10), the formula becomes as follows.

$$dv = da + \left(\gamma - \mu s_L^v\right)dk + \mu s_L^v dl. \tag{A.12}$$

In other words,

$$\begin{aligned} SR^v &\equiv dv - \left[\left(1 - s_L^v\right)dk + s_L^v dl\right] \\ &= da + s_L^v(\mu - 1)(dl - dk) + (\gamma - 1)dk. \end{aligned} \tag{A.13}$$

In the event of the existence of imperfect competition and economies of scale, $\mu > 1$ and $\gamma > 1$. Under these conditions, the value-added based Solow residual is not consistent with technological progress, and measurement bias occurs according to the degree of imperfect competition and economies of scale. Therefore, measurement bias according to imperfect competition and economies of scale also occurs for the effects of industrial agglomerations that are measured as an element of the Solow residual.

3. Gross output and value-added as the output element

Finally, the Solow residual is different when gross output is used as the output element compared to when value-added is used.

With gross output as Y and intermediate input goods as M, the respective share for labor and intermediate input goods on a total output basis are as follows.

$$s_L \equiv \frac{P_L L}{PY}, \; s_M \equiv \frac{P_M M}{PY}.$$

According to Basu and Fernald (1997, 2002), the value-added growth rate dv is expressed as follows.

$$dv = \frac{dV}{V} = \frac{PdY - P_M dM}{PY - P_M M} = \frac{dy - s_M dm}{1 - s_M}. \tag{A.14}$$

Then, introducing (A.7) into (A.14) and arranging it based on (A.8),

$$dy = (1 - s_M)\left[SR^v + \left\{\left(1 - s_L^v\right)dk + s_L^v dl\right\}\right] + s_M dm \tag{A.15}$$

is obtained.

Here, the gross-output based Solow residual (SR) is defined as follows.

$$SR \equiv dy - [(1 - s_L - s_M)dk + s_L dl + s_M dm]. \tag{A.16}$$

Therefore, arranging (A.15),

$$SR^{v} = \frac{1}{1 - s_M} SR \tag{A.17}$$

is established. This indicates that the Solow residual based on value-added is not independent of the variations in the share of intermediate input s_M.

4. Summary

As was shown above, as perfect competition and constant returns to scale are assumed when measuring the Solow residual, if producers face imperfect competition and possess production technologies providing increasing returns to scale, measurement bias occurs for the Solow residual. Further, when using value-added to measure the Solow residual, the value-added based Solow residual is affected by variations in the share of intermediate input. Therefore, it is judged highly likely that systematic bias occurs in the dynamic externalities evaluated using the value-added based production function because of the influence of the share of intermediate goods.

References

Arrow KJ. The economic implications of learning by doing. Rev Econ Stud. 1962;29(3):155–73.

Barro RJ. Economic growth in a cross section of countries. Q J Econ. 1991;106:407–43.

Bartelsman EJ, Caballero RJ, Lyons RK. Customer- and supplier-driven externalities. Am Econ Rev. 1994;84(4):1075–84.

Basu S, Fernald JG. Are apparent productive spillovers a figment of specification error? J Monet Econ. 1995;36(1):165–88.

Basu S, Fernald JG. Returns to scale in U.S. production: Estimates and implications. J Polit Econ. 1997;105(2):249–83.

Basu S, Fernald JG. Aggregate productivity and aggregate technology. Eur Econ Rev. 2002;46 (6):963–91.

Beeson PE. Total factor productivity growth and agglomeration economies in manufacturing, 1959–73. J Reg Sci. 1987;27(2):183–99.

Beeson PE. Sources of the decline of manufacturing in large metropolitan areas. J Urban Econ. 1990;28(1):71–86.

Benarroch M. Returns to scale in Canadian manufacturing: an interprovincial comparison. Can J Econ. 1997;30(4):1083–103.

Burnside C. Production function regressions, returns to scale, and externalities. J Monet Econ. 1996;37(2):177–201.

Caballero RJ, Lyons RK. Internal versus externalities in European industry. Eur Econ Rev. 1990;34(4):805–26.

Caballero RJ, Lyons RK. External effects in U.S. procyclical productivity. J Monet Econ. 1992;29 (2):209–25.

Carlino G, Kerr WR. Agglomeration and innovation. In: Duranton JH, Strange W, editors. Handbook of regional and urban economics, volume 5A. Amsterdam: Elsevier; 2015. p. 349–403.

Davis DR, Weinstein DE. Economic geography and regional production structure: an empirical investigation. Eur Econ Rev. 1999;43(2):379–407.

Dekle R. Industrial concentration and regional growth: evidence from the prefectures. Rev Econ Stat. 2002;84(2):310–5.
Duranton G, Puga D. Micro-foundations of urban agglomeration economies. In: Henderson JV, Thisse JF, editors. Handbook of regional and urban economics, vol 4. Amsterdam: Elsevier; 2004.
Fujita M, Thisse J. Economics of agglomeration. Cambridge: Cambridge University Press; 2002.
Fujita M, Krugman P, Venables A. The spatial economy: cities, regions, and international trade. Cambridge: MIT Press; 1999.
Gaspar J, Glaeser EL. Information technology and the future of cities. J Urban Econ. 1998;43 (1):136–56.
Glaeser EL, Kallal HD, Scheinkman JA, Shleifer A. Growth in cities. J Polit Econ. 1992;100 (6):1126–52.
Greene WH. Econometric analysis. 8th ed. New York: NY Pearson; 2017.
Griliches Z. The search for R&D spillovers. Scand J Econ. 1992;94(0):S29–47.
Grossman GM, Helpman E. Innovation and growth in the global economy. Cambridge MA: MIT Press; 1991.
Hall RE. Invariance properties of Solow's productivity residual. In: Diamond P, editor. Growth/ productivity/unemployment: essays to celebrate bob Solow's birthday. Cambridge, MA: MIT Press; 1990.
Hanson GH. Regional adjustment to trade liberalization. Reg Sci Urban Econ. 1998;28(4):419–44.
Henderson JV. Externalities and industrial development. J Urban Econ. 1997;42(3):449–70.
Henderson JV. Marshall's scale economies. J Urban Econ. 2003;53(1):1–28.
Henderson JV, Kuncoro A, Turner M. Industrial development of cities. J Polit Econ. 1995;103 (5):1067–90.
Hirschman JV. The strategy of economic development. New Haven: Yale University Press; 1958.
Jacobs J. The economy of cities. New York: Vintage Books; 1969.
Jaffe AB, Trajtenberg M, Henderson R. Geographic localization of knowledge spillovers as evidenced by patent citations. Q J Econ. 1993;108(3):577–98.
Knarvik KHM, Steen F. Self-reinforcing agglomerations? An empirical industry study. Scand J Econ. 1999;101(4):515–32.
Krugman P. Geography and trade. Cambridge, MA/London: MIT Press; 1991.
Lucas RE. On the mechanics of economic development. J Monet Econ. 1988;22(1):3–42.
Lucio JJ, Herce JA, Goicolea A. The effects of externalities on productivity growth in Spanish industry. Reg Sci Urban Econ. 2002;32(2):241–58.
Mano Y, Otsuka K. Agglomeration economies and geographical concentration of industries: a case study of manufacturing sectors in postwar Japan. J Jpn Int Econ. 2000;14(3):189–203.
Marshall A. Principles of economics. London: Macmillan; 1890.
McDonald JF. Fundamentals of urban economics. Upper Saddle River: Prentice Hall; 1997.
Otsuka A. Dynamic externalities of industrial agglomeration: a survey. Okayama Econ Rev. 2004;35(4):27–50. (in Japanese)
Oulton N. Increasing returns and externalities in UK manufacturing: myth or reality? J Ind Econ. 1996;44(1):99–113.
Porter ME. The competitive advantage of nations. New York: Free Press; 1990.
Porter ME. On competition. Boston: Harvard Business School Press; 1998.
Porter ME. Location, competition, and economic development: local clusters in a global economy. Econ Dev Q. 2000;14(1):15–34.
Rauch JE. Productivity gains from geographic concentration of human capital: evidence from the cities. J Urban Econ. 1993a;34(3):380–400.
Rauch JE. Does history matter only when it matters little? The case of city-industry location. Q J Econ. 1993b;108(3):843–67.
Romer PM. Increasing returns and long-run growth. J Polit Econ. 1986;94(5):1002–37.
Romer PM. Endogenous technical change. J Polit Econ. 1990;98(5):71–102.
Schumpeter JA. The theory of economic development. London: Oxford University Press; 1934.
Solow RM. Technical change and the aggregate production function. Rev Econ Stat. 1957;39 (3):312–20.

Chapter 6
A New Approach to Dynamic Externalities (I)

Abstract This chapter investigates how dynamic externalities promote industrial growth in Japanese manufacturing industries. In contrast to previous studies, this study characterizes dynamic externalities by total factor productivity. Using panel data of Japanese prefectures from 1985 through 2000, this study finds evidence of localization (MAR) externalities and urbanization (Jacobs) externalities. However, this study does not find clear evidence that dynamic externalities play the role of centripetal forces for industrial location.

Keywords Dynamic externalities • Industrial agglomeration • Total factor productivity • Imperfect competition • Economies of scale

6.1 Introduction

This chapter verifies the existence of dynamic externalities in Japan's manufacturing industries, and clarifies whether this effect contributes to industrial spatial agglomeration power. Following the 1985 Plaza Accord, international division of labor was progressed, and the hollowing-out continued in Japan's manufacturing industries. There was a greater need to form more competitive industrial clusters to improve international competitiveness, and so clarifying the effects of industrial agglomerations on productivity growth became extremely important. Mano and Otsuka (2000) found that a same-industry industrial agglomeration has a negative impact on growth. A new analysis in this chapter will clarify whether a similar tendency can be observed.

A feature of the analysis in this chapter is that it verifies the effects of industrial agglomerations from an analytical framework that is based on imperfect competition. Krugman (1991a, b) questioned the assumption of perfect competition for the market structure because if each product is produced under economies of scale, it is not rational for various firms to produce the same product. As discussed in the

This chapter is based on Otsuka (2003) "Dynamic externalities in Japanese manufacturing industries," Journal of Applied Regional Science (Vol. 8, No. 1, pp. 55–66, in Japanese).

A. Otsuka, *A New Perspective on Agglomeration Economies in Japan*,
New Frontiers in Regional Science: Asian Perspectives 20,
DOI 10.1007/978-981-10-6490-6_6

previous chapter, the effects of industrial agglomerations, which should inherently be uncorrelated with the monopoly power and production technologies, may be correlated under the assumptions of perfect competition and constant returns to scale. When imperfect competition is assumed, it becomes possible to explicitly present the relationship between the market structure and the effects of industrial agglomerations, which has not been done in existing research.

The empirical method is a panel data analysis using two-digit manufacturing industry classifications in the 47 prefectures of Japan. The measurements of the effects of industrial agglomerations in previous studies faced two potential problems; (1) the problem of endogeneity of the external effects variable, and (2) the handling of region-specific shocks to industry growth. In this chapter, a proxy variable is used to deal with the former and individual effects are used to deal with the latter. The panel data analysis makes an analysis of dynamic externalities possible while taking into consideration the effects of local characteristics on production activities.

A two-stage approach is employed for the analyses in this chapter. The external effects in the industry level are estimated in the first stage. In the second stage, the dynamic externalities that occur at the firm level using price markups are measured, and the relationship between the industry's powers of clustering and dispersion are considered.

6.2 Framework for the Analysis

This section attempts to clarify dynamic externalities through industry-level internalities and externalities. The model follows the formulation for total factor productivity from Hall (1988, 1990), Caballero and Lyons (1990, 1992), and Basu and Fernald (1995).

6.2.1 The Basic Model

It is assumed that the production function of a firm in a certain region is as follows.

$$Y = F(K, L, M, E, T), \tag{6.1}$$

where Y is the gross output, and K, L and M are the capital, labor, and intermediate goods inputs, respectively. Also, E represents externalities and T represents production technologies.[1,2] The firm's production function $F(K,L,M,E,T)$ is assumed to be γ degree-homogenous with regards to K, L, and M. There is no constraint that γ is equal to 1. In other words, it is not assumed that function F has constant returns to scale.[3] For simplicity, time notations are omitted.

Firms are price takers in the local production factors market, and act under the given production factor price P_J $(J=K,L,M)$. On the other hand, the firms have "monopoly power" in the production market. Firms are assumed to maximize profits based on price elasticity of demand ε (>1). Then profit maximization is as follows.

$$\max_{(K,L,M):F(K,L,M,E,T)=Y} PY - (P_K K + P_L L + P_M M).$$

In this case, the first-order condition for profit maximization becomes as follows.

$$P\frac{\partial F}{\partial K} = \mu P_K, \quad P\frac{\partial F}{\partial L} = \mu P_L, \quad P\frac{\partial F}{\partial M} = \mu P_M. \tag{6.2}$$

P is the output price, while μ $(\equiv\varepsilon/(\varepsilon-1))$ represents the price markup.

In the arbitrary variable X $(=Y,K,L,M,E,T)$ in (6.1), with $x=\ln X$, and performing a logarithmic total differential and transforming (6.1),

$$dy = \frac{\partial F}{\partial K}\frac{K}{Y}dk + \frac{\partial F}{\partial L}\frac{L}{Y}dl + \frac{\partial F}{\partial M}\frac{M}{Y}dm + \frac{\partial F}{\partial E}\frac{E}{Y}de + \frac{\partial F}{\partial T}\frac{T}{Y}dt \tag{6.3}$$

is obtained. Output growth (dy) is composed of each term representing the growth of capital input, labor input, intermediate goods input, externalities, and production technologies (dk, dl, dm, de, and dt, respectively).

---

[1] E is the spillover effects received from an agglomeration formed by individual producers in the same industry or different industries, and it incorporates technological progress embodied in the production factors, including the abilities of workers, the performance and quality of capital goods, and the quality of raw materials and intermediate input goods. This is in consideration of simultaneous growth, including from networks, externalities, complementarities, and economies of scale.

[2] It is assumed that E does not affect the marginal productivity of the production factor $J(=K,L,M)$.

[3] Generally, constant returns to scale are not established in the short term since it is not easy to adjust capital equipment and labor. To address this problem, one approach assumes that, in the short term, all capital stock are fixed factors and labor is variable. On the other hand, there is the approach in Nishimura et al. (1999) that handles the organizational structure of a firm and the existence of managers as semi-fixed factors. Both suggest the existence of some types of fixed costs in the short term. In this study, the cost function is not specified, but regardless of the cost structure envisaged, it does not have a direct effect on the derivations (Basu and Fernald 1997, 2002).

From the assumption of homogeneity for production factors K, L and M,

$$\gamma = \frac{\partial F}{\partial K}\frac{K}{Y} + \frac{\partial F}{\partial L}\frac{L}{Y} + \frac{\partial F}{\partial M}\frac{M}{Y} \tag{6.4}$$

is established. Therefore, from (6.2) and (6.4)

$$\gamma = \mu \frac{P_K K + P_L L + P_M M}{PY} \tag{6.5}$$

is obtained. When profit is a percentage of total income of firm s_π is defined as follows,

$$s_\pi \equiv \frac{PY - (P_K K + P_L L + P_M M)}{PY}, \quad 0 \leq s_\pi < 1,$$

(6.5) can be rewritten as follows.

$$\gamma = \mu(1 - s_\pi). \tag{6.6}$$

(6.6) shows the relationship between economies of scale and imperfect competition. When a firm's profit rate s_π is exceedingly small, γ and μ may become approximately equal.[4,5] In other words, if the economies of scale differ among firms due to differences in production technologies, then the price markup will also differ among firms.

Here, when s_J is the cost share of input factor J of total income and c_J is the cost share of input factor J of production factor costs, and when both are defined as follows,

$$s_J \equiv \frac{P_J J}{PY}, \quad c_J \equiv \frac{P_J J}{P_K K + P_L L + P_M M},$$

(6.5) can be rewritten as shown below.

$$\gamma c_K = \mu s_K, \quad \gamma c_L = \mu s_L, \quad \gamma c_M = \mu s_M. \tag{6.7}$$

From the above, from applying the relation between (6.2) and (6.7) to (6.3),

---

[4]According to Basu and Fernald (1997), the average profit rate of firms in imperfect competition is extremely small (approximately 3%). Klette (1999) estimated the margin rate for Norway's manufacturing industries, also obtaining the result that the margin rate was extremely small, economically.

[5]Although not explicitly shown in the model, the assumption that the profit rate is close to zero even under imperfect competition can be established by considering the existence of fixed costs.

$$\begin{aligned} dy &= \gamma[c_K dk + c_L dl + c_M dm] + de + dt \\ &= \gamma dx + de + dt \end{aligned} \tag{6.8}$$

is obtained. The fourth and fifth terms on the right side of (6.3) are set as *de* and *dt*. The above formula signifies that a firm's output growth (*dy*) depends on cost external effects (*de*) and technological shocks (*dt*), in addition to the input growth (weighted by cost share *dx*).

Growth in total factor productivity (TFP) at the firm level is expressed as follows.

$$\begin{aligned} d\ln TFP &\equiv dy - dx \\ &= (\gamma - 1)dx + de + dt. \end{aligned} \tag{6.9}$$

One part of a firm's productivity growth depends not only on the extent of returns to scale other than from technological progress (*dt*), but also on external effects (*de*), as clarified in (6.9).[6]

6.2.2 The Specification of Externalities

In this section, the concept of agglomeration economies is used to specify externalities. First, assuming firm *i* belongs to *j* industry, (6.8) is once again represented as follows.

$$dy_{ij} = \gamma_{ij} dx_{ij} + de_{ij} + dt_{ij}. \tag{6.8$'$}$$

Specifically, externalities are specified as the following linear function.

$$de_{ij} = \beta_{ij}^L dy_j + \beta_{ij}^U dy, y_j = \ln\left(\sum_i Y_{ij}\right) y = \ln\left(\sum_i \sum_j Y_{ij}\right). \tag{6.10}$$

The first term on the right side represents localization economies from a same-industry agglomeration (MAR-type externalities). Localization economies are when the transmission of technical knowledge occurs between firms in the same industry and they are internalized within that industry. If $\beta_{ij}^L > 0$, it means that positive external effects from the same-industry agglomeration are being actualized. The second term represents urbanization economies from a different-industry agglomeration (Jacobs-type externalities). Urbanization economies are when the transmission of technical knowledge occurs between industries and they are

[6]Assuming firm *i* is facing perfect competition, that production has constant returns to scale, and there are no effects from externalities, (9) will be consistent with the Solow residual.

internalized within the relevant urban area. If $\beta_{ij}^{U} > 0$, it indicates that positive effects from the industrial agglomeration itself are being actualized.

As a result, from (6.10), (6.8′) is expressed as follows.

$$dy_{ij} = \gamma_{ij} dx_{ij} + \beta_{ij}^{L} dy_j + \beta_{ij}^{U} dy + dt_{ij}, \quad \gamma_{ij} > 0. \tag{6.11}$$

6.2.3 The Internalization of Externalities

Externalities specified at the firm level are partially internalized when aggregated to the industry level. In accordance with Basu and Fernald (1997, 2002), the Divisia index is used for the aggregation of outputs and inputs. In other words, the industry-level aggregate output growth dy_j and the aggregate input growth dx_j are defined as follows.

$$dy_j \equiv \sum_i w_{ij}^{R} dy_{ij}, \tag{6.12}$$

$$dx_j \equiv \sum_i w_{ij}^{C} dx_{ij}, \tag{6.13}$$

where w_{ij}^{R} and w_{ij}^{C} are respectively the share of firm i in the gross output amount of j industry, and the share of firm i in the total cost amount of j industry.

Using the assumption that costs and income are about the same level for each firm that is a price taker in the production factor market,

$$dx_j = \sum_i w_{ij}^{C} dx_{ij} = \sum_i w_{ij}^{R} dx_{ij} \tag{6.14}$$

is established (Basu and Fernald 1997). On substituting (6.11) into (6.12),

$$dy_j = \sum_i w_{ij}^{R} \gamma_{ij} dx_{ij} + \sum_i w_{ij}^{R} \beta_{ij}^{L} dy_j + \sum_i w_{ij}^{R} \beta_{ij}^{U} dy + \sum_i w_{ij}^{R} dt_{ij} \tag{6.15}$$

is obtained. Next, $\overline{\gamma}_j$ and β_j^{L}, β_j^{U} and dt_j are respectively defined as the size of the weighted averages of the corresponding amounts for w_{ij}^{R} in industry j. In other words,

$$\overline{\gamma}_j \equiv \sum_i w_{ij}^{R} \gamma_{ij}, \quad \beta_j^{L} \equiv \sum_i w_{ij}^{R} \beta_{ij}^{L}, \quad \beta_j^{U} \equiv \sum_i w_{ij}^{R} \beta_{ij}^{U}, \quad dt_j \equiv \sum_i w_{ij}^{R} dt_{ij},$$

where $\overline{\gamma}_j > 0$. Further, when,

$$R_j \equiv \sum_i w_{ij}^{R} (\gamma_{ij} - \overline{\gamma}_j) dx_{ij},$$

(6.14) is used, (6.15) becomes as follows.

$$dy_j = \gamma_j dx_j + \beta_j dy + \delta_j R_j + \delta_j dt_j, \tag{6.16}$$

where,

$$\gamma_j = \frac{\overline{\gamma}_j}{1-\beta_j^L}, \quad \beta_j = \frac{\beta_j^U}{1-\beta_j^L}, \quad \delta_j = \frac{1}{1-\beta_j^L}.$$

The sign condition for the parameter of (6.16) is $\gamma_j > 0$.The sign conditions for β_j and δ_j are not confirmed because β_j^L and β_j^U can take either a positive or negative sign. The first term on the right side of (6.16) represents the economies of scale internalized for industry *j*. If $\gamma_j > 1$, it is considered that economies of scale are realized at the industry level. Their size depends on the average economies of scale ($\overline{\gamma}_j$) at the firm level within the industry, and the localization economies from the same-industry agglomeration (β_j^L). The second term represents the external effects that industry *j* receives from the relevant local industrial agglomeration itself, and it depends upon localization economies (β_j^L) and urbanization economies from the different-industry agglomeration (β_j^U). The third term considers the differences between firms' economies of scale, and the final term represents technological progress at the industry level.

6.3 Empirical Method and Results

6.3.1 The Estimation Method

The dynamic externalities are estimated by industry using (6.16). In the estimation formula, region and time are represented by *n* and *t* respectively. The estimation formula

$$dy_{nt} = \gamma dx_{nt} + \beta dx'_{nt} + \alpha_n + u_{nt}, \quad x'_{nt} = \ln\left(\sum_j X_{jnt}\right), \tag{6.17}$$

is used.[7] dx' represents the input growth for the entire region, and is used as the proxy variable for the output growth in the entire region dy. We face the problem of endogeneity for production factor inputs when estimating the production function.

[7]Since the *R* term in (6.16) includes the input growth of the industry and it is possible that it correlates with the explanatory variable, it is necessary to remove this term for the estimations. Therefore, there is no choice but to carry out a simplification that economies of scale in firms in the same industry are the same. If this simplification were not carried out, instrumental variables would be required in the estimations, but it would be difficult to find instrumental variables that do not correlate with the error term but do correlate significantly with the explanatory variable.

Klette and Griliches (1996) and Klette (1999) clarified that first, as productivity shocks affect production factor demand, they cause upward bias for the OLS estimated values, and second, that measurement errors cause downward bias in the OLS estimated values. In this chapter, these problems are dealt with by using a proxy variable. This is the method used in previous studies, including Caballero and Lyons (1990, 1992). Technological progress is assumed to be an individual effect that is constant over time (Oulton 1996).

γ represents economies of scale internalized at the industry level and it is assumed that $\gamma > 0$. β represents external effects that contribute to output growth in the industry and can take either a positive or negative sign. In other words, $\beta > 0$ signifies that external effects from the industrial agglomeration are being realized, while $\beta < 0$ indicates that the industrial agglomeration itself is having effects in the form of external diseconomies. For dynamic externalities, it is interpreted that local historical production environment has a certain effect on the industry's growth. In other words, it is assumed that estimation parameters γ and β are constant over time.[8]

α_n represents the "individual effects" for each region, and the region-specific technological shock variable that is normally unobservable.[9] If α_n is treated as a parameter, (6.17) becomes a "fixed effects model" and the estimations made using the Least Squares Dummy Variable (LSDV) model, which includes a dummy variable for the number of regions. Conversely, if α_n is treated as a random variable with mean 0 and variance σ_α^2, (6.17) becomes a "random effects model," and therefore the estimations use the generalized least squares method. u_{nt} is the error term, and when input growth and technological progress do not correlate, α_n and u_{nt} do not correlate with the explanatory variable.

The fixed effects model and the random effects model are selected based on the Hausman test. When $\mathbf{Z}_{nt}$ is the vector representing the explanatory variable, the null hypothesis used for the test becomes as follows.

$$H_0 : E(\alpha_n | \mathbf{Z}_{nt}) = 0.$$

The interpretation is that if the null hypothesis is not rejected, the random effects model should be adopted, and if it is rejected, it is preferable to adopt the fixed effects model. The test statistic follows a χ square distribution.

[8]Henderson (1997) conducted research on externalities considering differences at points in time, and confirmed that externalities have a certain degree of continuity and demonstrate the existence of dynamic externalities.

[9]From the results of the F test to consider individual effects, where the null hypothesis was that they do not exist, the null hypothesis was rejected in most of the industries at the significance level of 1%.

6.3.2 Data

The industries analyzed are manufacturing industries using two-digit classifications in the Japan Standard Industry Classifications. However, the classifications of petroleum and coal products, weapons, and miscellaneous manufacturing industries are excluded from the analysis due to an insufficient number of samples. The regions analyzed are the 47 prefectures in Japan, and the sample period is an annual time series starting in 1985, which is when the industry classifications were changed.[10] With regards to agglomerations that have external effects, all manufacturing industries in a region are assumed to be an industrial agglomeration.[11]

The data is from Statistics on Establishments with 30 or More Employees in the *Census of Manufactures,* and uses each year in an annual time series from 1985 to 2000.[12]

Output is the gross output from the *Census of Manufactures*. However, since these are nominal values, they are deflated using the output deflator in the *System of National Accounts*.

Capital input comprises the fixed capital stock adjusted by its rate of utilization. Fixed capital stock (K_t) are estimated using the following formula, as the Cabinet Office's benchmark of private-sector capital stock by regions.

$$K_t = I_t + (1 - \vartheta_t)K_{t-1},$$

where I_t is the investment amount, and ϑ_t is the depreciation rate. The investment amount is the total investment value in the *Census of Manufactures*. However, since these are also nominal values, they are deflated using the private fixed capital formation deflator in the *System of National Accounts*. The depreciation rate is calculated by dividing the depreciation amount in the *Census of Manufactures* by the tangible fixed assets at the start of the year, and the inter-region average values are used for the calculations. The utilization rate is the value by manufacturing industry in METI's indices of industrial production (IIP). As there is no data for several industries, the values for all manufacturing industries combined are used instead.

Labor input is the number of employees multiplied by the hours worked. The number of employees comes from the *Census of Manufactures*. Working hours are

---

[10] It is necessary to integrate the industry classifications when using data prior to 1985, but a new problem that arises in the process of integration is handling of concealment data.

[11] Conventionally, urbanization economies are considered to occur in all industries in urban areas, but here, due to data constraints, all manufacturing industries in a region are assumed as a body of industrial agglomeration.

[12] In this chapter, the possibility of series correlation is not considered. As it is an analysis of a log difference series, series correlations seem less likely to be a major problem compared to data level analysis.

the total number of actual working hours in establishments with 30 employees or more in the *Labor Statistics Annual Report*. However, as these are nationwide values, the hours worked are estimated based on data from the *Monthly Labor Survey* (Ministry of Health, Labour and Welfare) using the following procedure. First, the survey's index of hours worked is extracted as national-level data. Second, the deviation rate from the national level of actual hours worked is calculated for each prefecture. Third, the deviation rate is multiplied by the obtained national-level value to construct an index of the hours worked for each prefecture.

The intermediate goods input equals the raw materials usage amounts in the *Census of Manufactures*. The figures are deflated using the intermediate input deflator in the *System of National Accounts*.

Capital cost is calculated using the following formula.

$$capital\ \ cost = p_K(r + d)/(1 - \tau),$$

where the price of the capital good p_K is the private fixed capital formation deflator from the *System of National Accounts*. The interest rate r is the average contracted interest rate on loans and discounts of all banks. The deprecation rate d is calculated by dividing the depreciation amount in the *Census of Manufactures* by the private capital stock from the previous year. The corporate tax rate τ is calculated using the results of the *Company Sample Survey* in the *National Tax Agency Annual Statistics Report*. The wage rate is calculated by dividing the total cash earnings in the *Census of Manufactures* by the number of employees. The price of Intermediate goods is the intermediate input deflator by manufacturing industry in the *System of National Accounts*.

Concealed data is treated as missing values and an unbalanced panel data set is constructed. The classifications are integrated due to the inconsistencies in industry classifications that arose during the process of preparing the main statistical data. The integration of the classifications is in accordance with the correspondence tables for the various statistical reports.

In creating the growth rate series, the logarithm derivative is approximated using a discrete type. For example, output growth dy and input growth dx are calculated using

$$\begin{aligned} dy &\cong \ln Y_t - \ln Y_{t-1}, \\ dx &\cong c_K \cdot \ln\frac{K_t}{K_{t-1}} + c_L \cdot \ln\frac{L_t}{L_{t-1}} + c_M \cdot \ln\frac{M_t}{M_{t-1}}, \end{aligned}$$

respectively, and the Theil-Törnqvist index is used to measure input growth.

Table 6.1 shows the descriptive statistics for each variable. From the standard deviation, it can be observed that input growth does not change as much as output growth, suggesting the possibility of increasing returns to scale.

Table 6.1 Descriptive statistics

SIC	Industry name	Obs.	Output growth (dy_{nt}) Mean	Output growth (dy_{nt}) Std. Dev	Input growth (dx_{nt}) Mean	Input growth (dx_{nt}) Std. Dev
12	Food	705	0.015	0.052	0.012	0.040
13	Beverages, tobacco & feed	655	0.014	0.133	−0.010	0.081
14	Textile mill products	657	−0.068	0.231	−0.071	0.171
15	Apparel & other finished products made from fabrics & similar materials	705	−0.001	0.200	−0.030	0.115
16	Lumber & wood products	669	−0.014	0.166	−0.025	0.101
17	Furniture & fixtures	625	0.002	0.164	−0.014	0.108
18	Pulp, paper & paper products	705	0.014	0.099	0.010	0.064
19	Publishing, printing & allied industries	705	0.037	0.098	0.009	0.058
20	Chemical & allied products	659	0.030	0.095	0.009	0.050
22	Plastic products	678	0.033	0.123	0.021	0.077
23	Rubber products	595	0.020	0.156	−0.001	0.080
24	Leather tanning, Leather products & fur skins	360	−0.034	0.199	−0.039	0.121
25	Ceramic, stone & clay products	705	0.000	0.119	−0.013	0.061
26	Iron & steel	664	0.003	0.155	−0.010	0.072
27	Non-ferrous metals & products	532	0.025	0.227	0.013	0.101
28	Fabricated metal products	701	0.027	0.122	0.008	0.083
29	General machinery	684	0.031	0.157	0.003	0.093
30	Electrical machinery, equipment & supplies	677	0.085	0.112	0.012	0.062
31	Transportation equipment	654	0.036	0.174	0.003	0.089
32	Precision instruments & machinery	535	0.024	0.253	−0.007	0.139

6.3.3 Results

6.3.3.1 Internal Economies and Externalities

Based on the results of the Hausman test, the generalized least squares method is used for the random effects model. The estimation results are shown in Table 6.2. Economies of scale at the industry level are significant at the 1% level for all industries. With the null hypothesis being set as constant returns to scale, the results of the t test show that economies of scale are being actualized in most industries. There are 12 industries with economies of scale, centered on materials-type industries such as iron and steel and rubber products, and ceramic, stone, and clay products. In the materials-type industry, large-scale facilities are required for production activities, thus, it seems that this influence is reflected in the estimation result. Other than those industries, economies of scale are also conspicuous in apparel and other finished products made from fabrics and similar materials, as well as precision instruments and machinery. As apparel and other finished

Table 6.2 Estimation results (random effects model)

SIC	Industry name	Obs.	γ		Std. Error	β		Std. Error	Constant		Std. Error	$\bar{R}^2$	$H_0:\gamma_j=1$		Hausman
12	Food	705	0.7968	**	0.0418	–0.0673		0.0542	0.0051	*	0.0022	0.3608		**	0.346
					(19.06)			(–1.24)			(2.34)		(–4.86)		[0.841]
13	Beverages, tobacco & feed	655	0.7782	**	0.0552	–0.1858		0.1444	0.0198	**	0.0057	0.2157		**	0.781
					(14.10)			(–1.29)			(3.46)		(–4.02)		[0.677]
14	Textile mill products	657	1.1920	**	0.0236	0.0058		0.1317	0.0153	**	0.0053	0.7859		**	0.083
					(50.52)			(0.04)			(2.90)		(8.14)		[0.959]
15	Apparel & other finished products made from fabrics & similar materials	705	1.4190	**	0.0383	0.0098		0.1438	0.0415	**	0.0050	0.6653		**	0.561
					(37.07)			(0.07)			(8.30)		(10.94)		[0.756]
16	Lumber & wood products	669	1.1377	**	0.0448	0.2618		0.1484	0.0139	*	0.0055	0.4997		**	0.496
					(25.38)			(1.76)			(2.53)		(3.07)		[0.780]
17	Furniture & fixtures	625	1.1324	**	0.0377	0.5122	**	0.1343	0.0176	**	0.0044	0.6118		**	0.210
					(30.05)			(3.81)			(4.04)		(3.51)		[0.900]
18	Pulp, paper & paper products	705	0.9896	**	0.0460	0.2780	**	0.0952	0.0041		0.0031	0.4465			0.077
					(21.53)			(2.92)			(1.29)		(–0.23)		[0.962]
19	Publishing, printing & allied industries	705	1.1616	**	0.0482	0.3168	**	0.0909	0.0275	**	0.0030	0.5282		**	0.226
					(24.11)			(3.49)			(9.11)		(3.35)		[0.893]
20	Chemical & allied products	659	1.0081	**	0.0631	0.0279		0.1034	0.0198	**	0.0040	0.2901			1.106
					(15.99)			(0.27)			(4.99)		(0.13)		[0.575]
22	Plastic products	678	1.1777	**	0.0403	0.2804	**	0.1036	0.0086	*	0.0039	0.5880		**	0.131
					(29.23)			(2.71)			(2.22)		(4.41)		[0.937]
23	Rubber products	595	1.3853	**	0.0564	–0.0870		0.1489	0.0171	**	0.0047	0.5026		**	1.419
					(24.57)			(–0.58)			(3.60)		(6.83)		[0.492]

24	Leather tanning, Leather products & fur skins	360	1.0498	**	0.0487	–0.1950		0.1954	0.0035		0.0049	0.4137			0.174
					(21.54)			(–1.00)			(0.73)		(1.02)		[0.917]
25	Ceramic, stone & clay products	705	1.5793	**	0.0496	–0.1453		0.0982	0.0198	**	0.0033	0.6249		**	0.267
					(31.85)			(–1.48)			(5.94)		(11.68)		[0.875]
26	Iron & steel	664	1.5777	**	0.0680	–0.2782		0.1593	0.0172	**	0.0050	0.4968		**	0.070
					(23.19)			(–1.75)			(3.42)		(8.49)		[0.966]
27	Non-ferrous metals & products	532	1.0860	**	0.0797	0.3432		0.2608	0.0087		0.0074	0.2479			1.227
					(13.63)			(1.32)			(1.18)		(1.08)		[0.542]
28	Fabricated metal products	701	1.0653	**	0.0404	0.1015		0.1094	0.0188	**	0.0037	0.5400			0.043
					(26.37)			(0.93)			(5.09)		(1.62)		[0.979]
29	General machinery	684	1.2699	**	0.0455	0.4571	**	0.1366	0.0270	**	0.0041	0.6455		**	0.670
					(27.92)			(3.35)			(6.54)		(5.93)		[0.715]
30	Electrical machinery, equipment & supplies	677	0.9536	**	0.0678	0.7405	**	0.1347	0.0723	**	0.0038	0.4512			5.231
					(14.07)			(5.50)			(19.11)		(–0.68)		[0.073]
31	Transportation equipment	654	1.2116	**	0.0627	–0.0097		0.1823	0.0296	**	0.0057	0.3819		**	0.139
					(19.31)			(–0.05)			(5.18)		(3.37)		[0.933]
32	Precision instruments & machinery	535	1.3986	**	0.0443	0.2554		0.1990	0.0266	**	0.0065	0.5960		**	0.646
					(31.56)			(1.28)			(4.08)		(8.99)		[0.724]

Notes: The t-statistics are enclosed in parentheses and the p-statistics are enclosed in brackets
The Hausman is the test statistics from the Hausman test
** Significance at the 1% level; * significance at the 5% level

products made from fabrics and similar materials, and precision instruments and machinery do not require production equipment on as large a scale, it seems that they are can realize productivity growth through division of labor or from a same-industry agglomeration. Conversely, the results obtained for food, and for beverages, tobacco and feed show decreasing returns to scale. It is inferred that, in these industries, the firms' production technologies may produce decreasing returns to scale or that same-industry agglomeration may have a negative effect on growth.

Statistically significant values for external effects are obtained for six industries. External effects have the greatest influence on output growth in electrical machinery, equipment and supplies, followed by furniture and fixtures; general machinery; publishing, printing and allied industries; plastic products; and pulp, paper, and paper products. The external-effects parameter for electrical machinery, equipment and supplies is particularly large at 0.74, and external effects on production are considerable. No statistically significant values are obtained for the other industries.

6.3.3.2 Market Structure and Dynamic Externalities

At the industry level, internalities γ depend upon firm-level economies of scale $\overline{\gamma}$ and internalized localization economies (MAR-type externalities) β^L. On the other hand, externalities β depend upon β^L and urbanization economies (Jacobs-type externalities) β^U. From the assumption that firm-level economies of scale are approximately equal to the price markup μ, if the size of the price markup is clarified, it becomes possible to measure localization economies β^L and urbanization economies β^U occurring at the firm level.

When the industry-level estimated values for internalities and externalities are respectively $\widehat{\gamma}$ and $\widehat{\beta}$, localization economies β^L and urbanization economies β^U can be expressed as follows,

$$\beta^L = 1 - \frac{\mu}{\widehat{\gamma}}, \quad \beta^U = \widehat{\beta} \cdot \frac{\mu}{\widehat{\gamma}}, \quad \mu > 0.$$

The price markup becomes an averaged $\mu > 1$ in an imperfectly competitive market.[13] Therefore, assuming the existence of monopoly power compared to perfect competition, localization economies β^L become smaller and urbanization economies β^U become larger. For example, when considering monopoly power from the estimation results in Table 6.2, in the six industries with constant returns to scale, localization economies have a negative impact on output growth. If perfect competition is assumed, it appears that localization economies do not exist in these industries. In the empirical analyses, estimations using industry-level aggregate data are common due to publicly available data, so the effect of dynamic externalities on growth depends upon the assumptions about firm behaviors.

[13] Price markups tend to be linked to the business cycle. Refer to Hall (1988) for further details.

However, because firm-level data is not dealt with in this chapter, the size of firms' average price markup cannot be estimated. Therefore, the estimation results in Nishimura et al. (1999) are adopted as the benchmark. They estimate price markup as the ratio of price to marginal cost through the relational expression of (6.5), assuming the same firm behavior as in this chapter.[14] Their data is panel data, mainly of major firms, from 1971 to 1994.[15] The industrial classifications they used for the analysis are three-digit classifications and so are not consistent with the industry classifications in this chapter. Therefore, this study carries out sector integration. Five industries – lumber and wood products; furniture and fixtures; publishing, printing, and allied industries; plastic products; and leather tanning, leather products and fur skins – cannot be evaluated as price markup is not estimated for them.

Based on price markup, Table 6.3 shows the measurement results of dynamic externalities occurring at the firm level. When firms face imperfect competition, localization economies are actualized in eight industries; particularly in ceramic, stone, and clay products, but also in rubber products, iron and steel, precision instruments and machinery, apparel and other finished products made from fabrics and similar materials, general machinery, textile mill products, and transportation equipment. However, localization economies have a negative impact on output growth in several industries due to effects such as economies of scale, competition, and congestion.[16] When there are economies of scale at the firm level, it is difficult to realize benefits from the horizontal division of labor. Furthermore, if the firm's monopoly power is high, they have only a weak need to locate in an area where firms of the same industry agglomerate. For example, the monopoly power of firms is high in each of food; beverages, tobacco, and feed; and pulp, paper, and paper products, suggesting that economies of scale will be realized at the firm level. This suggests that their need to cooperate with firms in the same industry to achieve productivity growth will also be weak. In fabricated metal products and non-ferrous metals and products, the price markups are below 1.1, which suggests that the advantage of locating domestically has been declining due to intense international competition (Nishimura et al. 1999). Of course, it is necessary to be aware that this consideration depends on the estimation results in Nishimura et al. (1999).

---

[14]In other words, it is assumed that while each firm is a price taker in the production factors market, they face imperfect completion in the product market. However, Nishimura et al. (1999) used value-added production functions.

[15]The main data source is the Nikkei Needs database, which is based on companies' securities reports. As this is a database of listed companies, it is not consistent with the *Census of Manufactures*. To the best of my knowledge, there is no other research that attempted to estimate price markups at the firm-level, so it is adopted as the benchmark in this chapter.

[16]Mano and Otsuka (2000) conducted empirical research into dynamic externalities targeting metal products, general machinery, electric machinery, transportation equipment, and precision machinery from within the two-digit manufacturing industry classifications using the 47 prefectures in Japan. The results of their analysis clarify that, in each industry, localization economies have a negative effect on growth. Based on the product cycle hypothesis, they explained the ground of locational dispersion in these industries.

Table 6.3 Dynamic externalities

SIC	Industry name	Economies of scale/price markup		Localization economies/MAR-type externalities		Urbanization economies/ Jacobs-type externalities	
12	Food	1.213	(1.000)	–0.522	(–0.255)		
13	Beverages, tobacco & feed	1.213	(1.000)	–0.559	(–0.285)		
14	Textile mill products	1.133	(1.000)	0.050	(0.161)		
15	Apparel & other finished products made from fabrics & similar materials	1.133	(1.000)	0.202	(0.295)		
16	Lumber & wood products	NA	(1.000)	NA	(0.121)		
17	Furniture & fixtures	NA	(1.000)	NA	(0.117)	NA	(0.452)
18	Pulp, paper & paper products	1.259	(1.000)	–0.259	(0.000)	0.350	(0.278)
19	Publishing, printing & allied industries	NA	(1.000)	NA	(0.139)	NA	(0.273)
20	Chemical & allied products	1.146	(1.000)	–0.146	(0.000)		
22	Plastic products	NA	(1.000)	NA	(0.151)	NA	(0.238)
23	Rubber products	1.028	(1.000)	0.258	(0.278)		
24	Leather tanning, Leather products & fur skins	NA	(1.000)	NA	(0.000)		
25	Ceramic, stone & clay products	1.055	(1.000)	0.332	(0.367)		
26	Iron & steel	1.204	(1.000)	0.237	(0.366)		
27	Non-ferrous metals & products	1.097	(1.000)	–0.097	(0.000)		
28	Fabricated metal products	1.097	(1.000)	–0.097	(0.000)		
29	General machinery	1.048	(1.000)	0.175	(0.213)	0.377	(0.360)
30	Electrical machinery, equipment & supplies	1.305	(1.000)	–0.305	(0.000)	0.966	(0.740)
31	Transportation equipment	1.166	(1.000)	0.038	(0.175)		
32	Precision instruments & machinery	1.094	(1.000)	0.218	(0.285)		

Notes: The economies of scale (or the price markup) are from Nishimura et al. (1999)
Values in parentheses indicate the case of perfect competition
NA signifies that estimates could not be made due to data constraints
An empty entry signifies that no statistically significant value was obtained

Urbanization economies are particularly large in electric machinery, but are also seen in pulp, paper, and paper products, and in general machinery. The price markup of electrical machinery, equipment and supplies is the highest at 1.305. It is difficult to build cooperative relations between firms in same industries, thus localization economies are considered to have a negative impact on output growth. Conversely, urbanization economies are strongly evident. This suggests that productivity growth may be realized through cooperation among firms in different industries.

6.3.3.3 Industrial Distribution and Dynamic Externalities

Next, we will consider whether dynamic externalities contribute to the power of an industry to agglomerate spatially, from the perspective of the inter-regional distribution of industries. Table 6.4 shows the Hirschman-Herfindahl index (*HHI*) measurements. The formula defining *HHI* here is given as follows.

$$HHI_j \equiv \sum_n S_{jn}^2, \quad 0 < S_{jn} < 1,$$

where S_{jn} is the ratio of establishments and employees in region n and industry j compared to the ratio nationwide. The smaller this value, the greater the dispersion in the distribution of the industry. In other words, when this value is close to 0, it means that it has more of an even (decentralized) distribution, and when it is close to 1, it can be interpreted as having a more uneven (centralized) distribution. From the annual changes for 1985 to 2000, most manufacturing industries tend toward a decentralized distribution.

From Table 6.4, we can see a tendency toward specialization in transportation equipment over the years. This suggests that it is highly likely that localization economies influence the industry's locational pattern, and that dynamic externalities act as the centripetal forces.[17] Conversely, in the other industries where these effects are realized, the industrial distribution tends toward dispersion, so it cannot be said that dynamic externalities act as centripetal forces. The effects of urbanization economies on locational pattern do not appear noticeable in comparison to those of localization economies. The industrial distribution in each of electrical machinery, equipment, and supplies; pulp, paper, and paper products; and general machinery tends toward dispersion, so again, it cannot be said that they have effects as centripetal forces.

Ultimately, it is found from the relationship between industrial distribution and dynamic externalities that the only industry on which localization economies have a certain effect in terms of the centripetal forces is transportation equipment, and no tendency for urbanization economies to have any sort of effect on industrial agglomerations is observed. If firms face imperfect competition, localization

[17]In textile mill products and apparel, and other finished products made from fabrics and similar materials, the bias in the industrial distribution over time is noticeable. However, the rates of decrease in the number of establishments and employees in these industries over the analysis period were extremely high. For example, for the number of establishments and employees in textiles in 2000 compared to 1985, the rates of change were –67.6% and –71.2% respectively, which were the highest rates in all manufacturing industries. In apparel and other finished products made from fabrics and similar materials, these rates were –26.9% and –31.1%. These rates were high compared to transportation equipment (–3.3% and –11.2%) and as this industry is highly likely to transfer its bases overseas (particularly to China), it was judged unlikely that regional specialization within Japan would act as centripetal forces.

Table 6.4 Rates of change of *HHI*, the number of establishments, and the number of employees (%)

SIC	Industry name	Rates of change of *HHI*		Rates of change (nationwide)	
		Establishments base	Employees base	Number of establishments	Number of employees
12	Food	0.5	1.0	16.4	26.4
13	Beverages, tobacco & feed	–2.9	3.4	–10.9	–24.8
14	Textile mill products	40.1	32.9	–67.6	–71.2
15	Apparel & other finished products made from fabrics & similar materials	5.4	5.0	–26.9	–31.1
16	Lumber & wood products	–19.6	–17.0	–34.8	–35.1
17	Furniture & fixtures	–11.8	2.2	–31.5	–21.8
18	Pulp, paper & paper products	–11.4	–9.6	–4.2	–8.4
19	Publishing, printing & allied industries	–24.0	–18.2	10.0	10.6
20	Chemical & allied products	–12.2	–8.8	6.0	–8.3
22	Plastic products	–14.9	–15.3	26.5	19.1
23	Rubber products	–25.2	–15.5	–10.0	–18.6
24	Leather tanning, Leather products & fur skins	–4.6	28.4	–40.1	–48.3
25	Ceramic, stone & clay products	–9.4	–0.6	–26.6	–27.4
26	Iron & steel	–10.2	–9.9	–14.5	–41.5
27	Non-ferrous metals & products	–12.6	–8.2	1.5	–11.0
28	Fabricated metal products	–16.6	–18.3	2.4	–2.7
29	General machinery	–16.3	–11.9	–1.5	–7.2
30	Electrical machinery, equipment & supplies	–16.8	–23.5	–18.7	–12.3
31	Transportation equipment	6.7	15.5	–3.3	–11.2
32	Precision instruments & machinery	–24.8	–27.7	–30.0	–35.6
	All manufacturing industries	–7.2	–7.7	–10.8	–12.6

Source: METI's *Census of Manufactures*, Statistics for Establishments with 30 Employees or More

Notes: Missing values due to concealment were removed from the sample

The rates of change are the rates of change in 2000 compared to 1985

economies have a negative impact on output growth in several industries. This finding is a ground that the industrial distribution in Japan has the tendency toward dispersion over the years, and suggests that the industrial agglomeration effect in Japan's manufacturing industry may have declined.

6.4 Conclusion

This chapter attempted to explain dynamic externalities through a new analytical approach that uses the concept of total factor productivity. While localization economies (MAR-type externalities) tend to be relatively strongly observed in Japan's manufacturing industry, when imperfect competition is considered, cases were seen where localization economies had a negative impact on growth. This result suggests that agglomeration economies resulting from same-industry agglomerations are weakening in Japan, which is consistent with the results of Mano and Otsuka (2000) for some industries. On the other hand, unlike previous research, results indicated that urbanization economies (Jacobs-type externalities) have a positive effect on growth in several industries.

In the analysis, the relationship between market structure and dynamic externalities was reflected by explicitly taking into consideration the market conditions faced by firms. When the effects of industrial agglomerations realized based on imperfect competition and perfect competition are compared, we find that in imperfect competition, localization economies are underestimated. On the other hand, we find that urbanization economies tend to be overestimated when positive external effects exist at the industry level. It is highly likely that economies of scale will occur at the firm level in the short term, so sufficient consideration must be given to this point.

In terms of the relationship between dynamic externalities and centripetal or centrifugal forces of industry location, the results suggested that only in transportation equipment do localization economies have effects as centripetal forces. In all the industries, the effect of urbanization economies on output growth is weak, and it does not have a positive effect in terms of centripetal forces. In many of the industries, the industrial distribution tends to be dispersed over time, and in numerous cases localization economies had effects as centrifugal forces. One possibility from this result is that localization economies are structurally changing. In other words, as was pointed out by Mano and Otsuka (2000), it is inferred that the locational competitive advantage from existing agglomerations has been declining since 1985. To discuss this relationship in detail, it is necessary to analyze the statistical relations relating to dynamic externalities and industrial distribution, and as a prerequisite for this, the structural changes of dynamic externalities must also be considered.

References

Basu S, Fernald JG. Are apparent productive spillovers a figment of specification error? J Monet Econ. 1995;36(1):165–88.

Basu S, Fernald JG. Returns to scale in U.S. production: estimates and implications. J Polit Econ. 1997;105(2):249–83.

Basu S, Fernald JG. Aggregate productivity and aggregate technology. Eur Econ Rev. 2002;46 (6):963–91.

Caballero RJ, Lyons RK. Internal versus externalities in European industry. Eur Econ Rev. 1990;34(4):805–26.

Caballero RJ, Lyons RK. External effects in U.S. procyclical productivity. J Monet Econ. 1992;29 (2):209–25.

Hall RE. The relation between price and marginal cost in U.S. industry. J Polit Econ. 1988;96 (5):921–47.

Hall RE. Invariance properties of Solow's productivity residual. In: Diamond P, editor. Growth/ productivity/unemployment: essays to celebrate Bob Solow's birthday. Cambridge, MA/-London: MIT Press; 1990. p. 71–112.

Henderson JV. Externalities and industrial development. J Urban Econ. 1997;42(3):449–70.

Klette TJ. Market power, scale economies and productivity: estimates from a panel of establishment data. J Ind Econ. 1999;47(4):451–76.

Klette TJ, Griliches Z. The inconsistency of common scale estimators when output price are unobserved and endogenous. J Appl Econ. 1996;11(4):343–61.

Krugman P. Geography and trade. Cambridge, MA/London: MIT Press; 1991a.

Krugman P. Increasing returns and economic geography. J Polit Econ. 1991b;99(3):483–99.

Mano Y, Otsuka K. Agglomeration economies and geographical concentration of industries: a case study of manufacturing sectors in postwar Japan. J Jpn Int Econ. 2000;14(3):189–203.

Nishimura K, Ohkusa Y, Ariga K. Estimating the mark-up over marginal cost: a panel analysis of Japanese firms 1971–1994. Int J Ind Organ. 1999;17(8):1077–111.

Otsuka A. Dynamic externalities in Japanese manufacturing industries. J Appl Reg Sci. 2003;8 (1):55–66. (in Japanese)

Oulton N. Increasing returns and externalities in UK manufacturing: myth or reality? J Ind Econ. 1996;44(1):99–113.

Chapter 7
A New Approach to Dynamic Externalities (II)

Abstract This chapter examines the effects of industrial agglomeration on productivity growth in emerging industries. The analysis employs four-digit data of Japanese manufacturing industries, and shows that (1) ceramic, stone, and clay products, general machinery, and precision instruments and machinery enjoy the advantage generated by proximity to other industries; (2) new manufacturing technology sectors, such as industrial robots, tend to receive agglomeration effects, although information technology sectors do not; and (3) most emerging industries do not profit from economies of scale. These findings reveal that emerging industries benefit from agglomeration effects and face market competition.

Keywords Dynamic externalities • Industrial agglomeration • Product cycle • Emerging industry

7.1 Introduction

This chapter considers the industrial product cycle and analyzes dynamic externalities in emerging industries. The product cycle has been explained using the concept of a product's life cycle with regards to a firm's locational behavior (Vernon 1966). A product's lifecycle starts from when it is created, then moves to growth, maturity, and finally decline. The relevant product's production technologies mature, and the product is imitated as it moves through its life cycle. As a result, the product's sale price declines, so to maintain competitiveness, the firm relocates the plant to a late-developing area where low-cost production is possible (Scott 1988).

In accordance with the industrial product cycle, emerging industries locate in specific areas, where they benefit from the effects of industrial agglomerations. These benefits arise from their proximity to different industries, and the idea of innovation through cooperation among different industries. Conversely, conventional industries are expected to maintain cost competitiveness as a benefit from the

---

This chapter is based on Otsuka (2006) "Agglomeration economies in new growth sectors of Japanese manufacturing industry," The Economic Review (The Keizai Kenkyuu) (Vol. 57, No. 3, pp. 224–235, in Japanese).

A. Otsuka, *A New Perspective on Agglomeration Economies in Japan*,
New Frontiers in Regional Science: Asian Perspectives 20,
DOI 10.1007/978-981-10-6490-6_7

division of the production process, and the idea of efficiently carrying out mass production of standardized products. Wattes (1987) argued that the possibility of using universities, venture capital, specialist services, and other elements in the initial stage of R&D strongly affects product innovation. Based on data of cities in the United States, Henderson et al. (1995) noted that the benefits received from industrial agglomerations change in accordance with the product cycle, and showed that while emerging industries receive external effects from a variety of industries, in conventional industries, firms tend to receive external effects from their proximity to similar firms.

This chapter examines whether industrial agglomerations and product cycles are established in Japan's emerging industries using a comparison with the results obtained in the previous chapter on conventional industries. This chapter has the following two features. First, the analysis uses four-digit classification data of industries in Japan. This is because it is difficult to ascertain the industrial characteristics necessary to classify emerging industries in one- or two-digit classifications. Second, transmission pathways for the effects of industrial agglomerations are considered in the analytical framework. This chapter shows that the effects of industrial agglomerations on value-added productivity are determined based on how intensely intermediate goods are used in production, as well as economies of scale.

Section 7.2 identifies the trends in emerging industries. Section 7.3 presents the framework for the analysis, while Sect. 7.4 measures economies of scale in emerging industries and examines the effects of industrial agglomerations. The effects of industrial agglomerations on value-added productivity are also evaluated. Section 7.5 provides conclusions and discusses issues to be investigated in the future.

7.2 Trends in Emerging Industries

Emerging industries are classified in the Law for Facilitating the Creation of New Businesses. We find that there are 116 corresponding manufacturing industries included in the four-digit industry classifications, and in this chapter, each of these industries is classified as an emerging industry.

The production activities of emerging industries primarily consists of electrical machinery, equipment and supplies, general machinery, and transportation equipment (Table 7.1). Electrical machinery, equipment, and supplies contributes approximately 40% of the total of both product-shipments and value-added, followed by general machinery and transportation equipment, which each contribute around 20%. These three industries together represent approximately 80% of the total product-shipments and value-added for emerging industries. The growth rates from 1994 to 1999 for all manufacturing industries are 2.48% for product-shipments and 0.95% for value-added, while in contrast, the rates for all emerging industries for product-shipments and value-added are 20.13% and 12.09%,

Table 7.1 Trends in emerging industries in 2-digit classification (in %)

Industry name	Product-shipments Share	Growth rate	(growth contribution rate)	Value-added Share	growth rate	(growth contribution rate)
All manufacturing industries	–	2.48	–	–	0.95	–
All emerging industries	100.0	20.13	–	100.0	12.09	–
Chemical & allied products	5.4	–5.81	(–0.37)	6.7	–10.94	(–0.86)
Plastic products	4.0	2.45	(0.11)	4.5	3.30	(0.15)
Ceramic, stone & clay products	1.4	27.10	(0.37)	1.8	22.71	(0.39)
Non-ferrous metals & products	2.9	94.39	(1.66)	2.8	64.68	(1.18)
General machinery	18.6	7.74	(1.46)	21.5	6.77	(1.40)
Electrical machinery, equipment & supplies	45.6	38.66	(16.70)	42.5	23.69	(10.00)
Transportation equipment	18.6	0.45	(0.09)	16.0	–2.83	(–0.49)
Precision instruments & machinery	3.2	2.54	(0.09)	3.8	9.58	(0.34)
Miscellaneous manufacturing industries	0.2	9.80	(0.02)	0.4	–4.72	(–0.02)

Source: METI's *Census of Manufacture* 2-digit classification information
Notes: The share is the percentages for all emerging industries in 1999
The rates of growth and growth contributions are the rates of change and contributions in 1999 compared to 1994 respectively

respectively. These rates greatly exceed the manufacturing industries' growth rates. We also see high growth for both product-shipments and value-added in non-ferrous metals and products, but electrical machinery, equipment and supplies has the greatest contribution to total growth. The percentages that electrical machinery, equipment and supplies contributed to the growth of emerging industries are significantly larger than for other industries, at 16.70% and 10% for product-shipments and value-added, respectively. Even general machinery, which is the next most influential, contributes only 1.46% of product-shipments and 1.40% of value-added. Conversely, the percentage contributed by transportation equipment is small and is negative for value-added.

Therefore, we focus on electrical machinery, equipment and supplies and general machinery, and pick up the emerging industries. General machinery includes eight industries – metal machinists' precision tools; metal working machinery; parts and accessories for metal working machines and machine tools; machinists' precision tools; plastic working machinery and accessories;

Table 7.2 The growth rate of emerging industries and their locational distribution

Industry name	Growth rate (annual rate: 1994–1999): %				Gini coefficient
	Product-shipments	Value-added	Product shipment per employee	Value-added per employee	
Metal Machinists' precision tools	7.67	10.72	7.68	10.74	0.65
Metal working machinery	4.96	2.21	6.75	3.95	0.69
Parts & accessories for metal working machines & machine tools	2.97	2.51	2.05	1.60	0.62
Machinists' precision tools	1.58	1.43	1.15	1.00	0.69
Plastic working machinery & accessories	2.17	2.88	3.39	4.11	0.72
Semiconductor manufacturing equipment	14.82	12.87	–0.80	–2.49	0.68
Molds and dies, parts & accessories	4.78	3.60	3.14	1.99	0.68
Industrial robots	13.51	11.38	7.93	5.90	0.62
Communication equipment wired	7.99	2.05	10.15	4.09	0.62
Radio communication equipment	21.81	22.58	18.53	19.29	0.61
Computer	7.45	0.86	9.15	2.46	0.62
Semiconductor devices	6.11	4.04	4.96	2.92	0.52
Integrated circuits	12.39	9.53	13.98	11.07	0.45

Source: METI's *Census of Manufacture* 4-digit classification information

semiconductor manufacturing equipment; molds and dies, parts and accessories; and industrial robots – that are classified as "new manufacturing technology fields." Electrical machinery, equipment and supplies includes five industries – communication equipment wired, radio communication equipment, computer, semiconductor devices, and integrated circuits – that are classified as "information and communication technology fields." Growth in production activities of the new manufacturing technology fields is particularly noticeable in semiconductor manufacturing equipment (product-shipments, 14.82% and value-added, 12.87%) and industrial robots (13.51% and 11.38%); in the information and communication technology fields, in radio communication equipment (21.81% and 22.58%) and integrated circuits (12.39% and 9.53%) (Table 7.2). In these industries, the product shipments per employee and the value-added per employee are also growing, and productivity is improving along with the expansion in production scale. Specifically, radio communication equipment stands out at 18.53% and 19.29%, with these values being high compared to the other information and communication technology fields. The same type of growth can be observed in industries like industrial robots and metal machine tools in the new manufacturing technology fields.

The locational distribution of these industries appears to be geographically uneven, and they tend to conduct production activities in specific regions. When the Gini coefficients for the number of establishments by prefecture in 1999 are calculated, we find that in all emerging industries, values greatly exceed those of all manufacturing industries (0.32).[1] In the new manufacturing technology fields, plastic working machinery and accessories has the highest value at 0.72, while in the information and communication technology fields, communication equipment wired and computer have a value of 0.62. Although these are not as high as the values in the new manufacturing technology fields, they still exceed the value for all manufacturing industries. This result suggests that industrial agglomerations may affect the growth of emerging industries.

7.3 Framework for the Analysis

This section uses the production function at the establishment level to reveal the external effects of industrial agglomerations, and clarifies the dynamic externalities in emerging industries. In addition to the direct transmission of external effects, indirect transmission via the market is also established by considering the effects of industrial agglomerations on value-added productivity. Since value-added productivity is measured using the identity between total output and value-added, we will formulate the total-output based and the value-added based productivity as shown below.

7.3.1 Gross-Output Based Model

First, the production function of establishment i in j industry is defined as follows.

$$Y_{ij} = F^{ij}\left(K_{ij}, L_{ij}, M_{ij}, E_{ij}, T_{ij}\right), \tag{7.1}$$

where Y expresses the output, while K, L, and M are the capital, labor, and intermediate goods inputs, respectively. E represents externalities and T the technology level. The production function $F(K, L, M, E, T)$ is assumed to be γ degree homogenous with regards to K, L, and M. As there is no constraint that γ equals 1, function F does not necessarily indicate constant returns to scale. For simplicity, time notations have been omitted.

[1] The Gini coefficient expresses the bias in locational distribution and takes a value between 0 and 1. A larger value signifies greater bias in the locational distribution and indicates the tendency for an industry to be concentrated in a specific region.

Here, it is assumed that there are N number of establishments of the same scale within the industry. While each establishment is a price taker in the local production factor market, and act under the given production factor price P^J ($J = K, L, M$), it is assumed that each establishment has a certain degree of market power in the product market. In other words, each establishment carries out production based on price elasticity of demand ε (>1).

From the first-order condition for profit maximization,

$$P_j \frac{\partial F^{ij}}{\partial K_{ij}} = \mu_{ij} P_j^K, \quad P_j \frac{\partial F^{ij}}{\partial L_{ij}} = \mu_{ij} P_j^L, \quad P_j \frac{\partial F^{ij}}{\partial M_{ij}} = \mu_{ij} P_j^M$$

is established. P represents the price and μ ($\equiv \varepsilon/(\varepsilon - 1)$) the price markup. $\partial F/\partial J$ is the marginal productivity of production factor J ($= K, L, M$).

From the assumption of homogeneity for the production function,

$$\gamma_{ij} = \frac{\partial F^{ij}}{\partial K_{ij}} \frac{K_{ij}}{Y_{ij}} + \frac{\partial F^{ij}}{\partial L_{ij}} \frac{L_{ij}}{Y_{ij}} + \frac{\partial F^{ij}}{\partial M_{ij}} \frac{M_{ij}}{Y_{ij}} \tag{7.2}$$

is established. When establishment profit as a percentage of total income is defined as s^π, (7.2) is rewritten as follows.

$$\gamma_{ij} = \mu_{ij}\left(1 - s_{ij}^\pi\right), \quad 0 \le s_{ij}^\pi < 1. \tag{7.3}$$

(7.3) expresses the relationship between economies of scale and imperfect competition, and when an establishment's profit rate s^π is exceedingly close to zero, γ and μ become approximately equal.[2]

When the cost share of input J relative to total income in establishment i is s^J, and the cost share of input J relative to production factor costs is c^J,

$$\gamma_{ij} c_{ij}^K = \mu_{ij} s_{ij}^K, \quad \gamma_{ij} c_{ij}^L = \mu_{ij} s_{ij}^L, \quad \gamma_{ij} c_{ij}^M = \mu_{ij} s_{ij}^M \tag{7.4}$$

is obtained. Conducting a logarithmic total differential on (7.1) and using (7.2) and (7.4),

$$\begin{aligned} dy_{ij} &= \gamma_{ij}\left[c_{ij}^K dk_{ij} + c_{ij}^L dl_{ij} + c_{ij}^M dm_{ij}\right] + \frac{\partial F^{ij}}{\partial E_{ij}} de_{ij} + \frac{\partial F^{ij}}{\partial T_{ij}} dt_{ij} \\ &= \gamma_{ij} dx_{ij} + de_{ij} + dt_{ij} \end{aligned} \tag{7.5}$$

[2] In the analysis of listed companies by Nishimura et al. (1999), it was found that the price markup exceeded 1 in most of the manufacturing industries. Also from the analysis of Nakajima et al. (1998), who used data in the *Census of Manufactures*, economies of scale were observed in all manufacturing industries except textiles.

is derived. Terms four and five on the right side of (7.5) are once again set as *de* and *dt*. The lowercase variables represent the logarithm values of the uppercase variables, thus *dk*, *dl*, *dm*, *de*, and *dt* are the rates of change of the capital input *K*, labor input *L*, intermediate goods input *M*, external effects *E*, and technology level *T*, respectively. The above formula shows that a establishment's output growth (*dy*) depends upon the cost-share weighted input growth (*dx*), external effects (*de*), and technological shocks (*dt*).

The external effects in establishment *i* belonging to *j* industry are specified from the following linear function.

$$de_{ij} = \beta_{ij}^{S} dy_j + \beta_{ij}^{D} dy, \quad y_j = \ln\left(\sum_{k \neq i} Y_{kj}\right), \quad y = \ln\left(\sum_{l \neq j} Y_l\right). \tag{7.6}$$

The first term on the right side represents the effects of the same-industry agglomeration, or localization economies. This is from the transmission of technical knowledge among establishments in the same industry and its internalization within that industry. If $\beta_{ij}^{S} > 0$, it signifies that localization economies are being realized. The second term represents the effects of a different-industry agglomeration, or urbanization economies. This is from the transmission of technical knowledge between different industries and its internalization within all industries. $\beta_{ij}^{D} > 0$ identifies whether there are external effects from the industrial agglomeration itself.

On using (7.6), (7.5) becomes as follows.

$$dy_{ij} = \gamma_{ij} dx_{ij} + \beta_{ij}^{S} dy_j + \beta_{ij}^{D} dy + dt_{ij}, \quad \gamma_{ij} > 0. \tag{7.7}$$

Therefore, growth in total-factor productivity (*TFP*) is expressed as shown below.

$$\begin{aligned} d\ln TFP_{ij} &\equiv dy_{ij} - dx_{ij} \\ &= \left(\gamma_{ij} - 1\right) dx_{ij} + \beta_{ij}^{S} dy_j + \beta_{ij}^{D} dy + dt_{ij}. \end{aligned}$$

7.3.2 *Value-Added Based Model*

Next, the effects of industrial agglomerations on value-added productivity growth are investigated. According to Basu and Fernald (1997, 2002), when the growth rate of value-added is *dv*, the output growth rate *dy* is represented as follows.

$$dy_{ij} \equiv \left(1 - s_{ij}^{M}\right) dv_{ij} + s_{ij}^{M} dm_{ij}, \quad 0 < s_{ij}^{M} < 1.$$

The output growth rate is represented as the linear combination of the value-added growth weighted using intermediate input goods' distribution ratio share and intermediate input growth. On transforming the above formula, it becomes as follows.

$$dv_{ij} \equiv \frac{dy_{ij} - s_{ij}^{M} dm_{ij}}{1 - s_{ij}^{M}} \equiv dy_{ij} - \left(\frac{s_{ij}^{M}}{1 - s_{ij}^{M}} \right) \left(dm_{ij} - dy_{ij} \right). \tag{7.8}$$

Substituting (7.7) into (7.8) and arranging the formula, growth in value-added productivity (TFP^{v}) becomes:

$$\begin{aligned} d \ln TFP_{ij}^{v} &\equiv dv_{ij} - dx_{ij}^{v} \\ &= \left[\frac{\gamma_{ij} - 1}{1 - \gamma_{ij} s_{ij}^{M}} \right] dx_{ij}^{v} + a_{ij} \left(dm_{ij} - dy_{ij} \right) + b_{ij} \left(\beta_{ij}^{S} dy_j + \beta_{ij}^{D} dy + dt_{ij} \right). \end{aligned} \tag{7.9}$$

In this case,

$$a_{ij} \equiv \frac{\gamma_{ij} s_{ij}^{M}}{1 - \gamma_{ij} s_{ij}^{M}} - \frac{s_{ij}^{M}}{1 - s_{ij}^{M}}, \quad b_{ij} \equiv \frac{1}{1 - \gamma_{ij} s_{ij}^{M}}.$$

dx^{v} represents the primary factor input growth rate. This is defined as the linear combination of capital input growth and labor input growth weighted by the value-added based capital distribution ratio and labor distribution ratio. As shown in (7.9), value-added productivity is composed of changes to the primary factor input, changes to the raw materials output ratio ($dm - dy$), external effects from industrial agglomerations, and technological progress. The impact of changes in the raw materials output ratio on value-added productivity depends on economies of scale. If producers face perfect competition and production technologies provide constant returns to scale, this effect will not exist.

The effects of industrial agglomerations on value-added productivity (b) change according to the degree of intensity of intermediate goods (s^{M}) and economies of scale (γ). If the degree of intensity of intermediate goods increases from strengthened cooperation among establishments, this will cause value-added productivity to rise. For example, if production technology is constant returns to scale, the greater the degree of intensity of intermediate goods, the bigger the effects of industrial agglomerations will be. Knarvik and Steen (1999) defined external effects on a gross-output basis as "technological externalities" that are not mediated by the market. In contrast to this, they interpreted external effects on a value-added basis as "pecuniary externalities" that are mediated by the market. They argued that, under conditions of imperfect competition and increasing returns to scale, external effects through the intermediate goods market will affect the profitability of establishments, and ultimately this will be reflected in the producers' value-added. According to (7.9), where mutual external effects exist among establishments, an increase in the degree of intensity of intermediate goods because of strengthened cooperation among establishments will have a positive effect on value-added productivity growth.

7.4 Empirical Method and Results

7.4.1 The Estimation Method

This study estimates based on (7.7). The region and time are represented by r and t respectively, which gives the following estimation formula.

$$dy_{rt} = \gamma dx_{rt} + \beta dn_{rt} + \delta dx'_{rt} + \alpha + u_{rt}, \quad dx'_{rt} \equiv \sum_{l \neq j} w^c_{lrt} dx_{lrt}.$$

The data used for the analysis is converted into data per establishment by dividing the number of establishments by the output and inputs, respectively. Therefore, the rate of change for all establishments in the same industry, excluding the subject firms's establishments, is consistent with the rate of change of the number of establishments dn. dx' represents input growth excluding the subject industry j in the industrial field, and it is used as the proxy variable for other industries' output growth dy. As was described in Chaps. 2 and 4, we face the problem of endogeneity of the production factor input when estimating the production function. In this chapter, we deal with this problem, following Knarvik and Steen (1999), and substitute input growth for the output growth of other industries. Further, instrumental variables are used for the estimations. w^c is the individual establishment's share of the total cost for the industry, α is a constant term representing technological progress, and u is the error term.

Among the emerging industries, we identify cases pooled in each industry, cases pooled in the two-digit classification for manufacturing industries, and industries corresponding to the new manufacturing technology fields, and information and communication technology fields. The estimations are conducted using the GMM for these three categories. We use the constant term and the lag of the explanatory variables as instrumental variables.

The estimation parameters are γ, β, δ, and α. γ represents the extent of the average economies of scale at the level of establishments, and it is estimated that $\gamma > 0$. If establishments face imperfect competition, it is expected that $\gamma > 1$. β and δ represent localization and urbanization economies, respectively, and both could take either a positive or negative sign. For example, if $\beta > 0$, external effects between establishments in the same industry are being actualized, while if $\beta < 0$, the effects of improved productivity from the consolidation of establishments are being actualized. Similarly, if $\delta > 0$, external effects between different industries are being realized, while if $\delta < 0$, the effects of external diseconomies are being realized.

7.4.2 Data

The data is mainly from the industry four-digit classifications special table by prefecture in the *Census of Manufacture*. We can obtain data on the number of establishments, the number of employees, the total cash earnings, product-shipments, the production amount, the value-added amount, and tangible fixed assets from this table. The subjects of the survey in the *Census of Manufacture* are different in each observation year, but in principle, years ending in 0, 3, 5, and 8 in the Western calendar are the years in which all establishments are surveyed, and in all other years, establishments with four or more employees are surveyed. This study uses data from the surveys of establishments with four or more employees.

Output is the real value of production deflated by the manufacturing industry output price index (classification index broken down by sector).

Capital input comprises the fixed capital stock adjusted by its rate of utilization. Fixed capital stock (K_t) is estimated using the following formula.

$$K_t = I_t + (1 - \tau_t)K_{t-1}$$

The real balance of tangible fixed assets at the start of 1994, deflated by the deflator in the *System of National Accounts*, is set as the initial value. I_t is the real investment amount, and this is the acquisition value of tangible fixed assets deflated by the private fixed capital formation deflator in the *System of National Accounts*. τ_t is the separately calculated depreciation rate. The utilization rate is the value by manufacturing industry in METI's indices of industrial production (IIP).

Labor input is the number of employees multiplied by the hours worked. The number of working hours is from the index of total actual working hours for establishments with five or more employees in the *Monthly Labour Statistics Handbook*. As working hours are nationwide values, the hours worked are estimated based on data from the *Monthly Labour Survey* (Ministry of Health, Labour and Welfare) using the following procedure. First, we extract the survey's index of hours worked as national-level data. Second, the deviation rate from the national level of actual hours worked for each prefecture is calculated. Third, the deviation rate is multiplied by the obtained national-level value to construct an index of the hours worked for each prefecture.

Intermediate goods input is the raw materials usage amount, which is deflated by the manufacturing industry input price index (classification index broken down by sector).

Continuing, the cost of capital is calculated using the following formula.

$$capital\ \ cost_t \equiv \frac{p_{K,t-1}}{1-\tau_t}\left(r_t + d_t - \frac{p_{K,t} - p_{K,t-1}}{p_{K,t-1}}\right)$$

The purchase price of capital p_K is the private fixed capital formation deflator in the *System of National Accounts*, and the interest rate r is the average contracted interest rate on loans and discounts of all banks. The depreciation rate d is the value calculated by dividing the deprecation amount by private capital stock in the previous year, and τ is the corporate tax rate. In addition, the wage rate is calculated by dividing the total cash earnings by the number of employees. The intermediate goods price is the manufacturing industry input price index (classification index broken down by sector).

Due to inconsistencies in the industry classifications that occurred during the process of preparing the main statistical data, the classifications are integrated based on the correspondence tables for each statistical report. When preparing the growth rate series, in addition to using each real variable, Theil-Törnqvist type discrete approximations are used for the logarithmic derivative.

Table 7.3 shows the descriptive statistics. Each value is the value for each of the industry four-digit classifications pooled into the two-digit classifications. Here, excluding chemical and allied products and plastic products, the output growth rate of all industries is positive. As there are many cases where the number of establishments are declining, it is inferred that consolidation of establishments is taking place.

7.4.3 Results

First, considering the results of the GMM estimations of emerging industries evaluated based on the industry two-digit classifications, economies of scale are found to be significant in most industries at the 1% level (Table 7.4). The results of the t test on degree-homogeneity shows that economies of scale are being actualized in four industries: chemical and allied products, general machinery, electrical machinery, equipment and supplies, and precision instruments and machinery. There are constant returns to scale in the materials-type industries such as plastic products, ceramic, stone and clay products, and non-ferrous metals and products, as well as in transportation equipment. Although the results for economies of scale are different from those in the analysis of Nakajima et al. (1998) and Nishimura et al. (1999) for plastic products, and ceramic, stone, and clay products, they are consistent with previous results for chemical and allied products, general machinery,

Table 7.3 Descriptive statistics

Industry name	Obs.	dy_{rt} Mean	dy_{rt} Std. Dev	dx_{rt} Mean	dx_{rt} Std. Dev	dn_{rt} Mean	dn_{rt} Std. Dev
All emerging industries	6050	0.050	0.461	0.062	0.396	–0.010	0.221
Chemical & allied products	158	–0.003	0.343	0.034	0.260	–0.004	0.190
Plastic products	506	–0.022	0.326	0.000	0.296	–0.003	0.227
Ceramic, stone & clay products	320	0.041	0.406	0.055	0.324	0.005	0.224
Non-ferrous metals & products	379	0.013	0.350	0.044	0.297	–0.029	0.206
General machinery	2036	0.043	0.427	0.050	0.384	–0.001	0.225
Electrical machinery, equipment & supplies	1895	0.087	0.565	0.099	0.468	–0.020	0.224
Transportation equipment	282	0.037	0.338	0.054	0.330	0.000	0.211
Precision instruments & machinery	458	0.065	0.458	0.062	0.408	–0.025	0.207

electrical machinery, equipment and supplies, and precision instruments and machinery.

Localization economies and urbanization economies are observed in all emerging industries. When the estimated parameters are compared, the size of localization economies is 0.080, which is slightly more than urbanization economies at 0.070. Localization economies are observed in three industries: chemical and allied products, general machinery, and electrical machinery, equipment and supplies. Urbanization economies are also observed in three industries: ceramic, stone and clay products, general machinery, and precision instruments and machinery.

Table 7.5 compares the results of the analysis of emerging industries to the results of the analysis from Chap. 6, which were estimations based on aggregated data of the manufacturing industry two-digit classifications. The economies of scale in emerging industries are relatively small compared to all industries, except for in chemical and allied products and general machinery, and when compared to conventional industries, it is suggested that the extent of competition tends to be stronger in emerging industries. The effects of industrial agglomerations on emerging industries also tend to be different than effects on conventional industries. For example, localization economies are negative for all industries, including chemical and allied products, and electrical machinery, equipment, and supplies, but are positive for emerging industries. Further, urbanization economies are seen in ceramic, stone and clay products and precision instruments and machinery. Both localization economies and urbanization economies are observed in general machinery for emerging industries and all industries, so the conclusion is that general machinery is more strongly affected by industrial agglomerations.

Next, from the results of the GMM estimates of individual industries corresponding to new manufacturing technology fields, economies of scale are

Table 7.4 Estimation results

Industry name	Obs.	γ		β		δ		Constant		$\bar{R}^2$	$H_0: \gamma = 1$	
All emerging industries	6050	1.083	***	0.080	***	0.070	***	–0.027	***	0.867		***
		(87.82)		(6.17)		(3.13)		(–6.51)			(6.73)	
Chemical & allied products	158	1.270	***	0.172	*	0.021		–0.059		0.818		**
		(13.47)		(1.87)		(0.11)		(–1.83)			(2.86)	
Plastic products	506	1.021	***	0.048		0.058		–0.028	**	0.837		
		(22.48)		(1.09)		(1.04)		(–2.45)			(0.47)	
Ceramic, stone & clay products	320	0.976	***	0.073		0.238	**	–0.018		0.684		
		(10.90)		(1.35)		(1.94)		(–0.80)			(–0.26)	
Non-ferrous metals & products	379	0.950	***	0.037		0.068		–0.029	*	0.620		
		(15.38)		(0.61)		(0.77)		(–1.85)			(–0.80)	
General machinery	2036	1.055	***	0.055	***	0.070	**	–0.020	***	0.900		**
		(71.18)		(3.18)		(2.29)		(–3.75)			(3.72)	
Electrical machinery, equipment & supplies	1895	1.128	***	0.098	***	0.061		–0.032	***	0.890		**
		(59.51)		(3.75)		(1.47)		(–4.05)			(6.75)	
Transportation equipment	282	0.949	***	0.038		–0.044		–0.004		0.806		
		(16.13)		(0.97)		(–0.44)		(–0.26)			(–0.87)	
Precision instruments & machinery	458	1.061	***	0.064		0.143	**	–0.020	*	0.896		**
		(39.08)		(1.53)		(1.95)		(–1.71)			(2.25)	

Notes: The t-statistics are enclosed in parentheses
The constant term and lag of the explanatory variable are used for the instrumental variables
*** Significance at the 1% level; ** significance at the 5% level; * significance at the 10% level

Table 7.5 Comparison of the estimation results

Industry name	Economies of scale		Localization economies		Urbanization economies	
	Emerging industries	All industries	Emerging industries	All industries	Emerging industries	All industries
Chemical & allied products	1.270	1.146	+	–		
Plastic products	1.021	NA				
Ceramic, stone & clay products	0.976	1.055		+	+	
Non-ferrous metals & products	0.950	1.097		–		
General machinery	1.055	1.048	+	+	+	+
Electrical machinery, equipment & supplies	1.128	1.305	+	–		+
Transportation equipment	0.949	1.166		+		
Precision instruments & machinery	1.061	1.094		+	+	

Notes: The estimation results for all industries are the results from Chap. 6 targeting manufacturing industry 2-digit classifications
+ indicates positive external effects and – indicates negative external effects
NA. signifies that the estimation could not be made due to data constraints
An empty entry signifies that no statistically significant value was obtained

seen in three industries. Metal machine tools lead at 1.206, but they are also found in molds and dies, parts and accessories, and in metal working machinery. In the estimation results for information and communication technology fields, economies of scale are observed in only two industries, computer and radio communication equipment (Table 7.6). All other industries have constant returns to sale, and where economies of scale are found, they are small in many of the industries. Regarding external effects, urbanization economies are seen in three industries in the new manufacturing technology fields: parts and accessories for metal working machines and machine tools; molds and dies, parts, and accessories; and industrial robots. On the other hand, localization economies are not realized in any industry. Among all the industries, industrial robots have a comparatively high value of 0.299, which represents urbanization economies. As economies of scale are not actualized in this industry, competition is more intense within it, and it is more strongly affected by industrial agglomerations. In the information and communication technology fields, external effects are only observed in computer, so it cannot be said that the information and communication technology fields are greatly affected by industrial agglomerations.

Based on the results of the analysis, we next attempt to evaluate the effects of industrial agglomerations on value-added productivity. When evaluating these

Table 7.6 Estimation results by individual field

Industry name	Obs.	γ		β		δ		Constant		$\bar{R}^2$	$H_0:\gamma=1$	
New manufacturing technology fields												
Metal machine tools	87	1.206	***	0.131		0.137		–0.031		0.946		***
		(18.25)		(1.28)		(0.94)		(–1.44)			(3.12)	
Metal working machinery	66	1.090	***	–0.038		0.008		–0.001		0.936		***
		(34.50)		(–0.51)		(0.05)		(–0.03)			(2.86)	
Parts & accessories for metal working machines & machine tools	119	1.005	***	–0.133		0.258	**	–0.035		0.755		
		(18.12)		(–1.36)		(2.05)		(–1.48)			(0.08)	
Machinists' precision tools	88	1.020	***	0.055		0.190		–0.037	*	0.712		
		(15.17)		(0.56)		(1.31)		(–1.76)			(0.30)	
Plastic working machinery & accessories	50	0.904	***	–0.017		0.353		–0.046		0.807		
		(15.23)		(–0.26)		(1.48)		(–1.25)			(–1.62)	
Semiconductor manufacturing equipment	76	1.029	***	0.067		0.166		–0.063	**	0.958		
		(21.79)		(1.61)		(1.13)		(–2.57)			(0.61)	
Molds and dies, parts & accessories	120	1.131	***	–0.018		0.151	***	–0.024	**	0.845		**
		(17.84)		(–0.30)		(3.19)		(–2.18)			(2.06)	
Industrial robots	84	0.940	***	0.081		0.299	**	–0.041	*	0.911		
		(20.32)		(1.29)		(2.13)		(–1.82)			(–1.29)	
Information and communication technology fields												
Communication equipment wired	52	1.034	***	–0.122		–0.023		–0.029		0.916		
		(17.81)		(–1.59)		(–0.13)		(–0.79)			(0.58)	
Radio communication equipment	40	1.063	***	–0.075		–0.093		0.027		0.973		*
		(28.65)		(–0.96)		(–0.60)		(0.96)			(1.70)	
Computer	95	1.219	***	0.133	*	–0.008		–0.049		0.925		**
		(20.12)		(1.73)		(0.00)		(–1.28)			(3.62)	

(continued)

Table 7.6 (continued)

Industry name	Obs.	γ		β		δ		Constant		$\bar{R}^2$	$H_0: \gamma = 1$	
Semiconductor devices	51	0.966	***	0.033		0.008		–0.005		0.905		
		(35.27)		(0.59)		(0.05)		(–0.19)			(–1.24)	
Integrated circuits	64	1.076	***	0.123		0.311		–0.070		0.760		
		(7.47)		(0.87)		(1.02)		(–1.73)			(0.53)	

Notes: The t-statistics are enclosed in parentheses
The constant term and lag of the explanatory variable are used for the instrumental variables
*** Significance at the 1% level; ** significance at the 5% level; * significance at the 10% level

Table 7.7 The effects of industrial agglomeration on value-added productivity

Industry name	b_{ij} × industrial clusters effects		
	b_{ij} × localization economies (β)	b_{ij} × urbanization economies (δ)	$\bar{S}^M$
All emerging industries	0.235	0.208	0.61
Chemical & allied products	0.880	0.000	0.63
Ceramic, stone & clay products	0.153	0.497	0.53
Non-ferrous metals & products	0.093	0.000	0.63
General machinery	0.149	0.188	0.60
Electrical machinery, equipment & supplies	0.341	0.000	0.63
Precision instruments & machinery	0.167	0.373	0.58
New manufacturing technology fields			
Parts & accessories for metal working machines & machine tools	0.000	0.498	0.48
Molds and dies, parts & accessories	0.000	0.309	0.45
Industrial robots	0.000	0.789	0.66
Information and communication technology fields			
Computer	1.082	0.000	0.72

Notes: The intermediate input shares ($\bar{S}^M$) used for the calculations are the average values for the period

effects, the average values for the period are used for the degree of intensity of intermediate goods usage s_M (Tables 7.6 and 7.7). The results for the effects of industrial agglomerations on value-added productivity show that localization economies are 0.235, and urbanization economies are 0.208 in all emerging industries. In localization economies, the values of chemical and allied products and electrical machinery, equipment, and supplies exceed the values of all emerging industries, while in urbanization economies, the values of ceramic, stone and clay products and precision instruments and machinery exceed those of all emerging industries.

Looking at the results of the measurements for new manufacturing technology fields and information and communication technology fields, we see that the results for each of the industries greatly exceed the results in the manufacturing industry two-digit classifications. In urbanization economies in the new manufacturing technology fields, the values of industrial robots; parts and accessories for metal working machines and machine tools; molds and dies, parts and accessories each greatly exceed the values in the two-digit classifications. In the information and communication technology fields, localization economies are observed in computer, and the value exceeded 1, at 1.082. As a result, it is seen that in emerging industries, external effects tend to have a positive impact on value-added productivity growth, and it is highly likely that technical knowledge is transmitted via the market.

7.5 Conclusion

This chapter focused on emerging industries described by the Law for Facilitating the Creation of New Businesses, and quantitatively clarified the effects of industrial agglomerations based on data using the four-digit classifications of industries. The results of classifying and analyzing emerging industries and conventional industries suggest that the industrial product cycle hypothesis is established for Japan's manufacturing industry.

It was shown that the locational distribution of emerging industries tends to be concentrated in specific regions, which contrasts with the dispersion seen in conventional industries. Localization and urbanization economies are being realized in many of the emerging industries, with ceramic, stone and clay products, general machinery, and precision instruments and machinery benefiting from proximity to different industries. Urbanization economies were particularly remarkable in high productivity industries corresponding to new manufacturing technology fields, such as industrial robots, but were not observed in the information and communication technology fields.

The empirical results showed that economies of scale were relatively small compared to conventional industries, and production technologies in most of the emerging industries demonstrated constant returns to scale. When economies of scale are small, there are many firms that are small relative to the market, which promotes competition between firms. Conversely, when economies of scale are large, firms are also larger and there are fewer firms in the market, so these firms have stronger market power. From this viewpoint, many of the emerging industries are likely to face competitive markets due to their low economies of scale. On the other hand, no clear correspondence was seen between the size of economies of scale and the presence or absence of effects of industrial agglomerations.

As a result, it is highly likely that smoothing inter-firm transactions and promoting inter-firm cooperation in regions with industrial agglomerations will contribute to improving the producers' productivity. As both localization economies and urbanization economies tend to be high in new manufacturing technology fields, it could be extremely feasible to achieve productivity growth in these fields through inter-firm cooperation.

This chapter tried to explain the growth factors in emerging industries from the effects of industrial agglomerations, but the analysis still has issues. It is not clear whether the inter-firm transactions that are the source of the industrial agglomeration effect are intra-regional or inter-regional. In the future, it will be necessary to consider the relationship between industrial linkages and industrial agglomerations after fully investigating the situations for intra-regional and inter-regional transactional relations.

References

Basu S, Fernald JG. Returns to scale in U.S. production: estimates and implications. J Polit Econ. 1997;105(1):249–83.

Basu S, Fernald JG. Aggregate productivity and aggregate technology. Eur Econ Rev. 2002;46 (6):963–91.

Henderson JV, Kuncoro A, Turner M. Industrial development of cities. J Polit Econ. 1995;103 (5):1067–90.

Knarvik KHM, Steen F. Self-reinforcing agglomerations? An empirical industry study. Scand J Econ. 1999;101:515–32.

Nakajima T, Nakamura M, Yoshioka K. An index number method for estimating scale economies and technical progress using time-series of cross-section data: sources of total factor productivity growth for Japanese manufacturing, 1964–1988. Jpn Econ Rev. 1998;49(3):310–34.

Nishimura K, Ohkusa Y, Ariga K. Estimating the mark-up over marginal cost: a panel analysis of Japanese firms 1971–1994. Int J Ind Organ. 1999;17(8):1077–111.

Otsuka A. Agglomeration economies in new growth sectors of Japanese manufacturing industry. The Economic Review (The Keizai Kenkyuu). 2006;57(3):224–35. (in Japanese)

Scott AJ. Metropolis: from the division of labor to urban form. Berkeley/London: University of California Press; 1988.

Vernon R. International investment and international trade in the product cycle. Q J Econ. 1966;80 (2):190–207.

Wattes HD. Industrial geography. Harlow: Longman Scientific & Technical; 1987.

Chapter 8
Market Access, Agglomeration Economies, and Productive Efficiency (I)

Abstract This chapter examines whether agglomeration economies, market access, and public fiscal transfer have a positive or negative influence on the productive efficiency of Japanese regional industries. To accomplish the research objective, this chapter applies stochastic frontier analysis to a prefecture level Japanese data set that consists of estimated spatial and industrial economic activities. An empirical result obtained in this chapter indicates that both agglomeration economies and the improvement of market access have a positive influence on the productive efficiency of Japanese manufacturing and non-manufacturing industries. In contrast, public fiscal transfer has a negative impact on productive efficiency. These findings indicate that many prefectures that are characterized by weak market access and/or high dependence on public fiscal transfer are often associated with low productive efficiency.

Keywords Agglomeration economies • Productive efficiency • Market access • Fiscal transfer

8.1 Introduction

This chapter and the next chapter propose a new analytical approach to agglomeration economies, and examine whether agglomeration economies, market access, and public fiscal transfer have a positive or negative influence on the productive efficiency of Japanese regional industries. Many previous studies examined the impact of agglomeration economies on productivity, or so-called "technical efficiency" of firms or industries to empirically investigate the influence of agglomeration economies on productive efficiency. The results suggest a positive influence of agglomeration economies on the productivity of industries. The finding is important from the perspective of regional economies, because firms with high

This chapter is based on Otsuka et al. (2010) "Industrial agglomeration effects in Japan: Productive efficiency, market access, and public fiscal transfer," published in Papers in Regional Science (Vol. 89, No. 4, pp. 819–839).

A. Otsuka, *A New Perspective on Agglomeration Economies in Japan*, New Frontiers in Regional Science: Asian Perspectives 20, DOI 10.1007/978-981-10-6490-6_8

efficiency are expected to survive in a competitive market, and thus contribute to regional economic growth.

The purpose of this study is to extend the previous studies on agglomeration economies by examining two research hypotheses regarding their influence on industrial productivity at the level of Japanese prefectures. One of the two hypotheses (summarized below) measures how market access influences regional agglomeration economies. To examine this hypothesis, we distinguish market access from other conventional production factors related to agglomeration economies. We then estimate the influence of industrial agglomeration and market access on regional economies from the perspective of industrial productivity.

The effect of market access has been investigated in previous studies from the perspective of the managerial decision-making process regarding corporate location. For example, Hewings et al. (1998) observed that market orientation became a dominant factor in selecting a firm's location. In the theory of agglomeration economies, the best location for firms depends on market access, which consists of market size and transportation cost. For example, Fujita et al. (1999) and Fujita and Thisse (2002) indicated that market access affected the economic performance of firms through their linkages. The recent classification of agglomeration economies provided by Parr (2002) also incorporated linkage externalities, in addition to the related conventional regional and economic factors. Indeed, in their spatial economic analysis, Hewings and Parr (2007) argued that the degree of spatial interaction among regions was more influential and intricate than we can imagine. However, previous studies insufficiently examined the effect of market access from the perspective of industrial productivity, primarily because they could not access data sets with precise economic distance.

To overcome this research difficulty, this study attempts to provide new empirical evidence concerning agglomeration economies by fully utilizing a data set of market access in Japan that contains information on economic distance. The first hypothesis of this study is summarized as follows:

Hypothesis 8.1 Enhancement of industrial agglomeration and improvement in market access increase the productive efficiency of Japanese regional industries.

After examining the first hypothesis, this study investigates how governmental spending influences the productivity of regional industries. This analysis is motivated by the recent policy discussion on the Japanese fiscal deficit. In the 1990s, after the end of the bubble economy, Japanese policy makers believed that governmental spending could improve economic stagnation. Based on this belief, the Japanese government provided a large amount of public support for regional industries via local governments. For example, several highway systems were constructed in Japan during the observed period (1980–2002). It is true that this investment has improved market access for locations. However, as a negative consequence of the large amount of public spending, the Japanese fiscal balance continued to deteriorate until the total fiscal deficit increased to about 871 trillion yen.[1] How to maintain a fiscal balance and how to improve the efficiency of public

[1]The Nikkei (2010.02.11).

spending have become major policy issues for the Japanese government. Given this situation, it is necessary to examine the relationship between productive efficiency of regional industries and public spending for future economic growth in Japan. The Japanese government provides local governments with most of the funds for regional public spending. The political system often produces policy problems within local governments. For example, the fiscal transfer from the Japanese central government to local governments negatively affected the performance of local governments because governmental funding reduced their motivation to efficiently use taxpayers' money to supply public goods.[2]

Despite acknowledging the existence of this political problem, the Japanese government did not change its fiscal transfer policy, and local governments continued to inefficiently use fiscal resources. To provide an empirical perspective on the policy issue in Japan, this study investigates how the fiscal transfer to local governments has affected the productivity of regional industries. This policy concern is summarized by the second hypothesis:

Hypothesis 8.2 A fiscal transfer from the central government to local governments negatively affects productive efficiency of Japanese regional industries.

The remainder of this chapter is organized as follows. Section 8.2 briefly reviews literature on agglomeration economies, focusing on the relationship between agglomeration economies and industrial productivity. Section 8.3 summarizes the methodology used to measure productivity. Section 8.4 summarizes the characteristics of Japanese regional economies, along with a description of the data set and empirical model used in this study. The results of the empirical analysis are documented in Sect. 8.5. Section 8.6 concludes this study with policy implications for Japanese national land planning reforms.

8.2 Literature Review

TFP and productive efficiency: During the last two decades, many previous studies measured the impact of industrial agglomerations by total factor productivity (TFP), which is a conventional productivity measure of firms and industries (Combes and Gobillon 2015).[3] Previous studies indicated that the TFP of a given industry rose because of external economies resulting from the existence of

---

[2]This Japanese problem is often discussed as soft budget constraints (Otsuka et al. 2014). Previous studies also demonstrated that the fiscal transfer to local governments significantly affected the technical efficiency of regional economies, reducing their level of efficiency. For example, De Borger and Kerstens (1996) examined the efficiency of municipality finance in Belgium, and found that financial dependency on an intergovernmental subsidy reduced the efficiency of municipality finance. Otsuka et al. (2014) demonstrated that fiscal transfer to local governments significantly affected the cost efficiency of Japanese local governments.

[3]See Fried et al. (1993) for a detailed description of the measurement of productive or technical efficiency, empirical models, and their estimation techniques.

agglomeration economies. In other words, they suggested that an increased level of output, along with a reduced level of input, was achieved by agglomeration economies. Here, we need to mention that this study uses "productive efficiency" or technical efficiency as a productivity measure, and to distinguish between productive efficiency and conventional TFP. Our reason for the separation is that this study needs to identify two components that can enhance firms' TFP. One of the components is the improvement of an individual firm's productive efficiency. The other component is related to technological progress that advances industry-wide production technology. Technology advancement can produce an upward shift on an industrial production frontier. As a result, even if the first component (i.e., productive efficiency) does not exist in a firm, the firm can be efficient through technological advancement if it decreases the amount of input for a given level of output or increases the amount of output for a given level of input. The distinction between the two components is commonly accepted in production economics to avoid this methodological problem with TFP measurement. Furthermore, the measure of conventional TFP focuses on production activity of industries and it does not incorporate a level of utility into performance evaluation, such as an index to indicate people's living comfort. The methodological feature is problematic. Moreover, we need to measure the improvement in productive efficiency using each firm's decrease in distance from a production frontier over time, whereas technological progress means an advancement of the production frontier over time. The conventional research on TFP has difficulty distinguishing these when measuring the production frontier.

To overcome several methodological issues concerning the TFP-based measures, Beeson and Husted (1989) measured the productive efficiency of a manufacturing sector at the state level in the U.S. and found considerable variations in productive efficiency among samples. They explained that these variations were related to several factors, such as differences in labor-force characteristics and levels of agglomeration economies. Mitra (1999) estimated the firm-specific efficiency index by applying stochastic frontier analysis (SFA) to two Indian industries (i.e., electric machinery and cotton and cotton textiles), and verified the relationship between firms' efficiency and agglomeration economies. Moreover, Mitra (2000) measured TFP growth along with its components (i.e., technological progress and changes in productive efficiency) using regional data of industries in India. The author provided evidence for the existence of agglomeration economies, which made it possible for firms to obtain an economic benefit through improved quality of labor and enhanced utilization of resources.

Methodology: Considering research methodology in previous studies on agglomeration economies, we find that Mitra (1999) and some other studies have used two-stage regression to examine the relationship between technical (or productive) efficiency and agglomeration economies. They estimated a stochastic frontier production function and various efficiencies at the firm level. Then, the estimated efficiencies were regressed on several firm-specific variables to identify which factors explained differences in estimated efficiency measures among firms. Meanwhile, Driffield and Munday (2001), Tveteras and Battese (2006) and several other studies applied single-stage regression to the estimation of technical efficiency and its relationship with agglomeration economies. The single-stage regression method solved an inconsistency issue in the two-stage approach that was due to an assumption about the independence of inefficiency. For example, Driffield and Munday (2001) investigated both the impact of foreign manufacturing investment on productive efficiency of the UK's industries and the impact on industries' spatial agglomeration. They established the importance of industrial agglomeration. In the same research group, Tveteras and Battese (2006) examined the influence of regional agglomeration externalities on productivity of the Norwegian salmon aquaculture industry. They distinguished between the agglomeration effects on the production possibility frontier and the effects of productive inefficiency that are caused by "errors" in the optimization behavior of firms. Their study supported the existence of externalities for both the production frontier and productive inefficiency. Furthermore, Mitra and Sato (2007) examined the relationship between productive efficiency and agglomeration economies in the Japanese manufacturing sector. Their study indicated that the influence of agglomeration economies depended on the type of industries, and discussed a positive effect of agglomeration economies on productive efficiency.

Finally, the literature survey indicates a positive influence of agglomeration externalities on the productive efficiency of firms or industries. This study explores the policy concern by utilizing a SFA-based production frontier analysis (including the TFP measurement).

8.3 Research Methodology

As previously mentioned, this study applies the production-based SFA to a data set at the level of Japanese prefectures. The SFA was proposed by Meeusen and van den Broeck (1977); Aigner et al. (1977); and Battese and Corra (1977). Various types of SFA models for efficiency measurement of production activities were proposed by many researchers. A comprehensive survey, along with a variety of advanced models of SFA, can be found in Kumbhakar and Lovell (2000). Among the proposed SFA models, this study applies the model proposed by Battese and Coelli (1995) because it can examine the mean inefficiency of firms through a single-stage regression, using various explanatory variables for efficiency. The advantage of the SFA model is not limited to the methodological benefit obtained from using a single-stage estimation; it can also investigate the level of firm-specific efficiency. Furthermore, this study can provide a linkage between the SFA-based efficiency measure and regional components that can yield productivity growth. This methodological feature is important because this study uses a data set that has a panel structure with a time series aspect for each prefecture. It is commonly known that the productivity growth measure investigated in this study needs to be decomposed into several components, such as efficiency change and technological progress.[4] Thus, the proposed SFA approach is useful in dealing with a panel data set.

To describe the methodology proposed in this study, we use a production frontier model which can be specified by the following logarithmic form:

$$\ln Y_{jt} = \alpha_0 + \sum_{j=1,\ldots,J} \beta_j \cdot dum_j \cdot t + \sum_{i=1,\ldots,I} \alpha_i \ln X_{ijt} + v_{jt} - u_{jt}, \tag{8.1}$$

where Y_{jt} is the level of output for the jth ($j = 1,\ldots,J$) prefecture in the tth period and X_{ijt} are the level of the ith ($i = 1,\ldots,I$) input for the jth prefecture ($j = 1,\ldots,J$) in the period t. It is assumed that technological progress differs among prefectures because of differences in their regional industrial policies and their idiosyncratic conditions. To capture such a prefecture-specific condition, the dummy variable, dum_j, is multiplied by the time t as an independent variable in Eq. (8.1). The symbols (α and β) are parameter estimates. The parameter (α) indicates a constant parameter (α_0) and the other parameters represent a level of production technology ($\alpha_i,\ i=1,\ldots,I$), while β are parameters to capture technological progress that may vary across prefectures ($\beta_j,\ j=1,\ldots,J$). An error term ($v_{jt} - u_{jt}$) consists of two parts: an observational error term (v_{jt}) and a managerial error associated with productive inefficiency (u_{jt}). The error term (v_{jt}) is assumed to be *i.i.d.* $N\left(0, \sigma_v^2\right)$, as well as independent from the managerial error term (u_{jt}) and all regressors of the proposed production function. The u_{jt} is a non-negative random variable, which is assumed to be independently distributed as the truncation at zero of the $N\left(\mu, \sigma_u^2\right)$ distribution.

Given Eq. (8.1), productive efficiency, or TE_{jt}, is measured by the ratio of the observed output Y_{jt} to the estimated production frontier output y_{jt}. That is,

$$TE_{jt} = Y_{jt}/y_{jt} = e^{-u_{jt}}. \tag{8.2}$$

Equations (8.1) and (8.2) provide the following growth accounting:

$$\dot{Y}_{jt} = \sum_j \beta_j \cdot dum_j + \sum_i \alpha_i \dot{X}_{ijt} + \dot{TE}_{jt}, \tag{8.3}$$

where the dot on each variable indicates a percentage change of each variable. The equation measures an output growth that can be decomposed into three parts: (a) technological progress ($\sum_j \beta_j \cdot dum_j$), (b) input growth ($\sum_i \alpha_i \dot{X}_{ijt}$), and (c) change in productive efficiency ($\dot{TE}_{jt}$).

[4]See e.g., Färe et al. (1994). They use a nonparametric programming technique (activity analysis) to measure efficiency, while this study uses a parametric technique for the same purpose as a decomposition of productivity growth.

This study formulates the mean of productive inefficiency (μ_{jt}) in the following manner:

$$\mu_{jt} = \delta_0 + \sum_{Z} \delta_Z \ln Z_{jt}, \tag{8.4}$$

where Z are explanatory variables concerning mean inefficiencies. They depend upon regional industries over time. The symbols related to δ are parameters to be estimated. Because of the model structure, the estimated level of productive efficiency (TE_{jt}) is nonnegative with an upper bound of unity. That is,

$$TE_{jt} = E\left(\exp\left(-u_{jt}\right) \mid v_{jt} - u_{jt}\right), 0 < TE_{jt} \leq 1.$$

After substituting (8.4) into (8.3), the growth accounting is specified as follows:

$$\dot{Y}_{jt} = \sum_{j} \beta_j \cdot dum_j + \sum_{i} \alpha_i \dot{X}_{ijt} + \sum_{z} (-\delta_z)\, \dot{Z}_{jt}.$$

Thus, the growth rate of an observed output ($\dot{Y}_{jt}$) is measured by the sum of the three components: (a) the rate of technological progress ($\sum_{j} \beta_j \cdot dum_j$), (b) the weighted growth rate of inputs ($\sum_{i} \alpha_i \dot{X}_{ijt}$), and (c) the rate of productive efficiency change ($\sum_{Z} (-\delta_Z) \dot{Z}_{jt}$). By incorporating an error term ($\dot{v}_{jt}$) into the growth rate of TFP, this study can specify it in the following manner:

$$T\dot{F}P_{jt} = \sum_{j} \beta_j \cdot dum_j + \sum_{z} (-\delta_z)\, \dot{Z}_{jt} + \dot{v}_{jt}. \tag{8.5}$$

8.4 Data and Empirical Model

8.4.1 Data

The data set used in this study consists data from Japan's 47 prefectures for manufacturing and non-manufacturing industries from 1980 to 2002. Since there are many regional statistics, we compile the data set from various sources. The data set is mainly obtained from the *Annual Report on Prefectural Accounts*, prepared by the Economic and Social Research Institute, the Cabinet Office.

In the data set, an output (Y) for each prefecture is measured by a nominal value-added that is adjusted by the value-added deflator reported in the *System of National Accounts* (SNA). Labor input (L) is an estimate of man-hours. Capital input (K) is comprised of the fixed capital stock adjusted by its rate of utilization. Since the fixed capital stock at a regional level is not publicly available, this study uses the estimated value of capital stock for each prefecture, which is obtained from the Central Research Institute of Electric Power Industry's regional economic database.[5] The utilization rate in the manufacturing industries is obtained from a set of indices regarding operating ratios that is published by the Ministry of Economy, Trade, and Industry (METI). However, there is no publicly available data on the utilization rate in non-manufacturing industries. Therefore, this study estimates the deviation of the logarithm of the inverse of the capital coefficient from its time trend and then uses the deviation as a proxy variable for the utilization rate.[6]

This study employs population density (DENS) and market access (ACC) as proxy variables for agglomeration economies. They are used as explanatory variables for inefficiency. DENS is defined by the size of population divided by each inhabited area. Meanwhile, this study defines the following index as a proxy variable for market accessibility (ACC):

$$ACC_{jt} \equiv \sum\nolimits_{k \neq j} \left[\left(d_{jkt}^{-1} / \sum\nolimits_{k \neq j} d_{jkt}^{-1} \right) \cdot Q_{kt} \right],$$

where d_{jkt} represents automobile travel time between regions j and k in the period t,[7] and Q_{kt} is an amount of gross output by industry that represents the size of the local production market in the kth region (prefecture in this study) in the tth period. As described above, ACC changes over time because both automobile travel time and gross output vary over time. Specifically, a large-scale investment to build a road infrastructure was implemented during the observation period (1980–2002). This investment has significantly influenced the ACC variable because the development of the road infrastructure has decreased travel time between regions.

It is also important to note that production market size (gross amount of output) does not necessarily equal the demand size or the consumption in each region. The rationale for using gross output as market size is that our research is focused on examining productive efficiency of industries from the supply side of each regional

[5] In the CRIEPI regional economic database, capital stocks are constructed from gross investment by using the benchmark year method. The CRIEPI regional economic database provides fixed capital stock classified into manufacturing and non-manufacturing industries for each prefecture.

[6] It is expected that variations in the logarithm of the inverse of the capital coefficient, $\ln\left(\frac{Y}{K}\right)$, have a constant slope over time under the production system that employs capital intense technology for the long term. However, the value fluctuates every year in an observed data set. Hence, we assume the fluctuations in $\ln\left(\frac{Y}{K}\right)$ can be attributed to a change in capital utilization as well as to a time trend. Based on the assumption, a proxy of the capital utilization rate can be measured by a residual error term (ε) in the regression $\ln(Y/K) = \alpha + \beta T + \varepsilon$, where T is a time trend and β is a time-invariant slope of $\ln\left(\frac{Y}{K}\right)$.

[7] According to "Net Freight Flow Census (census logistics) 2000," 81.7% of total shipment cost is attributed to automobile transportation, while the shares of marine, air, and rail transportations are merely 13%, 4.2%, and 1.2%, respectively. These statistics suggest that using the travel time of automobile transportation is preferable for constructing measures of market access.

economy. Thus, the proposed definition is consistent with our research purpose, which is to examine industrial efficiency for each region's production. Furthermore, the production market in each region consists of the final goods' production market and the intermediate goods' production market. In this study, we use gross amount of output, which is the total of production in both markets.

An important characteristic of ACC is that the degree of market access is measured by production market size, which is combined with a transportation cost (travel time) of accessing the market. If the market size of the other region (Q_{kt}) increases, the corresponding variable increases. In contrast, if the travel time from one region to another region decreases, the market size of the region is considered to increase, so that the value of ACC increases.

In addition to these two variables, this study uses the fiscal transfer ratio (TRANS) as the third variable to explain productive efficiency. TRANS is defined as the ratio of local allocation tax to general finances. Here, local allocation tax implies a public fiscal transfer from the central government to a local government. The amount of the transfer is determined by the difference between fiscal expenditure and financial income in each municipality. The local allocation tax is included as part of general finances. In Japanese politics, general finances imply fiscal resources that the local government can spend without any restrictions on what they are used for.[8] In other words, if this ratio (i.e., local allocation tax divided by general finances) is high, local governments depend more on public fiscal transfer of arbitrary resources for uses such as road investments.

Japan invested a large amount of funds in local public infrastructure during the 1980s and the 1990s. Most of the local investments depended upon funds that the Japanese central government allocated to local governments through its financial transfer mechanism. The fiscal transfer policies resulted in an excessive amount of funds being allocated to low productivity regions from the 1970s to the 1990s (Yamano and Ohkawara 2000). Unfortunately, the public investment did not produce the expected return in terms of economic growth in the regions. The fiscal transfer systematically distorted local governments' investment in their public infrastructures. Moreover, the fiscal transfers were made without any serious evaluation of the cost-benefit impact of the projects being funded. As a political byproduct, local economies heavily depend upon funds from the central government. Thus, it is easy to imagine that public investment can save the local economy from temporarily deteriorating even if local governments do not make any serious effort toward economic growth. A consequence of the fiscal policy is that each local government continues to raise its ratio (the amount of public investment divided by economic activity), resulting in inappropriate use of public funds.

Figure 8.1 depicts the political relationship between the central government and local governments by comparing the share of public-sector fixed capital formation

[8]In Japan, the income of the local government is divided into fiscal resources that the local government can freely use without any purpose restrictions, and those constrained by a specific purpose.

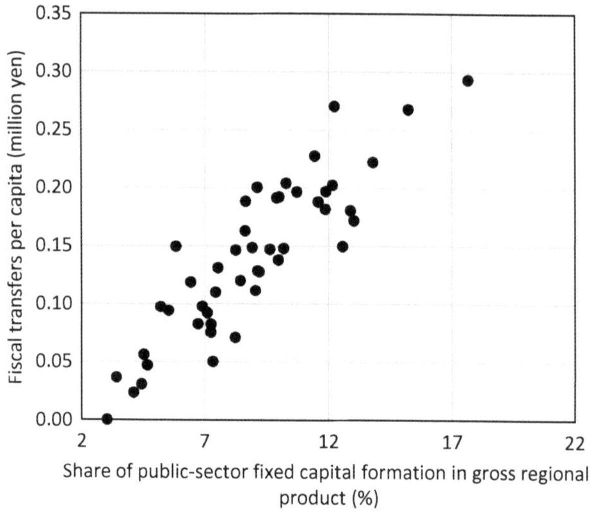

Fig. 8.1 Fiscal transfers and public-sector fixed capital formation in prefectures (2000)

in the gross regional product (on the horizontal axis) with the fiscal transfer per capita (on the vertical axis). The figure shows an increasing trend (or a positive correlation) between the share of public-sector fixed capital formation included in the gross regional product and the fiscal transfer per capita. In addition to Figs. 8.1 and 8.2 visually demonstrates a similar positive correlation between the share of the construction industry in the gross regional product (on the horizontal axis) and the fiscal transfer per capita (on the vertical axis). This figure shows that the ratio of the construction industry to total economic activity is higher in regions where local governments receive a large amount of allocated funds. As mentioned previously, Japanese local governments greatly depend upon the fiscal transfer from the central government. The funds obtained from the governmental fiscal transfer have long been allocated to the construction industry, which supports the regional economy by providing job opportunities. Because of this fiscal misallocation, local economies have been unsuccessful in decreasing their regional industrial structures' dependence on the construction industry. They have been unable to grow their industrial infrastructures using government funds because of inefficient resource allocation. This inefficiency is the result of a major policy problem of the regional economies in Japan.

8.4.2 An Empirical Model and Descriptive Statistics

Using the variables discussed in Sect. 8.4.1, this study uses the following SFA model that is comprised of a production function and an equation that expresses the level of inefficiency (due to managerial error):

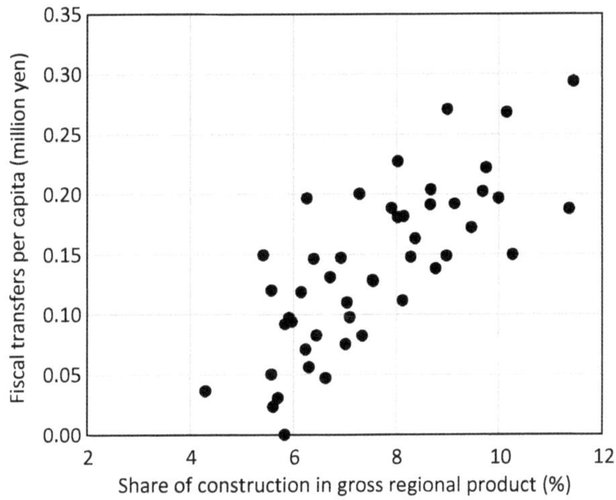

Fig. 8.2 Fiscal transfers and construction industry in prefectures (2000)

$$\begin{aligned} \ln Y_{jt} &= \alpha_0 + \sum_{j=1,\ldots,J} \beta_j \cdot dum_j \cdot t + \alpha_L \ln L_{jt} + \alpha_K \ln K_{jt} + v_{jt} - u_{jt} \\ \mu_{jt} &= \delta_0 + \delta_{dens} \ln DENS_{jt} + \delta_{acc} \ln ACC_{jt} + \delta_{trans} \ln TRANS_{jt}, \end{aligned} \quad (8.6)$$

where δ are parameters to be estimated. Note that if an explanatory variable improves the level of efficiency, then the parameter (δ) has a negative sign.

Tables 8.1a summarizes the descriptive statistics of the data set on value-added, capital, and labor, along with annual growth rates for five-year periods (1980, 1985, 1990, 1995, and 2000) as well as the entire period. The table highlights two important findings. First, the annual growth rate of value-added in the two types of industries (manufacturing and non-manufacturing) significantly increased during the 1980s. The average annual growth rate of manufacturing industries was 4.32% from 1980 to 1985 and 5.24% in the remaining periods of the 1980s. See the third column of Table 8.1a. The average annual growth rate of non-manufacturing industries was 2.74% from 1980 to 1985 and 5.30% in the remaining period. See the fourth column of Table 8.1a. However, the increasing trend was reversed in Table 8.1b. For example, during the 1990s, the annual growth rate of manufacturing industries decreased to 0.37% on average from 1990 to 1995 and 1.55% during the remaining period. Similarly, non-manufacturing industries' annual growth rate decreased to 1.46% (1990–1995) and 1.31% (1995–2000) on average. The annual average growth rate of value-added in the manufacturing industries was 2.41% and that of non-manufacturing industries was 2.50% from 1980–2002. This inconsistent trend in value-added was due to economic growth in Japan in the 1980s, followed by an economic recession in the 1990s.

Second, the growth rate of employees decreased during the 1990s, resulting in a negative growth rate for both types of industries. An exception was found in non-manufacturing industries from 1990 to 1995. In contrast, the private capital stock of the two industries attained a high growth rate during the 1980s and 1990s.

Table 8.1a Descriptive statistics

		Value-added (million yen)		Capital stock (million yen)		Labor (people)	
		Manufacturing	Non-manufacturing	Manufacturing	Non-manufacturing	Manufacturing	Non-manufacturing
1980	Mean	1,512,543	5,074,970	3,107,311	4,636,519	281,833	861,230
	Max	9,991,476	41,161,092	13,276,575	32,667,838	1,711,959	5,328,854
	Min	103,818	1,139,466	249,695	686,674	31,293	251,677
1985	Mean	1,868,359	5,810,479	4,117,898	6,768,035	297,289	897,056
	Max	10,846,149	49,895,711	18,071,001	52,527,728	1,712,526	5,892,715
	Min	120,706	1,290,891	386,764	1,219,206	32,574	244,207
	Annual growth rate (%, 1980–1985)	4.32	2.74	5.79	7.86	1.07	0.82
1990	Mean	2,412,051	7,522,333	5,526,015	9,794,408	311,546	950,111
	Max	11,880,503	71,011,441	26,149,136	88,470,383	1,718,244	6,556,556
	Min	160,517	1,494,293	486,512	1,973,412	31,964	240,828
	Annual growth rate (%, 1985–1990)	5.24	5.30	6.06	7.67	0.94	1.16
1995	Mean	2,457,165	8,085,906	6,873,736	13,023,203	288,431	1,021,231
	Max	11,164,328	72,467,285	32,792,296	121,266,218	1,498,047	6,876,558
	Min	175,557	1,585,674	615,874	2,636,974	31,434	249,503
	Annual growth rate (%, 1990–1995)	0.37	1.46	4.46	5.86	–1.53	1.45
2000	Mean	2,654,003	8,627,859	7,920,881	15,898,152	260,164	1,018,242
	Max	11,959,503	80,821,092	38,942,303	152,281,499	1,267,828	6,787,360
	Min	212,479	1,682,286	754,285	3,237,977	29,268	247,471
	Annual growth rate (%, 1995–2000)	1.55	1.31	2.88	4.07	–2.04	–0.06

1980–2002	Mean	2,180,130	7,191,132	5,742,417	10,521,764	288,003	958,813
	Max	13,070,375	82,168,043	40,494,703	164,615,821	1,741,519	6,926,722
	Min	103,818	1,139,466	249,695	686,674	27,243	240,248
	Annual growth rate (%, 1980–2002)	2.41	2.50	4.47	6.04	−0.81	0.73

Table 8.1b Descriptive statistics

		Population density (people per area)	Market access (million yen)		Fiscal transfer ratio (%)
			Manufacturing	Non-manufacturing	
1980	Mean	1298	24,291,364	20,649,683	0.48
	Max	7265	96,793,748	60,563,553	0.72
	Min	47	11,748,931	9,454,616	0.00
1985	Mean	1345	27,992,590	24,264,458	0.46
	Max	7434	114,695,747	70,796,316	0.73
	Min	47	12,974,102	10,605,441	0.00
	Annual growth rate (%, 1980–1985)	0.71	2.88	3.28	–0.89
1990	Mean	1366	36,275,856	31,350,769	0.46
	Max	7580	157,418,738	91,490,418	0.74
	Min	47	16,000,783	13,035,034	0.00
	Annual growth rate (%, 1985–1990)	0.31	5.32	5.26	–0.16
1995	Mean	1385	38,245,650	32,272,368	0.47
	Max	7579	163,606,099	90,437,085	0.73
	Min	47	17,274,156	14,236,184	0.00
	Annual growth rate (%, 1990–1995)	0.28	1.06	0.58	0.46
2000	Mean	1385	40,749,786	34,153,584	0.52
	Max	7469	183,807,692	95,978,950	0.74
	Min	47	18,587,850	15,223,498	0.00
	Annual growth rate (%, 1995–2000)	0.00	1.28	1.14	2.23
1980–2002	Mean	1363	34,182,924	29,023,754	0.48
	Max	7632	187,806,085	95,978,950	0.75
	Min	47	11,748,931	9,454,616	0.00
	Annual growth rate (%, 1980–2002)	0.31	2.37	2.23	0.49

The average annual growth rate of manufacturing industries was 4.47% and that of non-manufacturing industries was 6.04% from 1980 to 2002. The time trend of employees and capital stock implies a structural shift of Japanese industries from labor-intensive to capital intensive.

Looking at variables related to agglomeration economies, Table 8.1b indicates that the average annual growth rate of population density decreased from 0.71% from 1980 to 1985 to 0.00% from 1995 to 2000. The average annual growth rate of market access variables for the two Japanese industries decreased from the 1980s to the 1990s. However, a relatively high growth rate was maintained in the market access indices during the observation period. For example, see the bottom of Table 8.1b, which shows 2.37% and 2.23% for market access of the manufacturing and non-manufacturing industries, respectively. In contrast, the growth rate of the fiscal transfer ratio was negative in the 1980s, reflecting strong economic growth in Japan. It then shifted to an increasing trend in the 1990s, particularly from 1995 to 2000. The increase in fiscal transfer during the 1990s is attributed to the government's policy to increase the growth of regional economies, which had been stagnating since the so-called "bubble economy" at the end of the 1980s.

8.5 Results

Table 8.2 summarizes the estimation results of model (8.6). To estimate the proposed model, we use Frontier Version 4.1, which is an econometric software developed by Battese and Coelli (1995) for the specific purpose of estimating SFA models.

Table 8.2 indicates that technology parameters related to production (α_K and α_L) are statistically significant in each industry. All variance parameters ($\sigma_u^2 + \sigma_v^2$ and $\sigma_u^2/(\sigma_u^2 + \sigma_v^2)$) are also statistically significant. Since the degree of *TE* is calculated from information that is derived from the estimates of these variance parameters, it is very important that this study obtains statistically significant parameter estimates to demonstrate the validity of productive efficiency measures related to the two industries. Almost all parameters on technological progress (β_j) are significant and their signs and magnitudes are consistent with our expectations. The result confirms the validity of the assumption that technological progress varies among prefectures. Furthermore, population density (δ_{DENS}) and market access (δ_{ACC}) are the explanatory variables of productive efficiency. As shown in Table 8.2, the parameter estimates of those variables are negative and statistically significant. The result implies that the two variables (population density and market access) contribute to improving the efficiency of Japanese manufacturing and non-manufacturing industries. Conversely, the estimated parameter of fiscal transfer (δ_{TRANS}) is positive and statistically significant for both industries, implying that the fiscal transfer has a negative impact on productive efficiency. This result is important because it indicates that a productive efficiency loss is generated in regions where the central government provides a large amount of fiscal transfer. Thus, the two assumptions discussed in Sect. 8.1 are valid, and the results are consistent with the empirical evidence found by the previous studies on agglomeration economies.

Table 8.3 summarizes the average of productive efficiency measures and their changes for 11 regions during the period 1980–2002. The value for each region is obtained by calculating the arithmetic average of these efficiency measures for each prefecture. The comparison among regions in Table 8.4 indicates that the efficiency measures (*TE* for manufacturing and non-manufacturing) are relatively high in the

Table 8.2 Estimation results

	Manufacturing industries			Non-manufacturing industries		
α_0	0.2495	(0.1232)	*	0.6421	(0.0945)	**
α_K	0.3504	(0.0125)	**	0.2978	(0.0172)	**
α_L	0.6957	(0.0149)	**	0.7541	(0.0192)	**
$\beta_{1(Hokkaido)}$	0.0099	(0.0020)	**	0.0057	(0.0015)	**
$\beta_{2(Aomori)}$	0.0027	(0.0018)		0.0028	(0.0013)	*
$\beta_{3(Iwate)}$	0.0151	(0.0015)	**	0.0028	(0.0013)	*
$\beta_{4(Miyagi)}$	0.0219	(0.0015)	**	0.0078	(0.0014)	**
$\beta_{5(Akita)}$	0.0117	(0.0015)	**	0.0028	(0.0013)	*
$\beta_{6(Yamagata)}$	0.0126	(0.0015)	**	0.0002	(0.0014)	
$\beta_{7(Fukushima)}$	0.0183	(0.0015)	**	–0.0014	(0.0014)	
$\beta_{8(Niigata)}$	0.0035	(0.0014)	**	0.0029	(0.0013)	*
$\beta_{9(Ibaraki)}$	0.0176	(0.0016)	**	0.0045	(0.0011)	**
$\beta_{10(Tochigi)}$	0.0253	(0.0016)	**	0.0010	(0.0013)	
$\beta_{11(Gunma)}$	0.0214	(0.0014)	**	–0.0022	(0.0012)	
$\beta_{12(Yamanashi)}$	0.0195	(0.0017)	**	0.0001	(0.0015)	
$\beta_{13(Saitama)}$	0.0105	(0.0014)	**	0.0033	(0.0012)	**
$\beta_{14(Chiba)}$	0.0151	(0.0016)	**	0.0027	(0.0013)	*
$\beta_{15(Tokyo)}$	0.0208	(0.0012)	**	0.0096	(0.0017)	**
$\beta_{16(Kanagawa)}$	0.0188	(0.0017)	**	0.0026	(0.0014)	
$\beta_{17(Toyama)}$	0.0267	(0.0018)	**	0.0130	(0.0015)	**
$\beta_{18(Ishikawa)}$	0.0258	(0.0015)	**	0.0127	(0.0014)	**
$\beta_{19(Fukui)}$	0.0104	(0.0016)	**	0.0077	(0.0018)	**
$\beta_{20(Nagano)}$	0.0140	(0.0014)	**	–0.0014	(0.0012)	
$\beta_{21(Gifu)}$	0.0038	(0.0013)	**	0.0047	(0.0013)	**
$\beta_{22(Shizuoka)}$	0.0174	(0.0015)	**	–0.0029	(0.0011)	*
$\beta_{23(Aichi)}$	0.0155	(0.0015)	**	–0.0017	(0.0014)	
$\beta_{24(Mie)}$	0.0145	(0.0016)	**	0.0067	(0.0012)	**
$\beta_{25(Shiga)}$	0.0425	(0.0016)	**	0.0185	(0.0013)	**
$\beta_{26(Kyoto)}$	0.0253	(0.0015)	**	0.0116	(0.0014)	**
$\beta_{27(Osaka)}$	0.0073	(0.0013)	**	0.0069	(0.0015)	**
$\beta_{28(Hyogo)}$	0.0163	(0.0016)	**	0.0042	(0.0014)	**
$\beta_{29(Nara)}$	0.0273	(0.0017)	**	0.0138	(0.0015)	**
$\beta_{30(Wakayama)}$	0.0227	(0.0019)	**	–0.0028	(0.0014)	*
$\beta_{31(Tottori)}$	0.0259	(0.0016)	**	0.0067	(0.0014)	**
$\beta_{32(Shimane)}$	0.0117	(0.0016)	**	0.0031	(0.0014)	**
$\beta_{33(Okayama)}$	0.0232	(0.0017)	**	0.0081	(0.0012)	**
$\beta_{34(Hiroshima)}$	0.0113	(0.0015)	**	0.0132	(0.0013)	**
$\beta_{35(Yamaguchi)}$	0.0301	(0.0019)	**	0.0065	(0.0012)	**
$\beta_{36(Tokushima)}$	0.0321	(0.0016)	**	0.0053	(0.0015)	**
$\beta_{37(Kagawa)}$	0.0260	(0.0016)	**	0.0088	(0.0016)	**
$\beta_{38(Ehime)}$	0.0199	(0.0017)	**	0.0056	(0.0013)	**
$\beta_{39(Kochi)}$	0.0242	(0.0016)	**	0.0063	(0.0014)	**

(continued)

Table 8.2 (continued)

	Manufacturing industries			Non-manufacturing industries		
$\beta_{40(Fukuoka)}$	0.0131	(0.0016)	**	0.0058	(0.0014)	**
$\beta_{41(Saga)}$	0.0272	(0.0016)	**	0.0032	(0.0015)	*
$\beta_{42(Nagasaki)}$	0.0177	(0.0015)	**	0.0026	(0.0014)	
$\beta_{43(Kumamoto)}$	0.0226	(0.0015)	**	0.0012	(0.0014)	
$\beta_{44(Oita)}$	0.0441	(0.0018)	**	0.0023	(0.0015)	
$\beta_{45(Miyazaki)}$	0.0131	(0.0016)	**	0.0010	(0.0013)	
$\beta_{46(Kagoshima)}$	0.0192	(0.0015)	**	0.0023	(0.0014)	
$\beta_{47(Okinawa)}$	0.0114	(0.0018)	**	0.0037	(0.0014)	**
δ_0	4.4657	(0.3203)	**	3.0108	(0.1297)	**
δ_{DENS}	–0.0390	(0.0072)	**	–0.0137	(0.0039)	**
δ_{ACC}	–0.2330	(0.0184)	**	–0.1576	(0.0074)	**
δ_{TRANS}	0.0398	(0.0040)	**	0.0080	(0.0037)	*
$\sigma_u^2 + \sigma_v^2$	0.0079	(0.0004)	**	0.0024	(0.0001)	**
$\sigma_u^2/(\sigma_u^2 + \sigma_v^2)$	0.6316	(0.0485)	**	0.7259	(0.1430)	**
Log likelihood	1179.99			1758.03		
LR test	196.81			484.72		
Number of observations	1081			1081		

Notes: The standard error is listed within parentheses
** Significance at the 1% level; * significance at the 5% level
β_1: Hokkaido (Hokkaido); $\beta_2 - \beta_8$: Tohoku (Aomori, Iwate, Miyagi, Akita, Yamagata, Fukushima, Niigata); $\beta_9 - \beta_{12}$: Kita-Kanto (Ibaraki, Tochigi, Gunma, Yamanashi); $\beta_{13} - \beta_{16}$: Greater Tokyo Area (Saitama, Chiba, Tokyo, Kanagawa); $\beta_{17} - \beta_{19}$: Hokuriku (Toyama, Ishikawa, Fukui); $\beta_{20} - \beta_{24}$: Chubu (Nagano, Gifu, Shizuoka, Aichi, Mie); $\beta_{25} - \beta_{30}$: Kansai (Shiga, Kyoto, Osaka, Hyogo, Nara, Wakayama); $\beta_{31} - \beta_{35}$: Chugoku (Tottori, Shimane, Okayama, Hiroshima, Yamaguchi); $\beta_{36} - \beta_{39}$: Shikoku (Tokushima, Kagawa, Ehime, Kochi); $\beta_{40} - \beta_{46}$: Kyushu (Fukuoka, Saga, Nagasaki, Kumamoto, Oita, Miyazaki, Kagoshima); β_{47}: Okinawa (Okinawa)

three metropolitan areas of the Greater Tokyo Area (0.972, 0.947), Kansai (0.903, 0.842), and Chubu (0.904, 0.866), while the efficiency measures are relatively low in non-metropolitan areas such as Hokkaido (0.799, 0.764), Tohoku (0.769, 0.751), Hokuriku (0.748, 0.754), Chugoku (0.786, 0.781), Shikoku (0.738, 0.739), Kyusyu (0.762, 0.726), and Okinawa (0.733, 0.755). We can easily predict lower productive efficiency in non-metropolitan areas from the estimated parameters shown in Table 8.3. The non-metropolitan areas have low population density and relatively low market access. These areas received a relatively high level of fiscal transfer into their general finances during the entire observation period (1980–2002), which reduced the efficiency of their resource allocations. The geographical distribution pattern of efficiency measures corresponds to the regional structure in Japan, as described in Chap. 1.

Considering the change in productive efficiency, this study finds three important policy implications. First, the efficiency change of non-metropolitan areas, such as Hokkaido (15.4%, 5.1%) and Tohoku (10.2%, 7.5%,) is larger than that of the metropolitan areas, like the Greater Tokyo Area (3.4%, 3.0%) and Kansai (–2.9%, –

Table 8.3 Productive efficiency

	Manufacturing		Non-manufacturing	
11 regions	Average	Δ (1980–2002)	Average	Δ (1980–2002)
Hokkaido	0.799	0.154	0.764	0.051
Tohoku	0.769	0.102	0.751	0.075
Kita-Kanto	0.918	0.002	0.849	0.138
Greater Tokyo Area	0.972	0.034	0.947	0.030
Chubu	0.904	0.124	0.866	0.099
Hokuriku	0.748	0.081	0.754	0.001
Kansai	0.903	−0.029	0.842	−0.007
Chugoku	0.786	0.080	0.781	−0.021
Shikoku	0.738	0.055	0.739	0.015
Kyushu	0.762	0.026	0.726	0.059
Okinawa	0.733	0.153	0.755	−0.025
Total	0.827	0.056	0.799	0.043
Max	0.985	0.208	0.968	0.156
	(Tokyo)	(Gifu)	(Kanagawa)	(Gunma)
Min	0.686	−0.186	0.700	−0.154
	(Aomori)	(Shiga)	(Miyazaki)	(Hiroshima)
Coefficient of Variation	0.109	1.483	0.090	1.649

0.7%,) even though their average efficiency measures are lower than those of the metropolitan areas. The result implies that the efficiency change from 1980 to 2002 is different than the average efficiency. The difference between efficiency and efficiency change is because Japan constructed road networks mainly in non-metropolitan areas. Consequently, market access (ACC) improved in the non-metropolitan areas from 1980 to 2002. The investments in road construction were done under the government's economic policy that was intended to support regional economies by creating employment opportunities in local construction industries. Thus, improved traffic access to the Greater Tokyo Area positively influenced the growth of productive efficiency in non-metropolitan areas, but the increased dependence on fiscal transfer had a negative influence.

Here, it is important to note that the productive efficiency result provides an implication for policy that is partly consistent with previous studies that have claimed that highway investment increases the productivity of a region through enhanced accessibility to a market. For example, Montolio and Solé-Ollé (2009) examined whether public investment in road infrastructures increased TFP growth in Spanish provinces and found that road investment had a positive influence despite the negative effect of excessive use, or congestion. Otsuka (2017) also indicates social overhead capital contributes to TFP growth, and endorses improvements of social infrastructure to spur Japan's regional TFP growth.

The second implication for policy relates to the finding that the degree of average inefficiency in non-manufacturing industries is greater than that of manufacturing industries. For example, the efficiency loss of manufacturing

Table 8.4 Growth accounting (annual growth rate %) in 1980–2002

11 Regions	Output growth	Capital growth	Labor growth	Growth of total factor productivity (TFP)				
				Technological progress	Change in productive efficiency (TE)			Others
					DENS	ACC	TRANS	
(a) Manufacturing industries								
Hokkaido	1.97	0.88	–1.00	0.99	0.00	0.45	–0.03	0.68
Tohoku	3.49	1.81	–0.22	1.23	–0.01	0.52	–0.01	0.17
Kita-Kanto	3.61	2.04	–0.14	2.10	0.01	0.58	–0.02	–0.96
Greater Tokyo Area	1.62	1.09	–1.03	1.63	0.03	0.64	–0.07	–0.67
Chubu	3.56	1.69	–0.45	1.30	0.01	0.58	–0.12	0.55
Hokuriku	3.37	1.56	–0.74	2.10	0.01	0.56	–0.03	–0.09
Kansai	2.35	1.30	–0.92	2.36	0.01	0.47	–0.10	–0.77
Chugoku	2.79	1.25	–0.97	2.05	0.00	0.47	–0.03	0.02
Shikoku	2.95	1.25	–1.16	2.56	0.00	0.41	–0.01	–0.10
Kyushu	3.06	1.44	–0.62	2.24	0.01	0.45	–0.01	–0.45
Okinawa	3.03	1.60	–0.83	1.14	0.03	0.55	0.01	0.53
Average	2.89	1.45	–0.74	1.79	0.01	0.52	–0.04	–0.10
(b) Non-manufacturing industries								
Hokkaido	1.66	1.30	–0.49	0.57	0.00	0.34	–0.01	–0.05
Tohoku	1.86	1.59	–0.48	0.26	0.00	0.38	0.00	0.11
Kita-Kanto	2.46	1.47	0.00	0.09	0.00	0.41	0.00	0.49
Greater Tokyo Area	3.21	1.95	0.71	0.46	0.01	0.32	–0.01	–0.23
Chubu	2.40	1.70	0.01	0.11	0.00	0.43	–0.02	0.17
Hokuriku	2.14	1.34	–0.18	1.12	0.00	0.40	–0.01	–0.53
Kansai	2.41	1.60	0.09	0.87	0.00	0.28	–0.02	–0.41
Chugoku	1.82	1.74	–0.39	0.75	0.00	0.31	–0.01	–0.58
Shikoku	1.75	1.56	–0.48	0.65	0.00	0.27	0.00	–0.25
Kyushu	1.85	1.61	–0.42	0.27	0.00	0.32	0.00	0.07
Okinawa	2.68	2.14	0.51	0.37	0.01	0.34	0.00	–0.69
Average	2.20	1.64	–0.10	0.50	0.00	0.34	–0.01	–0.17

Note: "TFP" is calculated by (8.5). "Others" stands for "an unexplained efficiency change." "DENS," "ACC" and "TRANS" stand for population density, market access and fiscal transfer ratio, respectively

industries is approximately 17% (=(1−0.827) ×100) on average, while that of non-manufacturing industries is approximately 20% (=(1−0.799) ×100) on average. The result indicates that a significant efficiency loss occurred in both industries. The large difference occurs because there is a considerable efficiency difference between metropolitan and non-metropolitan areas. For instance, the level of efficiency ranges from 0.985 (Tokyo in the metropolitan) to 0.686 (Aomori in the non-metropolitan) in manufacturing industries, a difference of 0.299 (=0.985−0.686.) Meanwhile, efficiency ranges from 0.968 (Kanagawa in the metropolitan) to 0.700 (Miyazaki in the non-metropolitan) in non-manufacturing industries, a difference of 0.268 in their efficiency scores. This efficiency difference between metropolitan and non-metropolitan areas is consistent with the geographical distribution of industries depicted in Chap. 1.

Finally, to examine regional differences in productive efficiency further, this study calculates the coefficient of variation (CV) as summarized at the bottom of Table 8.3. There is no major difference in the CV of efficiency between the two industries. In contrast, there is a difference between them in the CV of efficiency change from 1980 to 2002. For example, the CV of efficiency change in non-manufacturing industries is 1.649, while that of manufacturing industries is 1.483. See the bottom of Table 8.3. Thus, the CV of non-manufacturing industries is larger than that of manufacturing industries. This indicates that the regional difference in the change of productive efficiency in non-manufacturing industries is larger than that of manufacturing industries.

Next, we pay attention to growth accounting. Table 8.4 summarizes the results of growth accounting. Table 8.4a summarizes the annual growth rate (%) of manufacturing industries. Table 8.4b summarizes that of non-manufacturing industries. The growth of TFP and its decomposed factors are described in the fifth to ninth columns in Table 8.4a, b.

In examining Table 8.4, we need to mention that the relationship between TFP growth and Z-variables is expressed by mean efficiency, as specified by Eq. (8.5). Since the relationship maintains a stochastic feature, the TFP growth incorporates an error term as in Eq. (8.5). Therefore, it may deviate from what is predicted by the explanatory variables, the Z-variables, and the dummy variables. When we measure a change between two periods, the change in the stochastic part (an error term) has a non-zero effect. Hence, we describe the missing element of an unexplained efficiency change as "others" in Table 8.4, according to Jacob and Los (2007).[9]

Table 8.4 presents three important findings. First, there is obvious technological progress during the observed period (1980–2002), and technological progress accounts for the largest portion of TFP growth. The contribution of technological progress ranges from 2.56% (Shikoku) to 0.99% (Hokkaido), indicating an overall average of 1.79% in manufacturing industries. See the fifth column of Table 8.4a. Meanwhile, technological progress ranges from 1.12% (Hokuriku) to 0.09% (Kita-Kanto), indicating an overall average of 0.50% in non-manufacturing industries. See the fifth column of Table 8.4b. The contribution of productive efficiency changes to TFP growth through the three factors (DENS, ACC, and TRANS) is smaller than that of technological progress. See the right-hand side of Table 8.4a, b. Meanwhile, enhanced market access (ACC) increases the average TFP growth by

[9]Jacob and Los (2007) label it as "unexplained assimilation," which could be translated in the current context as "unexplained efficiency change."

0.52% in manufacturing industries and 0.34% in non-manufacturing industries. This explicit contribution of market access (ACC) to the TFP growth is found in metropolitan areas as well as other areas.

Second, the contribution of the other factors (DENS and TRANS) is relatively small in manufacturing industries, being 0.01% and –0.04% on average, respectively. Their contributions are 0.00% (DENS) and –0.01% (TRANS) on average in non-manufacturing industries. In contrast, the impact of the fiscal transfer is not negligible in manufacturing industries. For instance, it ranges from –0.12% for Chubu to 0.01% for Okinawa. The impact in metropolitan areas is larger than that in non-metropolitan areas. This result implies that the loss of TFP growth caused by fiscal transfer in metropolitan areas is larger than the national average because the growth of fiscal transfer in metropolitan areas is larger than that of the other areas during the observed period (1980–2002). See the right-hand side of Table 8.4 explained later.

Finally, the third important finding is that the impact of population density (DENS) on TFP growth is negligible in this study, as it is less than 0.03% for all regions. In particular, the impact is almost zero in non-manufacturing industries.[10] See the sixth column of Table 8.4. Furthermore, we find that the degree of positive impact of market access exceeds that of the negative impact induced by the fiscal transfer so that productive efficiency change positively influences TFP growth, which is approximately 0.49% and 0.33% for manufacturing and non-manufacturing industries, respectively.[11]

Table 8.5 summarizes the degree of dependence on local allocation tax. Metropolitan areas have less dependence on public fiscal transfer than other areas. However, the growth rate of dependence in metropolitan areas is 1.47 from 1980 to 2002, which is larger than all other regions except for Kansai (1.70). See the right-hand side of Table 8.5. The level of dependence in most regions decreases during the period from 1980 to 1990 and increases in the remaining other periods, as indicated in Table 8.5.

[10]An exception is the Greater Tokyo Area, which shows contributions of 0.03% for manufacturing industries; however, the total average is 0.01%. Hence, the effect of population density is negligible in this study.

[11]Table 8.4 indicates that the "Other" factor is calculated from residuals as unexplained efficiency change. The value of the "Other" factor is not small enough to be negligible. Thus, it implies that there are some regional differences that cannot be identified by the proposed model. Since our main research concern is to examine the impact of agglomeration economies and fiscal transfer on TFP, we do not explore the residuals further in this study.

Table 8.5 Degree of dependence on local allocation tax (%)

11 Regions	1980 (%)	1985 (%)	1990 (%)	1995 (%)	2000 (%)	2002 (%)	2002/1980
Hokkaido	50.6	53.8	56.1	54.3	57.3	58.2	1.15
Tohoku	58.5	58.2	58.6	54.7	59.5	60.7	1.04
Kita-Kanto	42.3	36.3	35.0	39.0	45.7	47.0	1.11
Greater Tokyo Area	7.2	5.4	3.5	6.1	11.8	10.5	1.47
Chubu	24.6	20.4	19.7	23.8	32.1	32.3	1.31
Hokuriku	50.5	48.9	49.0	48.4	57.1	58.5	1.16
Kansai	24.2	19.7	18.5	28.1	37.8	41.2	1.70
Chugoku	49.8	49.6	49.5	51.1	56.3	58.7	1.18
Shikoku	62.3	60.7	61.0	61.8	63.7	65.3	1.05
Kyushu	56.1	56.6	56.9	55.6	58.8	60.3	1.07
Okinawa	72.0	68.1	69.1	70.3	70.7	69.3	0.96

8.6 Conclusion and Future Extensions

There is an ongoing policy discussion about national land planning reforms. The Japanese government has been facing a large fiscal deficit. The government needs to implement an effective economic policy to support regional economic growth at the level of prefectures. To examine the influence of agglomeration economies and fiscal transfer on productive efficiency of regional industries, this study suggested two assumptions, as summarized in Sect. 8.1.

Two policy implications arise from this empirical study. The first implication is that agglomeration economies positively influenced productive efficiency, and market access contributed to the improvement of productive efficiency for manufacturing and non-manufacturing industries. The second is that public fiscal transfer or local allocation tax negatively influenced productive efficiency of Japanese industries.

In addition to the policy implications, it is important to mention that the data set used in this study is comprised of panel data with time series on each prefecture. The effects of regional factors on productive efficiency enhanced the total factor productivity growth over time.

The empirical evidence found in this study showed that enhanced market access contributed to TFP growth through improved productive efficiency, while the public fiscal transfer had no or negative influence on TFP growth through diminished productive efficiency. Such effects were particularly evident in manufacturing industries. The decrease in efficiency linked to the public fiscal transfer was caused by a reduced incentive for managerial efforts in local governments and industries. Furthermore, we found that the negative impact of fiscal transfer on TFP growth in metropolitan areas was larger than in non-metropolitan areas because the degree of dependence on local allocation tax in metropolitan areas increased faster than in non-metropolitan areas, particularly since the late 1990s. These findings were consistent with previous studies on metropolitan areas.

As future extensions of this study, we envision four research agendas. First, we will have to investigate the policy implications of the impact of agglomeration economies on economic growth in Japan. This an important future extension of this study because the Japanese government is expected to implement the most effective spatial policy based on a cost-benefit analysis of each economic project without any political bias. Second, it is important for Japan to support industries so that they can achieve more efficient spatial patterns of firms' locations; an extension of this study could explore this policy issue. Third, it is necessary for Japan to develop a traffic system that improves inter-regional access because an economic loss often occurs when there is limited market access and an inefficient transport network to metropolitan areas. Such limitations become serious policy issues because of the impact on regional industries. Therefore, these policy issues need to be investigated in the future. Fourth, it is necessary for us to design a more efficient system of fiscal transfer. The new system should include managerial incentives for local governments and industries to achieve growth in regional economies.

References

Aigner DJ, Lovell C, Schmidt P. Formulation and estimation of stochastic frontier production function model. J Econ. 1977;6(1):21–37.

Battese GE, Coelli TJ. Model for technical inefficiency effects in a stochastic frontier production function for panel data. Empir Econ. 1995;20(2):325–32.

Battese GE, Corra GS. Estimation of a production frontier model: with application to the pastoral zone of Eastern Australia. Aust J Agric Econ. 1977;21(3):169–79.

Beeson PE, Husted S. Patterns and determinants of productive efficiency in the state manufacturing. J Reg Sci. 1989;29(1):15–28.

Combes PP, Gobillon L. The empirics of agglomeration economies. In: Duranton G, Henderson JV, Strange W, editors. Handbook of regional and urban economics, volume 5A. Amsterdam: Elsevier; 2015.

De Borger B, Kerstens K. Cost efficiency of Belgian local governments: a comparative analysis of FDH, DEA and econometric approaches. Reg Sci Urban Econ. 1996;26(2):145–70.

Driffield N, Munday M. Foreign manufacturing, regional agglomeration and technical efficiency in UK industries: a stochastic production frontier approach. Reg Stud. 2001;35(5):391–9.

Färe R, Grosskopf S, Norris M, Zhang Z. Productivity growth, technical progress, and efficiency change in industrialized countries. Am Econ Rev. 1994;84(1):66–83.

Fried HO, Lovell CAK, Schmidt SS. The measurement of productive efficiency: techniques and applications. New York: Oxford University Press; 1993.

Fujita M, Thisse J. Economics of agglomeration: cities, industrial location, and regional growth. Cambridge: Cambridge University Press; 2002.

Fujita M, Krugman P, Venables A. The spatial economy: cities, regions, and international trade. Cambridge: MIT Press; 1999.

Hewings GJD, Parr JB. Spatial interdependence in a metropolitan setting. Spat Econ Anal. 2007;2(1):7–22.

Hewings GJD, Israilevich PR, Schindler GR, Sonis M. Agglomeration, clustering and structural change: interpreting changes in the Chicago regional economy. In: Steiner M, Cappellin R, editors. From agglomeration economies to innovative clusters. London: Pion; 1998.

Jacob J, Los B. Absorptive capacity and foreign spillovers: a stochastic frontier approach. In: Frenken K, editor. Applied evolutionary economics and economic geography. Cheltenham: Edward Elgar; 2007.

Kumbhakar SC, Lovell CAK. Stochastic frontier analysis. Cambridge: Cambridge University Press; 2000.

Meeusen W, van den Broeck J. Efficient estimation from Cobb-Douglas production functions with composed error. Int Econ Rev. 1977;18(2):435–44.

Mitra A. Agglomeration economies as manifested in technical efficiency at the firm level. J Urban Econ. 1999;45(3):490–500.

Mitra A. Total factor productivity growth and urbanization economies: a case of Indian industries. Rev Urban Reg Dev Stud. 2000;12(2):97–108.

Mitra A, Sato H. Agglomeration economies in Japan: technical efficiency, growth and unemployment. Rev Urban Reg Dev Stud. 2007;19(3):197–209.

Montolio D, Solé-Ollé A. Road investment and regional productivity growth: the effects of vehicle intensity and congestion. Pap Reg Sci. 2009;88(1):99–118.

Otsuka A. Regional determinants of total factor productivity in Japan: stochastic frontier analysis. Ann Reg Sci. 2017;58(3):579–96.

Otsuka A, Goto M, Sueyoshi T. Industrial agglomeration effects in Japan: productive efficiency, market access, and public fiscal transfer. Pap Reg Sci. 2010;89(4):819–39.

Otsuka A, Goto M, Sueyoshi T. Cost-efficiency of Japanese local governments: effects of decentralization and regional integration. Reg Stud Reg Sci. 2014;1(1):207–20.

Parr JB. Missing elements in the analysis of agglomeration economies. Int Reg Sci Rev. 2002;25 (2):151–68.

Tveteras R, Battese GE. Agglomeration externalities, productivity, and technical inefficiency. J Reg Sci. 2006;46(4):605–25.

Yamano N, Ohkawara T. The regional allocation of public investment: efficiency or equity? J Reg Sci. 2000;40(2):205–29.

Chapter 9
Market Access, Agglomeration Economies, and Productive Efficiency (II)

Abstract This chapter examines the impacts of agglomeration economies and fiscal transfer on productive efficiency in Japanese regional industries. Two popular methodologies, stochastic frontier analysis and data envelopment analysis, are applied to measure productive efficiency. The empirical findings are summarized as follows: (1) Agglomeration economies improve productive efficiency. (2) Fiscal transfer negatively influences productive efficiency. (3) Those two findings are observed for aggregated manufacturing and non-manufacturing industries, and for sectors in manufacturing industries. (4) The importance of agglomeration economies for regional industries has increased in recent years. Based on these results, this chapter discusses effective regional policy for Japan.

Keywords Productive efficiency • Agglomeration economies • Market access • Fiscal transfer • Stochastic frontier analysis • Data envelopment analysis

9.1 Introduction

This chapter re-examines the impacts of agglomeration economies and fiscal transfer systems on the productive efficiency of industries to enable a discussion regarding effective regional policy in Japan that will improve the productive efficiency of regional industries.

It is well known that industry agglomeration positively influences productive efficiency and the productivity of firms, as discussed in Chap. 8. For example, firms can benefit from their locations by securing capital equipment and human resources with highly specialized knowledge for production activities, especially if they are in areas with high population density. In addition, if a firm is in an area close to a large-scale market, then it has the advantage of having access to market information at any time. Agglomeration economies can therefore help corporate leaders avoid poor decision-making that may cause inefficiency in firms (Scott and Storper 2003).

This chapter is based on Otsuka and Goto (2015) "Regional policy and the productive efficiency of Japanese industries," published in Regional Studies (Vol. 49, No. 4, pp. 518–531).

A. Otsuka, *A New Perspective on Agglomeration Economies in Japan*,
New Frontiers in Regional Science: Asian Perspectives 20,
DOI 10.1007/978-981-10-6490-6_9

The positive effects of agglomeration economies on productive efficiency in various countries have been shown in recent empirical studies; for example, Beeson and Husted (1989); Mitra (1999); Tveteras and Battese (2006); Mitra and Sato (2007); Yamamura and Shin (2007). Driffield and Munday (2001) examined the impacts of foreign direct investment and agglomeration economies on productive efficiency of UK industries. Otsuka et al. (2010) examined productive efficiency of Japanese manufacturing and non-manufacturing industries using a data set from the 1980s to the 1990s, and revealed positive influences of agglomeration economies. In particular, they indicated the importance of market access to improve productive efficiency of regional industries. The importance of market access for regional economic growth is also discussed in a case from the U.S. Midwest in Parr et al. (2002).

In addition, Otsuka et al. (2010, 2014) examined how fiscal transfer influenced productive or cost efficiency of regional economies in Japan. The analysis was motivated by serious on-going fiscal problems in Japan, which were magnified by large-scale public investments implemented in all regions in Japan after the collapse of the bubble economy. Public investments were made to avoid a rapid economic downturn in the 1990s, but instead they exacerbated fiscal conditions in Japan. For example, the rate of government debt to GDP in Japan in 2010 was greater than 200%, larger than that of Greece (approximately 150%) or Italy (approximately 125%). Despite the deterioration of the government fiscal condition, there has been very little research on the effectiveness of the current regional policy, particularly from the perspective of the productive efficiency of industries. For a policy assessment of the fiscal transfer system, it is necessary to consider two aspects of the construction investments that are partly funded by the fiscal transfer from national to local governments. First, road construction, which is partly funded by fiscal transfer, improves access to other regional markets. Second, the fiscal transfer policy hinders the dynamism of the economy because the system discourages the necessary shift of industrial structure from traditional (but unproductive) sectors to more productive ones.

The study in this chapter extends Otsuka et al. (2010) in three ways. First, the data set is extended from 1980–2002 to 1980–2005. Second, the previous study only distinguished two categories of industries: manufacturing and non-manufacturing. Because there are many different sectors in those industries, this was a significant limitation in terms of policy implications. To overcome the limitation of the previous study, this study subdivides the manufacturing industry into individual industrial sectors and examines the influences of agglomeration economies and fiscal transfer on productive efficiency for each subdivided industry sector. Third, to check the robustness of the empirical results, this study uses two different methodologies: stochastic frontier analysis (SFA) and data envelopment analysis (DEA). The use of two different methodologies allows us to determine whether methodology bias exists, as it is often argued that different methodologies produce different results in empirical studies. Therefore, it is necessary to check the robustness of the results using multiple methodologies to provide important policy implications. In addition, this study compares the results with those of the previous study.

At the heart of this empirical study are two hypotheses on industries' productive efficiency.

Hypothesis 9.1 Agglomeration economies improve the productive efficiency of Japanese regional industries.

Hypothesis 9.2 The fiscal transfer system, from the national government to local governments, negatively affects productive efficiency of Japanese regional industries.

The remainder of this chapter is structured as follows: Section 9.2 reviews the two methodologies used in this study, SFA and DEA. Section 9.3 describes the data used in the empirical analysis. Section 9.4 describes the two empirical models, SFA and DEA, and the empirical results. The two hypotheses are also discussed in this section regarding the empirical results. This study concludes in Section 9.5.

9.2 Research Methodology

9.2.1 Stochastic Frontier Analysis

SFA was initiated by Meeusen and Van den Broeck (1977), Aigner et al. (1977) and Battese and Corra (1977). Following these three studies, researchers have proposed various models using different assumptions to measure the productive efficiency of firms and industries.[1] This study uses a model proposed by Battese and Coelli (1995), which examines the effects of various factors on the mean inefficiencies of firms through an integrated regression of production frontier and inefficiency functions. The advantage of the model is that it is possible to estimate the parameters for productive inefficiency along with those for the production function without assuming the same trajectory for all firms under the panel data setting.

In logarithmic form, the production frontier model can be written as follows:

$$\ln Y_{jt} = \alpha_0 + \sum_{j=1,\ldots,n} \beta_j \cdot dum_j \cdot t + \sum_{i=1,\ldots,m} \alpha_i \ln X_{ijt} + v_{jt} - u_{jt}, \tag{9.1}$$

where Y_{jt} is the level of output for the jth ($j = 1,\ldots,n$) region in period t, and X_{ijt} is the level of the ith ($i = 1,\ldots,m$) input for the jth region ($j = 1,\ldots,n$) in period t ($t = 1,\ldots,T$). It is assumed that technological progress differs across regions. To capture technological progress for each region by parameters, the regional dummy variable, dum_j is multiplied by the time trend t in Eq. (9.1). The parameters to be

[1]Comprehensive surveys and various advanced models of SFA can be obtained from Kumbhakar and Lovell (2000).

estimated are denoted by α and β, and α includes the constant parameter (α_0) and the parameters of production technology (α_i), while β denotes parameters to capture technological progress, which can vary across regions. A combined error term ($v_{jt} - u_{jt}$) consists of two parts: a random term v_{jt}, and a term associated with productive inefficiency u_{jt}. In addition, v_{jt} is assumed to be i.i.d. $N(0, \sigma_v^2)$, and independent of u_{jt} and all regressors, and u_{jt} is a non-negative random variable, which is assumed to be independently distributed with truncations at zero of the $N(\mu, \sigma_u^2)$ distribution.

Given the specification in (9.1), the corresponding measure of productive efficiency PE_{jt}, which is the ratio of the observed output Y_{jt} over the production frontier output y_{jt}, is given as follows:

$$PE_{jt} = Y_{jt}/y_{jt} = e^{-u_{jt}}.$$

Here, the mean of productive inefficiency, μ, is formulated as follows:

$$\mu_{jt} = \delta_0 + \sum_Z \delta_Z \ln Z_{jt},$$

where Z_{jt} indicates variables that possibly depend on regional industries and time, and δ indicates parameters to be estimated. From the construction of the frontier function, the estimated productive efficiency PE_{jt} is positive with an upper bound of unity, that is,

$$PE_{jt} = E\left(\exp(-u_{jt}) \mid v_{jt} - u_{jt}\right), 0 < PE_{jt} \leq 1.$$

9.2.2 Two-Stage Approach Using DEA

To examine the effects of agglomeration economies and fiscal transfer on productive efficiency of Japanese regional industries, this study uses DEA as an additional methodology. The DEA approach has long served as an important methodology to evaluate the performance of various organizations in public and private sectors (for example, see Emrouznejad et al. 2008, who summarized DEA contributions over the past three decades). A major contributor to DEA was Professor William W. Cooper (University of Texas at Austin). Glover and Sueyoshi 2009, discussed Professor Cooper's DEA theories, models, and algorithms dating back to the eighteenth century.

A two-stage approach is used for the DEA application. The first stage is a bootstrap DEA, and the second stage is a panel data Tobit regression (Cameron and Trivedi 2005, chapter 23.5).[2] The first stage produces DEA efficiency scores for Japanese industries in each region, and the second stage uses the efficiency score as a dependent variable. This study uses bootstrap DEA as proposed by Simar and Wilson 1998, because the bootstrap technique provides DEA with the capability of statistical inference.

This study assumes an output-oriented BCC model (Banker et al. 1984) for the bootstrap DEA to measure the productive efficiency of the specific hth decision making unit (DMU—a regional industry in this study) among n DMUs. The output-oriented BCC model is mathematically expressed using the following formulation:

$$\max \{\theta \mid \mathbf{x_h} - \mathbf{X}\boldsymbol{\lambda} \geq 0, \ \ \mathbf{Y}\boldsymbol{\lambda} \geq \theta\, \mathbf{y_h}, \ \ \mathbf{i}\boldsymbol{\lambda} = 1, \ \ \boldsymbol{\lambda} \geq 0\}, \tag{9.2}$$

where θ is a DEA efficiency score (Farrell output efficiency estimate), which is greater than or equal to 1, $\mathbf{i}$ is a $1 \times n$ unit vector and $\boldsymbol{\lambda}$ is an $n \times 1$ weight vector connecting all the data points in the form of a convex hull. In addition, $\mathbf{x_h}$ is an $m \times 1$ input vector of the hth DMU, $\mathbf{y_h}$ is an $s \times 1$ output vector of the hth DMU, $\mathbf{X}$ is an $m \times n$ matrix representing m inputs ($i = 1,\ldots,m$) of n DMUs and $\mathbf{Y}$ is an $s \times n$ matrix representing s outputs ($r = 1,\ldots,s$) of n DMUs.

Applying the bootstrap DEA method proposed by Simar and Wilson (1998) to model (9.2), it is possible to obtain the bias-corrected DEA efficiency score, θ^*. Because of the way the DEA model is constructed, efficiency does not distribute below 1. In other words, efficiency is censored at unity and it may concentrate on unity. Hence, efficiency becomes a limited dependent variable of the Tobit regression in the second stage of the proposed approach. Here, it is important to note that if ordinary least squares regression is used at the second stage, the estimated parameters are biased because the standard regression needs to assume a normal and homoscedastic distribution for its disturbance and a dependent variable. Therefore, this study applies a censored Tobit model (Tobin, 1958) at the second stage regression due to the distribution of efficiency.

To apply the Tobit model, the efficiency score is transformed from θ^* to $\theta^* - 1$, which produces a normalized inefficiency index (NIE). This transformation is for the computational convenience of the censored Tobit regression where the censoring point is 0. Because of the normalization, the inefficiency index (NIE) has a distribution with $[0, \infty]$ where the censoring point is 0. The censoring point corresponds to full efficiency in the DEA efficiency measurement. Because the data set has a panel data structure, this study applies the random effects panel data Tobit model to the NIE index. Therefore, the inherent aspects of each region are absorbed in the random effects parameter. Consequently, the proposed two-stage DEA approach provides us not only with the level of productive efficiency but also with empirical evidence on what factors increase productive efficiency as measured by DEA. The computational flow of the two-stage approach is depicted in Fig. 9.1.

[2]See Charnes et al. (1988) and Sueyoshi (1996) for a combined use of DEA and regression analysis.

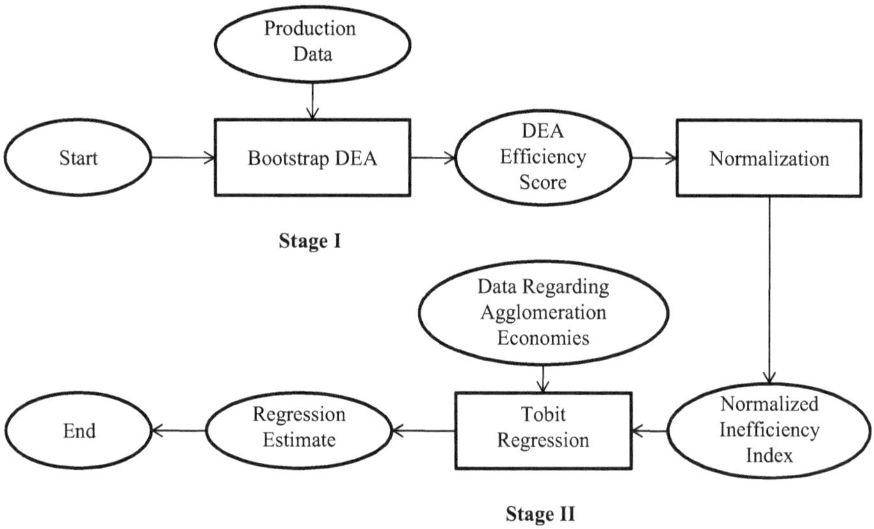

Fig. 9.1 Computational flow of two-stage approach

9.3 Data

Using data pertaining to Japan's 47 prefectures, productive efficiency is estimated for manufacturing and non-manufacturing industries as a whole, and 13 individual manufacturing sectors (Table 9.1) over the period 1980–2005.

The output is defined by value-added, and the inputs are labor and capital. Value-added (Y) for each prefectural industry is measured by the nominal value-added reported in the *Annual Report on Prefectural Accounts*, deflated by the value-added deflator reported in the *System of National Accounts* (SNA). Labor input (L) is measured by an estimate of working hours. Capital input (K) is fixed capital stock adjusted by its rate of utilization. Fixed capital stock is constructed from gross investment, which applies the benchmark year method. The data source of capital input is the Regional Economic Database from the Central Research Institute of Electric Power Industry. The rate of utilization for the manufacturing industry is derived from a set of indices of operating ratios published by the Ministry of Economy, Trade, and Industry (METI). Because there is no publicly available data on the rate of utilization for non-manufacturing industries, a "deviation rate" is used as a proxy variable for the rate, which is calculated by the inverse of the capital coefficient.

In addition to the basic variables for production inputs and output, this study uses three variables to explain productive efficiency. First, population density (DENS) and market access (ACC) are used as the indexes of agglomeration economies.

The most widely known indices of agglomeration are the Ellison-Glaeser Index (EGI) and the Herfindahl-Hirschman Index (HHI) (Capello and Nijkamp 2009). Ellison and Glaeser (1997) suggested the former index and it expresses the spatial

Table 9.1 List of manufacturing industry sectors

Code	Sector
1	Food products
2	Textile mill products
3	Pulp, paper and allied products
4	Chemical industry
5	Petroleum and coal products
6	Stone, clay and glass products
7	Primary metal products
8	Metal products
9	General machinery
10	Electrical machinery
11	Transportation equipment
12	Precision machinery
13	Miscellaneous manufacturing

Note: This list is based on the classification of economic activities from the *Annual Report on Prefectural Accounts*

agglomeration of the industry. Calculation of this index requires individual data of firms, which is generally not available. The latter index is defined as:

$$HHI_j = \sum_i S_{ij}^2,$$

where $S_{ij}$is a composition ratio of industry i in region j. This indicates that the smaller the index, the more diversified the industrial structure.

As diversity is the foundation of agglomeration economies, the HHI is often used to indicate agglomeration. However, calculation of this index requires employment data by industry and by region. In Japan, the index uses national census data, which is published in 5-year increments. However, population density, which is published every year, is found to have a high correlation with the HHI. In fiscal year 2005, the correlation between population density and the HHI calculated using the three-digit industry classification was –0.74, which is statistically significant at the 5% level. Therefore, we employ population density (DENS) as a variable indicating diversity in industrial structure because we can interpret that the higher the population density, the more diversified the industrial structure. Population density is calculated by dividing population by the inhabited area.

The effect of market access on corporate location decisions has long been debated in empirical research. Spatial economics demonstrate that a firm's best location depends on market access, which is defined to include market size and transportation costs. For instance, Fujita et al. (1999) and Fujita and Thisse (2002) point out that the development of high-speed traffic networks reduces transportation costs, which improves market access, thus improving agglomeration economies. Fujita et al. (1999) show theoretically that reduced transport costs accelerate agglomeration. This study employs market access (ACC) as the second variable of agglomeration economies to empirically verify the effect. The second index of agglomeration economies, market access, is defined as follows:

$$ACC_{jt} \equiv \sum_{k \neq j} \left[\left(d_{jkt}^{-1} / \sum_{k \neq j} d_{jkt}^{-1} \right) \cdot Q_{kt} \right],$$

where d_{jkt} represents the economic distance from region j to k in period t. Gross output Q_{kt} is used to capture the size of the local production market in region k in period t. The statistics are based on automobile travel costs.[3] Please note that only market access within Japan is considered in this study. Normally global linkages should be considered in measuring market access because Japan has an export-dependent economic structure. However, there is no data about Japanese exports that specifies both exporting region and importing country. Moreover, it is currently difficult to create time–distance data among overseas regions. Therefore, the variables in this study refer to local market access.

Second, the ratio of fiscal transfer (TRANS) is used as the third variable to explain productive efficiency, and is defined by the ratio of local allocation tax to general finances. The local allocation tax is a public fiscal transfer from the national government to local governments. General finances are fiscal resources that a local government can use without any restrictions as to purpose. The ratio is relatively high for regions that depend heavily on fiscal transfer to finance public investment.

9.4 Empirical Analysis

9.4.1 SFA

The following equations describe an empirical SFA model. Equation (9.3) is a production frontier function and Eq. (9.4) is a function to estimate productive efficiency.

$$\ln Y_{jt} = \alpha_0 + \sum_{j=1,\ldots,n} \beta_j \cdot dum_j \cdot t + \alpha_L \ln L_{jt} + \alpha_K \ln K_{jt} + v_{jt} - u_{jt}, \tag{9.3}$$

$$\mu_{jt} = \delta_0 + \delta_{DENS} \ln DENS_{jt} + \delta_{ACC} \ln ACC_{jt} + \delta_{TRANS} \ln TRANS_{jt}. \tag{9.4}$$

Labor is denoted by L, and K is capital, while δ represents parameters for each variable of the agglomeration economies and public fiscal transfer used to explain

[3]According to the "Net Freight Flow Census (census logistics) 2005," 84.02% of the total shipment cost is automobile transportation, while marine, air, rail, and other types of transportation account for only 11.86%, 0.008%, 0.84% and 3.26%, respectively. These statistics suggest that using travel costs of automobile transportation is preferable for constructing data on economic distance.

Table 9.2 Estimation results of SFA

	Chapter 8				Estimation results			
	Manufacturing industries		Non-manufacturing industries		Manufacturing industries		Non-manufacturing industries	
α_0	0.2495		0.6421		–0.1522		0.6893	
	(2.03)	**	(6.79)	**	(–1.49)		(8.01)	**
α_K	0.3504		0.2978		0.3278		0.3014	
	(28.10)	**	(17.32)	**	(29.89)	**	(17.34)	**
α_L	0.6957		0.7541		0.7515		0.7436	
	(46.62)	**	(39.20)	**	(58.23)	**	(37.99)	**
δ_0	4.4657		3.0108		3.1438		4.1510	
	(13.94)	**	(23.21)	**	(8.54)	**	(19.65)	**
δ_{DENS}	–0.0390		–0.0137		–0.1724		–0.1339	
	(–12.63)	**	(–3.49)	**	(–13.84)	**	(–20.43)	**
δ_{ACC}	–0.0398		–0.1576		–0.1130		–0.1843	
	(9.85)	**	(–21.18)	**	(–4.89)	**	(–14.76)	**
δ_{TRANS}	0.0398		0.0080		0.0383		0.0128	
	(9.85)	**	(2.18)	**	(2.85)	**	(2.42)	**
$\sigma_u^2 + \sigma_v^2$	0.0079		0.0024		0.0087		0.0022	
	(17.85)	**	(21.22)	**	(25.74)	**	(20.05)	**
$\sigma_u^2/(\sigma_u^2 + \sigma_v^2)$	0.6316		0.7259		0.5658		0.4293	
	(13.04)	**	(5.08)	**	(10.83)	**	(6.99)	**
Log likelihood	1179.99		1758.03		1274.91		2035.50	
LR test	196.81		484.72		195.19		753.49	
Mean efficiency	0.8271		0.7989		0.8406		0.8121	
Number of observations	1081		1081		1222		1222	

Notes: For a concise presentation, parameters of interest are indicated and the results of time-trend terms are omitted
The *t*-statistics are enclosed in parentheses
** Significance at the 1% level; * significance at the 5% level

productive efficiency. If the sign of the parameters (δ_{DENS}, δ_{ACC}, δ_{TRANS}) is negative, then the variable improves the level of efficiency.

Table 9.2 shows the estimation results of the model formulated with Eqs. (9.3) and (9.4) for manufacturing and non-manufacturing industries. This study uses Frontier Version 4.1 developed by Battese and Coelli (1995) for the estimation. Prefecture-specific fixed effects are introduced in the estimation to consider unique regional characteristics of the production environment. Table 9.2 also shows the estimation results from Chap. 8 to enable a comparison with the results of this study.

Table 9.2 shows that the parameters (α_K and α_L) of the production functions for each industry are statistically significant. The results also indicate that the variance parameters ($\sigma_u^2 + \sigma_v^2$, $\sigma_u^2/(\sigma_u^2 + \sigma_v^2)$) for error terms are statistically significant, which implies the estimated values of productive efficiency are valid for performance evaluation of manufacturing and non-manufacturing industries. Furthermore, population density (δ_{DENS}) and market access (δ_{ACC}) are negative and statistically significant. These results suggest that both population density and market access contribute to improving the efficiency of the industries. Conversely, the parameter of fiscal transfer (δ_{TRANS}) is positive and statistically significant. This result indicates that fiscal transfer has a negative influence on productive efficiency for both industries. In other words, loss of productive efficiency occurs in regions that have higher ratios of fiscal transfer. These results are consistent with Hypotheses 9.1 and 9.2.

When these results are compared with those of Chap. 8, it is evident from the larger size of the estimated parameters in this study that the magnitude of the impact of population density has increased for both manufacturing and non-manufacturing industries. At the same time, the effect of market access has also grown stronger. This result shows that the agglomeration economies were more influential on productive efficiency from the 1990s to the 2000s. On the other hand, the effect of fiscal transfer has weakened somewhat for manufacturing industries, but strengthened for non-manufacturing industries.

In addition, according to Chap. 8, the mean productive efficiency for Japan's 47 prefectures was 0.827 for manufacturing industries and 0.799 for non-manufacturing industries, whereas efficiency in this study improved to 0.841 and 0.812 for manufacturing and non-manufacturing industries, respectively. These improvements in efficiency suggest that the positive influences of agglomeration economies have become more significant compared with the negative influences caused by fiscal transfer.

Next, Table 9.3 shows the estimation results for the 13 individual sectors of the manufacturing industries. For all sectors, except general machinery (code 9), the parameters (α_K and α_L) of the production functions are statistically significant. In addition, for all sectors, excluding stone, clay, and glass products (code 6) and general machinery (code 9), the variance parameters ($\sigma_u^2 + \sigma_v^2$, $\sigma_u^2/\left(\sigma_u^2 + \sigma_v^2\right)$) are statistically significant.

Population density (δ_{DENS}) and market access (δ_{ACC}) are negative and statistically significant for most of the industry sectors. With respect to population density, the estimated parameter with the largest absolute value is –1.515 for primary metal products (code 7), followed by –1.111 for chemical industry (code 4). That is, the effects of industry agglomeration are stronger for material industries. On the other hand, of the processing/assembly industries, only transportation equipment (code 11) has a large estimated parameter value at –0.833. Compared with population density, there are more sectors that are significantly influenced by market access, and the range of the effects is broad. The degree of influence is approximately the same for both material industries and processing/assembly industries. In particular, the chemical industry (code 4) has a large absolute value at –5.994, followed by pulp, paper, and allied products (code 3) at –4.115 and petroleum and coal products (code 5) at –1.764. These are all material industries. Meanwhile, for processing/

Table 9.3 Estimation results of SFA (manufacturing sectors)

Code	α_0	α_K	α_L	δ_0	δ_{DENS}	δ_{ACC}	δ_{TRANS}	$\sigma_u^2+\sigma_v^2$	$\frac{\sigma_u^2}{\sigma_u^2+\sigma_v^2}$	Log likelihood	LR test	Mean efficiency
1	2.6303	0.4344	0.4600	9.3563	−0.3407	−0.4966	0.0797	0.0406	0.6221	361.89	201.83	0.7517
	(12.88)**	(13.60)**	(11.65)**	(7.35)**	(−10.88)**	(−5.46)**	(8.36)**	(15.20)**	(15.07)**			
2	−0.9332	0.3474	0.7049	10.8062	−0.0975	−0.8157	−0.0018	0.0533	0.7700	143.94	368.63	0.5605
	(−4.64)**	(17.60)**	(29.91)**	(19.30)**	(−3.22)**	(−17.73)**	(−0.12)	(18.73)**	(9.95)**			
3	0.5499	0.2279	0.8608	50.1410	−0.4531	−4.1149	0.0411	0.4394	0.9749	444.19	257.00	0.8680
	(5.56)**	(15.80)**	(48.87)**	(4.31)**	(−4.90)**	(−4.21)**	(0.71)	(4.29)**	(181.62)**			
4	−1.6596	0.4008	0.8349	69.4937	−1.1114	−5.9937	0.1861	7.1634	0.9979	−430.23	1852.91	0.7417
	(−11.43)**	(14.07)**	(23.29)**	(14.19)**	(−5.51)**	(−11.27)**	(2.21)*	(20.91)**	(3041.3)**			
5	2.5014	0.2685	0.8647	−38.3905	−0.2399	−1.7638	0.1239	59.5212	0.9979	−1545.45	1131.17	0.5490
	(17.23)**	(13.68)**	(22.11)**	(−5.93)**	(−0.27)	(−4.62)**	(1.36)	(10.58)**	(3119.9)**			
6	0.5129	0.5176	0.4922	8.0917	−0.1854	−0.5165	−0.0113	0.0169	0.4053	764.32	356.98	0.6198
	(3.39)**	(29.53)**	(22.84)**	(17.30)**	(−11.33)**	(−14.01)**	(−1.53)	(23.52)**	(1.59)			
7	1.8161	0.2480	0.7121	22.2351	−1.5146	−1.0304	0.0745	0.4233	0.9511	26.03	269.52	0.8111
	(19.60)**	(13.60)**	(32.89)**	(7.68)**	(−36.52)**	(−4.56)**	(11.20)**	(15.12)**	(136.98)**			
8	0.2259	0.5755	0.4382	10.2044	−0.0442	−0.7631	−0.0120	0.0479	0.9455	541.49	423.57	0.7769
	(2.22)**	(29.15)**	(19.18)**	(14.24)**	(−1.95)	(−13.66)**	(−0.82)	(9.00)**	(67.74)**			
9	−0.1675	0.5611	0.5141	0.0143	0.0094	−0.0061	0.0349	0.1050	0.0205	−347.78	0.42	0.9724
	(−0.17)	(0.93)	(0.69)	(0.02)	(0.05)	(−0.05)	(0.03)	(3.80)**	(0.10)			
10	−1.2756	0.5365	0.4983	31.3095	0.0567	−2.8632	0.2363	1.7743	0.9794	−146.20	910.73	0.8306
	(−9.53)**	(17.57)**	(12.79)**	(10.04)**	(0.52)	(−12.77)**	(9.22)**	(11.56)**	(400.90)**			
11	0.8965	0.4871	0.4871	58.0063	−0.8329	−4.2182	0.1991	1.6720	0.9851	−144.62	895.49	0.7988
	(9.58)**	(16.73)**	(14.05)**	(30.51)**	(−12.21)**	(−30.52)**	(3.06)**	(11.51)**	(553.44)**			

(continued)

Table 9.3 (continued)

Code	α_0	α_K	α_L	δ_0	δ_{DENS}	δ_{ACC}	δ_{TRANS}	$\sigma_u^2 + \sigma_v^2$	$\frac{\sigma_u^2}{\sigma_u^2 + \sigma_v^2}$	Log likelihood	LR test	Mean efficiency
12	0.7313	0.3766	0.6284	57.4249	–0.5821	–5.4501	0.0507	3.4323	0.9906	–434.49	477.46	0.7569
	(7.60)**	(18.16)**	(21.45)**	(29.94)**	(–2.07)*	(–13.70)**	(2.19)*	(8.92)**	(695.58)**			
13	–0.0239	0.4581	0.6176	0.5497	–0.0422	–0.0306	0.1127	0.0404	0.8772	1007.18	75.18	0.9179
	(–0.32)	(29.28)**	(34.42)**	(2.61)*	(–3.91)**	(–1.62)	(10.82)**	(4.31)**	(23.75)**			

Notes: For a concise presentation, parameters of interest are indicated and the results of time-trend terms are omitted
The *t*-statistics are enclosed in parentheses
** Significance at the 1% level; * significance at the 5% level

assembly industries, the estimated parameter of precision machinery (code 12) is large at –5.450, which is followed by transportation equipment (code 11) at –4.218, and electrical machinery (code 10) at –2.863.

Furthermore, positive effects of agglomeration economies (population density and market access) are widely observed in manufacturing industries compared with the negative effects of fiscal transfer. More specifically, there are only seven sectors where fiscal transfer has a significantly negative effect on productive efficiency: food products (code 1), chemical industry (code 4), primary metal products (code 7), electrical machinery (code 10), transportation equipment (code 11), precision machinery (code 12), and miscellaneous manufacturing (code 13).

Thus, industry agglomeration has a significantly positive effect on the productive efficiency of material industries. In addition, the positive effects of market access are strong for both material and processing/assembly industries, and the effects are widely observed among individual manufacturing sectors. Therefore, adopting a regional policy to improve market access provides benefits for a broad range of sectors in manufacturing industries. For example, it is claimed that an investment in a high-speed transportation network increases the productivity of a region via enhanced access to the market. This claim is consistent with Montolio and Solé-Ollé (2009) and Otsuka (2017) who examined whether public investment in social infrastructure increased productivity growth in Spanish and Japanese provinces respectively. Both studies identified a positive influence on productivity from public investment, even though the negative impact of excessive use or congestion was considered in the evaluation.

Meanwhile, the effects of fiscal transfer on productive efficiency are weaker than those of the industry agglomeration, and the estimated parameter is not statistically significant for most sectors. This may be attributed to the policy change to gradually reduce tax allocations to local governments, which was planned and implemented as part of the Trinity Reform under the Liberal Democratic Party administration in the early 2000s during the Koizumi cabinet. More specifically, tax allocations to local governments were reduced from 2003 to 2006 due to the Trinity Reform, and the degree of fiscal transfer gradually decreased over the period. As a result, it is reasonable to infer that the effect of fiscal transfer on productive efficiency was weakened for manufacturing industries.

Finally, the average value of productive efficiency for the 47 prefectures is calculated for each manufacturing sector. Here, interpretation is not possible for general machinery (code 9) and stone, clay, and glass products (code 6) because the variance parameter is not significant for these sectors, but there is considerable variation on average efficiency among the other sectors. For example, there are many sectors with high productive efficiency in processing/assembly industries, such as miscellaneous manufacturing (code 13), electrical machinery (code 10), transportation equipment (code 11), and precision machinery (code 12), where the estimated productive efficiencies range from 0.8 to 0.9. In contrast, for material sectors such as petroleum and coal products (code 5) and stone, clay, and glass products (code 6), the average productive efficiency is only approximately 0.5–0.6.

Therefore, regional policy that improves productive efficiency in material sectors is important to improve the overall efficiency of manufacturing industries.

9.4.2 DEA

Bias-corrected efficiency values are obtained from a bootstrap DEA in the first stage. Those values are converted to the normalized inefficiency index (*NIE*). Then in the second stage, Eq. (9.5) is estimated using a random effects panel data Tobit model (see Fig. 9.1).

$$NIE_{jt}^{*} = \gamma_j + \gamma_{DENS} \ln DENS_{jt} + \gamma_{ACC} \ln ACC_{jt} + \gamma_{TRANS} \ln TRANS_{jt} + \varepsilon_{jt}, \quad (9.5)$$

where, NIE_{jt}^{*} indicates the estimated *NIE* of region *j* in period *t*. If $NIE_{jt}^{*} > 0$, then $NIE_{jt} = NIE_{jt}^{*}$, and if $NIE_{jt}^{*} \leq 0$ then $NIE_{jt} = 0$. In (9.5), it is assumed that $\varepsilon_{jt} \sim N\left[0, \sigma_e^2\right]$ and $\gamma_j \sim N\left[0, \sigma_u^2\right]$.

First, let us compare the results for manufacturing and non-manufacturing industries (Table 9.4). Just like SFA, a negative sign for the estimated parameters ($\gamma_{DENS}, \gamma_{ACC}, \gamma_{TRANS}$) indicates that the variable improves productive efficiency.

The variance factor σ_u is larger than σ_e, and both are statistically significant. This implies that the panel data model is appropriate for the data so that random effects are properly absorbed in the model. The estimated parameters of population density and market access are negative and statistically significant for both manufacturing and non-manufacturing industries. The results show that agglomeration economies do have positive influences on productive efficiency. On the other hand, fiscal transfer has a negative impact on efficiency for both types of industries. These results for agglomeration economies and fiscal transfer are consistent with Hypotheses 9.1 and 9.2. However, whereas the estimated parameter for non-manufacturing industries is statistically significant, it is not significant for manufacturing industries. As the influence of fiscal transfer changes depending on industries, its influence is not as strong compared to that of agglomeration economies.

Next, we examine the results for each individual sector in manufacturing industries (Table 9.5).

Population density positively influences productive efficiency for most sectors, which includes food products (code 1), textile mill products (code 2), stone, clay, and glass products (code 6), primary metal products (code 7), metal products (code 8), general machinery (code 9), transportation equipment (code 11), and precision machinery (code 12). In other words, the positive effects of population density are apparent in life-style goods industries, material industries, and processing/assembly industries. Among these industries, general machinery (code 9) is most strongly influenced by population density because the absolute value of the estimated parameter is the largest at –3.747. In addition, the absolute values of estimated parameters exceed 1 for life-style goods industries such as food products (code 1) at

Table 9.4 Estimation results of DEA

	Manufacturing industries		Non-manufacturing industries	
γ_{DENS}	–0.1337		–0.1016	
	(–2.98)	**	(–4.39)	**
γ_{ACC}	–0.2609		–0.2183	
	(–2.25)	**	(–3.85)	**
γ_{TRANS}	0.0144		0.0143	
	(1.35)		(2.99)	**
σ_u	0.1927		0.1015	
	(9.32)	**	(9.21)	**
σ_e	0.1383		0.0620	
	(47.44)	**	(47.4)	**
ρ	0.6599		0.7281	
	(0.56)		(0.64)	
Wald test	755.75		89.7	
Log likelihood	565.24		1497.69	

Notes: The *z*-statistics are enclosed in parentheses
** Significance at the 1% level; * significance at the 5% level

–1.171 and textile mill products (code 2) at –1.059, which also indicates that population density strongly influences the productive efficiency of those sectors. The chemical industry (code 4) and petroleum and coal products (code 5) satisfy the expected sign conditions for population density, but are not statistically significant.

The effects of market access are apparent for five material industries and processing/assembly industries: pulp, paper, and allied products (code 3), stone, clay, and glass products (code 6), primary metal products (code 7), general machinery (code 9) and transportation equipment (code 11). It is evident that the development of market access has had a positive impact on productive efficiency. The estimated parameter for general machinery (code 9) has an extremely large absolute value of –10.058. Among the other sectors, food products (code 1), textile mill products (code 2), chemical industry (code 4), petroleum and coal products (code 5), precision machinery (code 12), and miscellaneous manufacturing (code 13) satisfy expected sign conditions for market access, but are not statistically significant.

Finally, let us consider the effects of fiscal transfer. These effects are not apparent in several sectors, except for pulp, paper, and allied products (code 3) and general machinery (code 9). Of these, general machinery (code 9) has a large parameter value of 2.244, which suggests that an increase in fiscal transfer greatly decreases productive efficiency. The other sectors—chemical industry (code 4), petroleum and coal products (code 5), stone, clay, and glass products (code 6), primary metal products (code 7), metal products (code 8), electrical machinery (code 10), transportation equipment (code 11) and miscellaneous manufacturing (code 13)—satisfy the sign conditions, but are not statistically significant. Overall, the effects of fiscal transfer are weaker than those of agglomeration economies for

Table 9.5 Estimation results of DEA (manufacturing sectors)

Code	γ_{DENS}	γ_{ACC}	γ_{TRANS}	σ_u	σ_e	ρ	Wald test	Log likelihood
1	–1.1709	–0.7772	–0.0033	1.1239	0.4412	0.8664	440.92	–824.85
	(–4.90)**	(–1.14)	(–0.97)	(9.34)**	(47.30)**	(0.81)		
2	–1.0593	–0.6839	–0.1659	1.2524	1.4726	0.4197	129.91	–2181.82
	(–3.21)**	(–1.07)	(–1.50)	(8.80)**	(47.24)**	(0.31)		
3	0.0749	–0.6690	0.1203	0.3350	0.4793	0.3282	86.35	–860.72
	(0.85)	(–2.64)**	(3.38)**	(8.72)**	(47.42)**	(0.23)		
4	–0.3982	–3.7215	0.8079	4.2835	17.2711	0.0580	51.60	–4973.92
	(–0.25)	(–0.79)	(0.83)	(5.66)**	(47.15)**	(0.03)		
5	–3.2274	–10.3878	4.5462	31.3699	1888.4320	0.0270	24.20	–7529.04
	(–0.21)	(–0.25)	(0.45)	(3.77)**	(3.77)**	(0.01)		
6	–0.2456	–0.9698	0.0797	0.3752	–0.8225	0.1723	92.69	–1476.19
	(–2.22)*	(–2.21)*	(1.38)	(8.07)**	(–47.46)**	(0.11)		
7	–0.3334	–1.0823	0.1401	0.4770	1.1372	0.1496	80.90	–1851.49
	(–2.31)*	(–2.07)*	(1.78)	(7.82)**	(47.32)**	(0.09)		
8	–0.1608	0.1700	0.0147	0.2614	0.2685	0.4866	1029.73	–195.92
	(2.50)*	(1.05)	(0.72)	(8.56)**	(47.3)**	(0.37)		
9	–3.7473	–10.0580	2.2442	3.4578	18.4331	0.0340	74.22	–5064.27
	(–2.40)*	(–2.96)**	(2.00)*	(4.44)**	(47.01)**	(0.01)		
10	0.0915	0.4151	0.6451	2.5196	10.9347	0.0504	123.11	–4470.28
	(0.09)	(0.24)	(1.04)	(5.24)**	(47.24)**	(0.10)		
11	–0.3725	–0.6808	0.0453	0.4758	0.9040	0.2169	68.04	–1590.62
	(–2.83)**	(–2.51)*	(0.79)	(8.34)**	(47.34)**	(0.14)		
12	–0.9223	–0.4135	–0.0188	1.3696	2.7617	0.1974	57.64	–2861.8
	(–2.39)*	(–0.76)	(–0.11)	(8.21)**	(47.1)**	(0.13)		
13	0.3171	–0.7383	0.4069	1.2111	8.5672	0.0196	24.73	–4189.84
	(0.48)	(–0.60)	(0.80)	(3.22)**	(47.46)**	(0.01)		

Notes: The *z*-statistics are enclosed in parentheses
** Significance at the 1% level; * significance at the 5% level

all individual manufacturing sectors, as seen with the aggregated manufacturing industries.

9.4.3 Comparison of SFA and DEA

The stochastic frontier analysis (SFA) and the data envelopment analysis (DEA) each have both strengths and weaknesses. One of the strengths of SFA is that when a production value is very high (an "abnormal value") in comparison to the other samples, the stochastic frontier in production can absorb most of the effect of the abnormal value in a symmetrical error term. Therefore, even abnormal values in productivity should not make the estimation of the production function unstable.

On the other hand, the weaknesses of SFA are that we are required to have a priori assumptions about the type of frontier function and the distribution of productive inefficiency. Normally, the function type—Cobb Douglas or translog—and the distribution of productive inefficiency—half normal, exponential or gamma—are assumed. However, SFA does not have any particular economic theoretical basis for selecting the type of function and distribution. Even when the same data set is used, the estimated production frontier depends on the assumption of the function type and distribution of productive inefficiency. Furthermore, there is variation in the estimation of productive inefficiency level. Moreover, when there are several products, the distance function must be considered and expanded.

The strength of data envelopment analysis (DEA) is that the non-parametric estimation of a production frontier does not initially require a particular production function or productive inefficiency distribution data. Additionally, it can easily be applied even when there are several products or several inputs.

On the other hand, DEA has certain weaknesses. First, this approach does not consider statistical errors. Therefore, when a sample contains an abnormal value that is difficult to compare to other samples, DEA cannot absorb the effects in the error term, which may substantially affect the results. While the SFA has the same problem, DEA's results could be more seriously affected because of its lack of consideration of error terms. However, the bootstrap DEA used in this study statistically modifies bias in the efficiency value by repeat sampling of the data to alleviate, if not solve, this problem. Second, while DEA is effective at measuring relative efficiency by comparing the sample with a reference set close to the decision-making units (DMU), there is a problem with comparing whole samples. For instance, when several samples are evaluated with the efficiency value 1 (most efficient), it is difficult to determine which sample is better or worse among them. Another weakness is that DEA functions poorly for statistical hypothesis tests because it is a non-parametric method.

As described above, because SFA and DEA have both strengths and weaknesses, it is better to compare their analytical results to verify the robustness of the empirical findings. We should particularly be aware of biases introduced by the method when analyzing important political issues. A careful comparative analysis using multiple techniques is optimal.

Therefore, this study investigates the relationship between efficiencies measured using SFA and DEA to check the robustness of the results obtained from the two methodologies. If both methodologies provide the same results on the direction of effects from agglomeration economies and fiscal transfer, then we can use them as the basis for our policy implications. This study applies Spearman's rank correlation test to all industries examined in this study. Each industry consists of efficiency-based rankings for all prefectures and years measured by SFA and DEA. As the absolute values of efficiency measured by each methodology cannot be compared directly, it is useful to apply a rank correlation test to their rankings of efficiency. In addition, there is an advantage in using Spearman's rank correlation test for this study because the test is nonparametric so that we do not need an assumption of a normal distribution of variables or rankings. Table 9.6 shows the

Table 9.6 Spearman rank-correlation coefficient

	Spearman rank-correlation coefficient
Manufacturing industries	0.578
Code 1: Food products	0.664
Code 2: Textile mill products	0.281
Code 3: Pulp, paper and allied products	0.671
Code 4: Chemical industry	0.502
Code 5: Petroleum and coal products	0.453
Code 6: Stone, clay and glass products	0.632
Code 7: Primary metal products	0.785
Code 8: Metal products	0.678
Code 9: General machinery	0.576
Code 10: Electrical machinery	0.569
Code 11: Transportation equipment	0.715
Code 12: Precision machinery	0.562
Code 13: Miscellaneous manufacturing	0.361
Non-manufacturing industries	0.669

results of the test. The null hypothesis is that two groups of rankings measured by SFA and DEA are mutually independent.

According to the results, the null hypothesis is rejected at the 1% level of significance for all industries. These results imply that there is a correlation between the efficiency-based rankings with SFA and DEA. In other words, the methodologies are consistent in terms of evaluation of efficiency for each industry. Therefore, there is no significant methodological bias regarding the results of this study.

Next, let us further compare the results of SFA and DEA (Table 9.7).

Using SFA, the results show that increases in the variables of agglomeration economies, that is, population density and market access, contribute to the improvement of productive efficiency for both manufacturing and non-manufacturing industries, but that increases in fiscal transfer decrease efficiency. The same effect is observed in DEA regarding population density and market access. However, the results differ between SFA and DEA on the effects of fiscal transfer. In particular, fiscal transfer decreases productive efficiency for both industries in SFA. On the other hand, fiscal transfer decreases the productive efficiency of non-manufacturing industries in DEA, which is consistent with SFA, but the SFA and DEA results differ for manufacturing industries. Consequently, population density and market access increase productive efficiency for both manufacturing and non-manufacturing industries, and the fiscal transfer decreases productive efficiency of non-manufacturing industries in both SFA and DEA measurements.

Furthermore, we compared the results for each individual sector of manufacturing industries. With both SFA and DEA, population density influences most sectors. That is, population density has a positive effect on productive efficiency with SFA for food products (code 1), textile mill products (code 2), pulp, paper, and allied products (code 3), chemical industry (code 4), stone, clay, and glass products (code 6),

Table 9.7 Comparison of estimation results between SFA and DEA

	Population density		Market access		Public fiscal transfer	
	SFA	DEA	SFA	DEA	SFA	DEA
Manufacturing industries	+	+	+	+	–	
Code 1: Food products	+	+	+		–	
Code 2: Textile mill products	+	+	+			
Code 3: Pulp, paper and allied products	+		+	+		–
Code 4: Chemical industry	+		+		–	
Code 5: Petroleum and coal products			+			
Code 6: Stone, clay and glass products	+	+	+	+		
Code 7: Primary metal products	+	+	+	+	–	
Code 8: Metal products		+	+			
Code 9: General machinery		+		+		–
Code 10: Electrical machinery			+		–	
Code 11: Transportation equipment	+	+	+	+	–	
Code 12: Precision machinery	+	+	+		–	
Code 13: Miscellaneous manufacturing	+				–	
Non-manufacturing industries	+	+	+	+	–	–

Notes: The sign in the table shows the effect of statistically significant estimated parameters on productive efficiency. That is, the sign in the table is opposite to the sign of the estimated parameter. ("+" = Effect that increases productive efficiency. "–" = Effect that decreases productive efficiency)

primary metal products (code 7), transportation equipment (code 11), precision machinery (code 12), and miscellaneous manufacturing (code 13). Meanwhile, a positive influence from population density is observed for food products (code 1), textile mill products (code 2), stone, clay, and glass products (code 6), primary metal products (code 7), metal products (code 8), general machinery (code 9), transportation equipment (code 11), and precision equipment (code 12) in DEA. In comparing SFA and DEA, this study concludes that the results are robust for food products (code 1), textile mill products (code 2), stone, clay, and glass products (code 6), primary metal products (code 7), transportation equipment (code 11), and precision equipment (code 12).

Next, market access also increases productive efficiency in most manufacturing sectors, although the results are not as strong as for population density. That is, in SFA, market access has a positive effect on productive efficiency for all sectors, except for general machinery (code 9) and miscellaneous manufacturing (code 13), while in DEA it improves efficiency for pulp, paper, and allied products (code 3), stone, clay, and glass products (code 6), primary metal products (code 7), general machinery (code 9), and transportation equipment (code 11). Consequently, the results for market access are robust for all the above listed sectors, except for general machinery (code 9).

Finally, let us compare the effects of fiscal transfer on each manufacturing sector. Fiscal transfer decreases productive efficiency for food products (code 1), chemical industry (code 4), primary metal products (code 7), electrical machinery (code 10), transportation equipment (code 11), precision machinery (code 12), and miscellaneous manufacturing (code 13) in SFA. However, under DEA, no sectors are consistent with SFA. Therefore, the results are not robust regarding the impacts of fiscal transfer. This implies that the effects of fiscal transfers on productive efficiency are extremely limited in terms of policy implications for each sector of the various manufacturing industries.

9.5 Conclusion and Policy Implications

It has been recognized in academic and practical discussions that agglomeration economies are important for regional economic growth (Rosenthal and Strange 2004; Combes and Gobillon 2015). However, local governments and politicians often complain that production activities have been over-concentrated in the Japanese capital, centered in the Greater Tokyo Area. They are seriously concerned that only the capital area will grow, and that it will grow at the expense of local economies. Hence, to boost regional economies and to ensure balanced economic growth nationwide, the Japanese government has supported the regional policy of public investment that increased from the 1980s to the 1990s. To implement this policy, a large amount of tax revenue was allocated from the national government to local governments. As a result, tax allocations to local governments expanded. Unfortunately, a negative impact of the policy was that tax allocations possibly resulted in stiffening the industrial structure of regional economies and negatively affected the productive efficiency of regional industries.

For Japan, it is important to implement effective economic policies to achieve regional economic growth. Improving productive efficiency of regional industries is essential for economic recovery because, given the huge fiscal deficit, we cannot continue to depend on tax allocations from the government. To address concerns regarding regional economies, this study analyzed the effects of agglomeration economies and fiscal transfer on productive efficiency of regional industries.

As a result, two hypotheses (Hypotheses 9.1 and 9.2) were verified for manufacturing and non-manufacturing industries, and individual sectors of manufacturing industries. The major findings of this study are as follows: First, agglomeration economies have a positive effect on productive efficiency, significantly assisted by improvements in market access. Second, fiscal transfer has a negative impact on productive efficiency. Furthermore, it was confirmed that those results are generally applicable to individual sectors of manufacturing industries. Both SFA and DEA showed that population density increased productive efficiency in most of the manufacturing industries. Similarly, market access positively influenced productive efficiency for the majority of manufacturing industries. As a practical example, we see the development of a high-speed transportation network as contributing to economic growth through improvement in productive efficiency of regional industries. On the other hand, fiscal transfer negatively influenced productive efficiency for several manufacturing industries and non-manufacturing industries in SFA, whereas DEA results showed that the influence of fiscal transfer was limited to only a few sectors of manufacturing industries and non-manufacturing industries. Therefore, regarding the impacts of fiscal transfer, the results for SFA and DEA were consistent for non-manufacturing industries, but not robust for individual sectors of manufacturing industries. The differences in the results are attributed to the different methodologies and such differences are often observed in empirical analysis. Hence, it is important to check the robustness of results using multiple techniques, particularly to evaluate important policy issues.

The Japanese government needs to consider the importance of agglomeration economies to implement effective regional economic policy, which is essential for future economic growth. All regions in Japan are facing depopulation. In this context, it is essential to increase population concentration in areas within each region to realize regional economic growth. To do this, it is necessary to enhance the economies of agglomeration. Regional industrial agglomeration can be strengthened by promoting collaboration among industries, academia, and the government to enhance the Industrial Cluster Plan, so that human capital in the region is developed and utilized simultaneously. Additionally, improvement of regional productivity requires the enhancement of economies of agglomeration by developing a high-speed traffic network and reducing transportation costs. The development of a high-speed traffic network reduces the time and distance of conveyance between regions, thus improving market access and strengthening agglomeration economies. Through this, regional economic efficiency will eventually be enhanced. The effects of population density and market access on productive efficiency have grown stronger in recent years. That is, economic policy that properly makes use of the positive influence of agglomeration economies has become increasingly important in Japan.

References

Aigner DJ, Lovell CAK, Schmidt P. Formulation and estimation of stochastic frontier production function model. J Econ. 1977;6(1):21–37.

Banker RD, Charnes A, Cooper WW. Some models for estimating technical and scale inefficiencies in data envelopment analysis. Manag Sci. 1984;30:1078–92.

Battese GE, Coelli TJ. A model for technical inefficiency effects in a stochastic frontier production function for panel data. Empir Econ. 1995;20(2):325–32.

Battese GE, Corra GS. Estimation of a production frontier model: with application to the pastoral zone of Eastern Australia. Aust J Agric Econ. 1977;21(3):169–79.

Beeson PE, Husted S. Patterns and determinants of productive efficiency in the state manufacturing. J Reg Sci. 1989;29(1):15–28.

Cameron AC, Trivedi PK. Microeconometrics: methods and applications. New York: Cambridge University Press; 2005.

Capello R, Nijkamp P. Handbook of regional growth and development theories. Cheltenham: Edward Elgar; 2009.

Charnes A, Cooper WW, Sueyoshi T. A goal programming/constrained regression: review of the bell system breakup. Manag Sci. 1988;34:1–26.
Combes PP, Gobillon L. The empirics of agglomeration economies. In: Duranton G, Henderson JV, Strange W, editors. Handbook of regional and urban economics, volume 5A. Amsterdam: Elsevier; 2015. p. 247–348.
Driffield N, Munday M. Foreign manufacturing, regional agglomeration and technical efficiency in UK industries: a stochastic production frontier approach. Reg Stud. 2001;35(5):391–9.
Ellison G, Glaeser EL. Geographic concentration in US manufacturing industries: a dartboard approach. J Polit Econ. 1997;105:889–927.
Emrouznejad A, Parker BR, Tavares G. Evaluation of research in efficiency and productivity: a survey and analysis of the first 30 years of scholarly literature in DEA. Socio Econ Plan Sci. 2008;42:151–7.
Fujita M, Thisse J. Economics of agglomeration. Cambridge, MA: Cambridge University Press; 2002.
Fujita M, Krugman P, Venables A. The spatial economy: cities, regions, and international trade. Cambridge, MA: MIT Press; 1999.
Glover F, Sueyoshi T. Contributions of Professor William W. Cooper in operations research and management science. Eur J Oper Res. 2009;197:1–16.
Kumbhakar SC, Lovell CAK. Stochastic frontier analysis. Cambridge: Cambridge University Press; 2000.
Meeusen W, van den Broeck J. Efficient estimation from Cobb-Douglas production functions with composed error. Int Econ Rev. 1977;18(2):435–44.
Mitra A. Agglomeration economies as manifested in technical efficiency at the firm level. J Urban Econ. 1999;45(3):490–500.
Mitra A, Sato H. Agglomeration economies in Japan: technical efficiency, growth and unemployment. Rev Urban Reg Dev Stud. 2007;19(3):197–209.
Montolio D, Solé-Ollé A. Road investment and regional productivity growth: the effects of vehicle intensity and congestion. Pap Reg Sci. 2009;88(1):99–118.
Otsuka A. Regional determinants of total factor productivity in Japan: stochastic frontier analysis. Ann Reg Sci. 2017;58(3):579–96.
Otsuka A, Goto M. Regional policy and the productive efficiency of Japanese industries. Reg Stud. 2015;49(4):518–31.
Otsuka A, Goto M, Sueyoshi T. Industrial agglomeration effects in Japan: productive efficiency, market access, and public fiscal transfer. Pap Reg Sci. 2010;89(4):819–40.
Otsuka A, Goto M, Sueyoshi T. Cost-efficiency of Japanese local governments: effects of decentralization and regional integration. Reg Stud Reg Sci. 2014;1(1):207–20.
Parr JB, Hewings GJD, Sohn J, Nazara S. Agglomeration and trade: some additional perspectives. Reg Stud. 2002;36(6):675–84.
Rosenthal SS, Strange WC. Evidence on the nature and sources of agglomeration economies. Handb Urban Reg Econ. 2004;4:2119–71.
Scott AJ, Storper M. Regions, globalization, development. Reg Stud. 2003;37(6&7):579–93.
Simar L, Wilson P. Sensitivity analysis of efficiency scores: how to bootstrap in nonparametric frontier models. Manag Sci. 1998;44:49–61.
Sueyoshi T. Divestiture of Nippon telegraph & telephone. Manag Sci. 1996;42:1326–51.
Tobin J. Estimation of relationships for limited dependent variables. Econometrica. 1958;26 (1):24–36.
Tveteras R, Battese GE. Agglomeration externalities, productivity, and technical inefficiency. J Reg Sci. 2006;46(4):605–25.
Yamamura E, Shin I. Dynamics of agglomeration economies and regional industrial structure: the case of the assembly industry of the Greater Tokyo Region, 1960–2000. Struct Chang Econ Dyn. 2007;18(4):483–99.

Chapter 10
Market Access, Agglomeration Economies, and New Firm Formation

Abstract This chapter analyzes the determinants of regional variations in new firm formation by industry, using the data of 47 prefectures in Japan. The results of this study reveal the following findings: (1) market access is the factor that promotes new firm formation in all industries, although the impact on new firm formation is greater in the service industry than in the manufacturing industry; (2) industrial agglomeration contributes to stimulating new firm formation in the manufacturing industry; and (3) while average wage is an important factor in the manufacturing industry, it is not significant in the service industry.

Keywords New firm formation • Firm creation • Agglomeration economies • Market access

10.1 Introduction

Determinant factors of new firm formation have been explored in the theoretical and empirical literature. A long tradition of studies on the determinants of regional variation has focused on tax rates, transportation costs, and scale economies at the plant level (Kieschnick 1981; Bartik 1989). More recently, a growing body of literature has sought to uncover the determinants of regional variation in new firm formation (Reynolds 1994; Audretsch and Fritsch 1994; Keeble and Walker 1994; Reynolds et al. 1994; Sutaria 2001). The results of empirical studies reveal that new firms create jobs, stimulate technological progress, and contribute to regional economic growth. Therefore, the promotion of new firm formation is an important policy issue for regional governments. In Japan, the support infrastructure, such as venture capital and incubation facilities, was developed between the 1980s and 1990s. However, the start-up rate in Japan for the period 1996–2001 was sluggish at approximately 3.8%, and the policy of promoting new firm formation has not achieved the expected result.

This chapter is based on Otsuka (2008) "Determinants of new firm formation in Japan: A comparison of the manufacturing and service sectors," published in *Economics Bulletin* (Vol. 18, No. 4, pp. 1–7).

A. Otsuka, *A New Perspective on Agglomeration Economies in Japan*,
New Frontiers in Regional Science: Asian Perspectives 20,
DOI 10.1007/978-981-10-6490-6_10

This study examines the difference in firm creation patterns in Japan between the 1980s and 1990s, and verifies the effects of market access and agglomeration economies on firm creation. The location of new firms is analyzed using reduced form count data models that relate the probability of acquiring a new firm to a set of potential location factors. The decision factors of firm creation were identified using the regional data of Japan, and verified by small and medium enterprise agencies (Small and Medium Enterprise Agency 1999, 2002). Though these empirical studies demonstrate the determinants of spatial variations in new firm formation, they neglect the differences in determinants across industries. There is no consensus as to whether manufacturing and service industries exhibit the same location patterns. This study expands the scope of industrial details beyond those covered in previous studies, most of which were limited to manufacturing industries.

Firm location patterns can be distinguished by industrial sector, based on different industrial characteristics. Each industry might differ in its sensitivity to local market conditions. For example, while new local services firms are more dependent on regional demand in their supply requirements, manufacturing industries may have a greater need for labor. That is, it appears that the influence of demand trends in a region differs for manufacturing and service industries. Almost all the demand for manufacturing comes from beyond the border, while demand for service industries depends on domestic regional demand. Therefore, identifying the differences between the two types of industries can help identify which location characteristics are more important for new firms.

The rest of the chapter is organized as follows. Section 10.2 reveals the spatial patterns of start-ups in Japan. Section 10.3 presents a framework for analysis, and describes the determinants of firm creation. Section 10.4 analyzes the influence of regional factors on new firm formation. Finally, Sect. 10.5 concludes the study and presents research topics for the future.

10.2 Firm Creation in Japan

Firm creation between the 1980s and 1990s is identified using the *Establishment and Enterprise Census of Japan* conducted by the Ministry of Internal Affairs and Communications (MIC). The dataset consists of firm- and plant-level information. New firms in a year are those firms that appeared in the database for the first time that year, and include both new firms and relocation of existing establishments. The geographical details of the data permit a regional analysis at the prefectural level. Major regional industrial policies in Japan are being implemented in prefectures, not municipalities. Therefore, prefectures are the economic areas that are best suited to capture the geography of firm formation from the viewpoint of industry policy.

Firm creation is studied in one-digit classification industries. Table 10.1 provides the start-up rates and the share of start-ups for the period 1981–2001. The start-up rate is the ratio of the average annual number of new firms to the number of

Table 10.1 Rates and shares of start-ups in Japan (%)

	1981–1986	1986–1991	1991–1996	1996–2001
Construction	3.2	3.2	2.4	2.0
	(6.1)	(7.1)	(6.9)	(5.3)
Manufacturing	3.1	2.8	1.4	1.6
	(9.3)	(9.4)	(5.8)	(4.7)
Transportation and telecommunication	4.5	4.5	3.3	4.6
	(2.1)	(2.5)	(2.6)	(3.3)
Wholesale, retail, and restaurant	5.1	4.0	3.6	4.7
	(52.6)	(46.8)	(51.4)	(53.5)
Finance and insurance	6.4	5.2	3.4	4.7
	(1.8)	(1.9)	(1.7)	(2.1)
Real-estate	4.5	5.3	2.8	2.2
	(3.7)	(5.2)	(3.8)	(2.7)
Service	5.3	4.6	3.5	4.0
	(24.2)	(26.8)	(27.4)	(28.1)
All industries	4.7	4.0	3.1	3.8
	(100.0)	(100.0)	(100.0)	(100.0)

Source: Establishment and Enterprise Census of Japan (Ministry of Internal Affairs and Communications (MIC))
Note: The proportions of the number of new firms are presented in parentheses

establishments at the beginning of the period. The share of start-ups represents each industry's share of the total number of new firms. While the start-up rate for manufacturing industries and the construction industry is low at about 2%, the rates for finance and insurance, the service industry, wholesale-retail trade, and the restaurant industry are high. Further, for each period, the relative size of the industries varies considerably. In terms of share of new firms, wholesale and retail industries are the largest, with a combined 53.5% of new firms in 1996-2001. The share of new firms in service industries, at 28.1%, is the next largest, followed by the construction industry's share at 5.3%, and that of manufacturing industries at 4.7%. In fact, these industries account for 91.6% of the total of new firms. The share of manufacturing industries, which was about 9% in the first half of the 1980s, decreased to about 5% after the 1990s; on the other hand, the share of service industries, which was 24.2% in the 1980s, increased by about 4% in the 1990s. Since the service industry supports the formation of other industries, the importance of this industry in new firm start-ups is increasing.

There have been considerable spatial variations in the location of new firms. Figure 10.1 illustrates the spatial distribution of newly formed firms in the service industry over the period 1996–2001. The picture depicts a highly-polarized distribution in Tokyo and Osaka, the metropolitan areas of the country. Together with the regions in their vicinity, these two cities stand out as having the highest number of service firms. The start-up rate in non-metropolitan areas is relatively low, especially in the Fukui and Shimane prefectures at 2.4%, which is about half of the rate in the Tokyo metropolitan area.

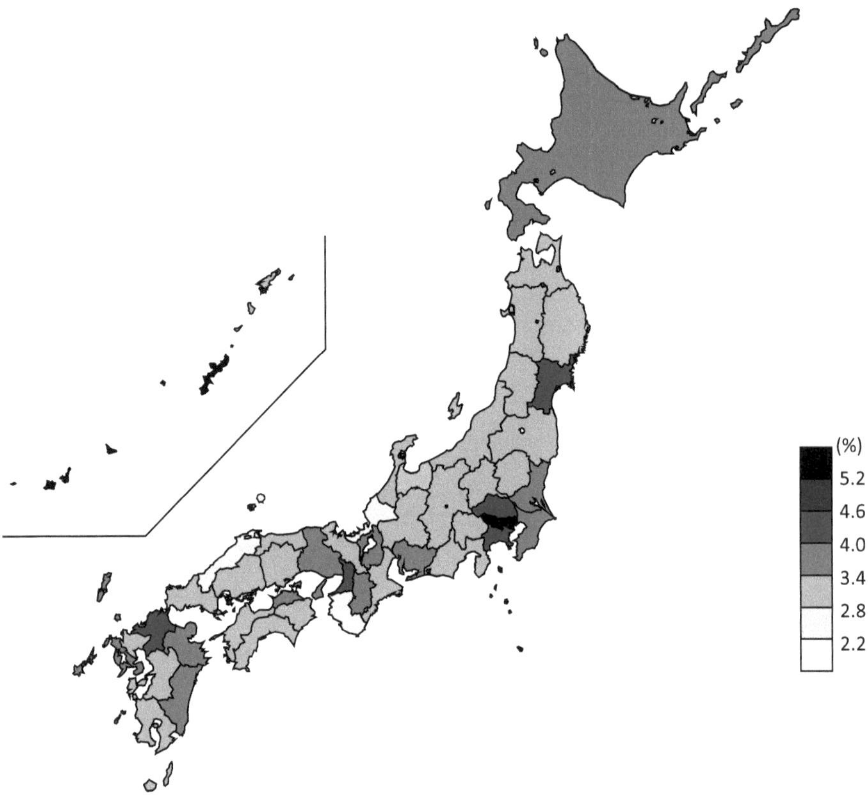

Fig. 10.1 Start-up rates for service industries in 1996–2001

Figure 10.2 shows the differences in the spatial location pattern of manufacturing plant start-ups, revealing that the location pattern is different from that of service industries. Manufacturing industries are concentrated in the non-metropolitan areas. Hokkaido, Iwate, and Miyagi prefectures have the highest rate of new manufacturing firms. High rates of firm creation are observed in the non-metropolitan areas that do not have large populations. Therefore, the pattern that emerges indicates that there are, indeed, differences between the location choices of new manufacturing plants and service industries.

We observe the change in regional disparities of new firms by the coefficient of variation. The coefficient of variation in the manufacturing industry has been at a high level compared to the service industry (Table 10.2). Firm creation in the manufacturing industry has large regional disparities, and continues to be high. On the other hand, the coefficient of variation of the service industry is small, and the disparity in the start-up rate has been shrinking. However, the start-up rate for manufacturing industries in the 1990s declined in most prefectures. For example, the Nara prefecture decreased by −1.0% points, and the Aomori and Tokushima prefectures declined by −0.5% points. Only the Oita prefecture (+0.3%) saw an

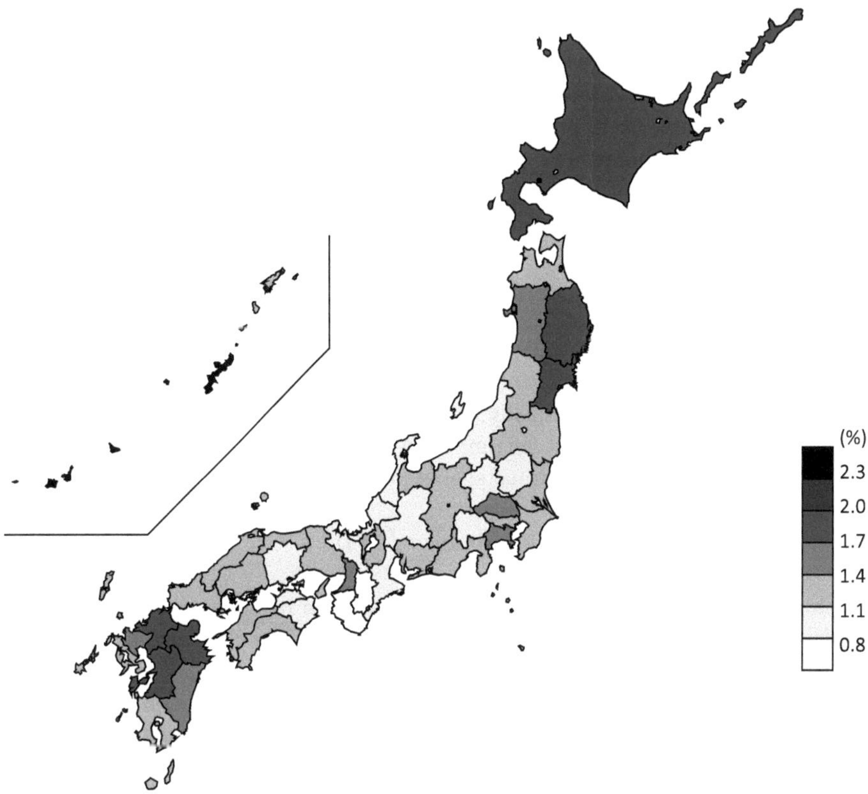

Fig. 10.2 Start-up rates for manufacturing industries in 1996–2001

Table 10.2 Coefficient of variation in start-ups in Japan

	1981–1986	1986–1991	1991–1996	1996–2001
Manufacturing	0.254	0.260	0.246	0.303
Service	0.199	0.187	0.187	0.189

increase in the start-up rate. Meanwhile, the start-up rate for the service industry has increased in most prefectures. The Tokyo, Iwate, and Oita prefectures increased by 0.5% points each. There are only nine prefectures where the start-up rate for the service industry has declined.

These findings show that the disparities in firm creation between metropolitan areas and non-metropolitan areas is expanding in the manufacturing industry, while new firm creation is active nationwide in the service industry. To develop effective regional economic policies, it is necessary to analyze the factors that cause differences in the location patterns of these industries. This study clarifies location factors in manufacturing and service industries.

10.3 Modeling Firm Creation

The decision on where to locate a new establishment depends on the profit that the firm expects to earn in alternative locations. Profit will depend on the characteristics of the location as well as firm characteristics. Expected profits π_{ijt} that a firm in industry *i* derives from locating an establishment in region *j* at time *t* can be written as

$$\pi_{ijt} = \beta' x_{jt} + \varepsilon_{ijt}, \tag{10.1}$$

where x_{jt} is a vector of the locational environment that affects profits in the region, ε_{ijt} is the usual random component, and β is a parameter to be estimated.

To analyze start-ups empirically, the probability of observing a count of new firms n_{ijt} in industry *i* in region *j* in time *i* can be written as a function of the location characteristics that affect the firms' spatial profit function

$$prob(n_{ijt}) = f_i(x_{jt}). \tag{10.2}$$

With the number of new firms started in each region being a nonnegative integer with zeros as a frequent and natural outcome, Eq. (10.2) is estimated using a count data model.

Table 10.3 categorizes the locational environment variables that influence start-ups. Definitions and data sources for each variable are summarized in this table. Following previous firm location studies, three groups of location determinants can be identified: (1) market demand, (2) agglomeration economies, and (3) factor costs and market conditions.

10.3.1 Market Demand

First, this study verifies the influence of regional domestic demand on start-ups as a demand factor. Other things being equal, areas with a greater market demand are expected to offer greater profit opportunities for new firms. Local market characteristics have been found to influence business locations (Keeble and Walker 1994). If the regional domestic demand can be expected to increase, then it would provide those who might potentially locate to the region with an incentive to start a business there. This study uses the lag of the growth rate of population (RPOP) to investigate this influence. Population growth rate is the average annual rate of increase in population in the region during a previous period. This implies that the behavior of firm founders follows adaptive expectations regarding regional domestic demand.

Firm demand is also a function of domestic demand and size of markets in other locations. The size of market in other locations considers that transportation costs make distant markets more difficult and costly to serve. That is, the location

Table 10.3 Description of independent variables

Variables	Abbreviation	Definition	Expected effects	Data source
Market demand				
Local market demand:	RPOP	Lag of the variable of the growth rate of population	+	National Census
Market potential:	ACC	Regional market access index	+	CRIEPI Database
Agglomeration economies				
Localization economies:	LQ	Location quotient (manufacturing, service)	±	Establishment and Enterprise Census of Japan
Urbanization economies:	DENSE	Density of the office	+	Establishment and Enterprise Census of Japan
Factor costs and market condition				
Factor costs:	WAGE	Average annual wages for workers	−	Monthly Labour Survey
Local market condition:	UNEMP	Unemployment rate	±	National Census

Note: CRIEPI database stands for the Central Research Institute of Electric Power Industry's Regional Economic Database

potential should include the influence of transportation costs that are required for access, in addition to the demand size of other places. This study employs a market access index (ACC), which considers traffic access to markets in other locations as an index of the market potential measurement. In the classic gravity-type measure, the potential between two locations is positively related to their size and negatively related to the distance between them as described below.

$$ACC_j \equiv \sum_k \left[\frac{d_{jk}^{-1}}{\sum_k d_{jk}^{-1}} \cdot P_k \right],$$

where P is the size of population as a measure of the market size of destination k, and d_{jk} is the distance between origin j and destination k. The location of each region is related to the highway network over the period of analysis. d_{jk} is calculated as the shortest travel time in hours along the highway network from each of the 47 prefectures to the main markets, represented by the 228 largest cities. This market access index reflects the ease of access to consumer markets. Higher values indicate greater accessibility.

Accessibility variables are expected to have a stronger influence on new manufacturing firms because they are likely to have a larger activity space, as suggested by Taylor (1975), and therefore greater transportation requirements. Manufacturing plants can benefit from easy access to flows of potential clients and suppliers. In contrast, new firms in service industries should be more strongly influenced by local market conditions.

10.3.2 Agglomeration Economies

Locating in industrial agglomerations with more firms nearby can provide advantages through agglomeration economies (Rosenthal and Strange 2004; Otsuka et al. 2010; Otsuka and Goto 2015a, b; Combes and Gobillon 2015). Agglomeration economies can be divided into localization economies and urbanization economies (McCann 2001). Localization economies are the external economies that stem from the co-location of firms in industrial sectors, which offer higher productivity in terms of obtaining specialized inputs, labor, or information, particularly in some sectors. Urbanization economies are attained across industries in a location by maximizing the potential for a diverse range of information and inputs at a lower cost.

This study adopts the logarithm value of the density of offices (DENSE) as a proxy variable for urbanization economies, and the location quotient (LQ) according to the industry as a proxy variable of localization economies. Industrial density refers to the number of establishments divided by the region's population. The greater the number of establishments relative to the population, the more spillovers should be facilitated (Ciccone and Hall 1996). Therefore, it is assumed that the density of offices positively influences a new opening, because a firm located in industrial agglomerations can easily procure talent, information, and capital. Density influences the intensity of agglomeration forces by increasing the potential of finding both industrial inputs and intermediate output markets locally (Henderson et al. 1995). In addition, local density can be important for the "spin-off" of new firm founders, as most entrepreneurs starting a new business remain in the same sector (Storey and Jones 1987). On the other hand, a firm located in an industrial agglomeration of the same industry suffers the disadvantage of competition while enjoying the convenience of agglomeration. Therefore, location quotient is assumed to be able to take either sign.

10.3.3 Factor Costs and Market Condition

Factor costs negatively influence firm profits, and hence, other things being equal, a firm can be assumed to be less likely to locate in areas with higher wage costs. The variable "wages," which are the average annual wages for workers (WAGE), is hypothesized to have a negative effect on new firms.

When deciding where to locate, firms will not only examine wage levels but also differences in labor market conditions that might impact the firm's profit. This study verifies the influence of the unemployment rate (UNEMP) as a labor market condition factor. The unemployment rate is the traditional calculation for the first year of our start-up measurement period—the average number of unemployed divided by the labor force. Audretsch and Fritsch (1994), Guesnier (1994), and Reynolds et al. (1994) have used this measure. It is assumed that this variable exerts both positive and negative influences on start-ups. A region where the unemployment rate is high is not preferred as a business environment because of recession. However, the firm in question can easily secure talent there because of the availability of many potential workers in the region. In addition, it is possible to open a business for self-employment, in which case the availability of workers is not important.

To test the degree to which new firms are attracted by different sets of location characteristics, models with the following basic specification are estimated:

$$\begin{aligned} n_{ijt} = \beta_0 + \beta_1 RPOP_{jt-1} + \beta_2 ACC_{jt} + \beta_3 DENSE_{jt} \\ + \beta_4 LQ_{jt} + \beta_5 WAGE_{jt} + \beta_6 UNEMP_{jt} + u_{ijt}. \end{aligned} \tag{10.3}$$

where n_{ijt} is the number of new firms started in region j at time t and is a function of location-specific attributes as in Eq. (10.2). u_{ijt} is the error term. The dependent variable is a count variable with zeros as frequent and natural outcomes. Here, the standard model is the Poisson model and the more general negative binominal model.

β is a parameter to be estimated. If $\beta_k > 0$ with respect to element k, the element has a positive influence on start-ups. Conversely, if $\beta_k < 0$, then element k has a negative impact on start-ups.

Descriptive statistics of the variables are summarized in Table 10.4.

10.4 Results and Discussion

Table 10.5 presents the results of the Poisson and negative binominal estimations for new manufacturing and service industries in Japanese prefectures from 1981 to 2001. Overall, the results for the independent variables demonstrate high levels of significance. Table 10.5 also includes the results of an over-dispersion test of the Poisson models, where the models are supported for the negative binominal estimations. The coefficients estimated in the Poisson models closely resemble the estimates from the negative binominal models. The estimations conducted separately for manufacturing industries and service industries reveal a considerable variation in the effects of the independent variables.

The importance of the spatial patterns of market areas is similar for both industries. Market access variables exhibit a positive effect on a new location. Both industries exhibit a clear tendency to locate close to the newly constructed interregional highways. Manufacturing industries are much more attracted by the new transportation corridors, as shown by the much stronger market potential. These results are like those of Holl (2004a, b, c) for manufacturing plant locations

Table 10.4 Descriptive statistics

Variable	Unit	Mean	Std.Dev.	Min	Max
n (manufacturing)	–	397	532	34	3421
n (service)	–	1393	1614	273	11,079
RPOP	Percentage	2.48	2.79	–2.73	14.13
ACC	In hundred thousands	5.41	2.55	3.18	15.25
LQ (manufacturing)	–	1.01	0.26	0.31	1.54
LQ (service)	–	1.00	0.11	0.81	1.29
DENSE	Logarithm	2.86	0.93	1.23	5.88
WAGE	In hundred thousands	3.47	0.46	2.61	5.13
UNEMP	Percentage	3.19	1.24	1.23	10.26

Table 10.5 Estimation results

	Poisson model		Negative binominal model	
	Manufacturing	Service	Manufacturing	Service
Constant	6.0471**	6.6438**	5.7273**	5.7322**
	(0.397)	(0.421)	(0.331)	(0.390)
Lag of the variable of the growth rate of population (RPOP)	–0.0223	0.0000	0.0193	0.0128
	(0.014)	(0.008)	(0.016)	(0.010)
Regional market access index (ACC)	0.2349**	0.2668**	0.3154**	0.2928**
	(0.048)	(0.022)	(0.024)	(0.016)
Location quotient (LQ)	0.9155**	−0.3747	0.5796**	0.2645
	(0.221)	(0.281)	(0.193)	(0.276)
Density of the office (DENSE)	0.4996**	0.0574	0.3030**	0.0599
	(0.148)	(0.057)	(0.062)	(0.042)
Average annual wages for workers (WAGE)	−1.1062**	–0.3642**	–0.8899**	–0.3124**
	(0.172)	(0.090)	(0.127)	(0.084)
Unemployment rate (UNEMP)	–0.0473	0.1065**	–0.0824*	0.0695**
	(0.054)	(0.026)	(0.040)	(0.025)
Observations	188	188	188	188
Log likelihood	–8042.36	−11,975.4	−1154.16	−1339.49
Over dispersion test	9.578**	7.228**		

Notes: All regressions include unreported annual time dummies
The standard error is listed within parentheses
** Significance at the 1% level; * significance at the 5% level

in Spain and Portugal, and suggest spillover effects in the sense that a new highway increases the attractiveness of regions in the new transportation corridors. Even the local population shows no significant effect on plant creation. Overall, the results suggest that new plants are less dependent on local market demand, tending to operate over wider geographical areas.

As predicted by spatial economics, agglomeration economies are strongly positive and statistically significant (Krugman 1991a, b). Localization economies that were measured in terms of location quotients have the expected positive and significant effects on manufacturing plant openings. In addition, the very large positive coefficients estimated for manufacturing plants indicate that labor density has become markedly more attractive for new firms. The greater importance of urbanization economies for a plant's opening is consistent with the "nursery city" argument of Duranton and Puga (2004), which posits that new manufacturing plants prefer diversified areas where they can realize increased opportunities to learn about different processes from a variety of activities. These results are also consistent with those of Audretsch and Fritsch (1994), Keeble and Walker (1994), and Reynolds (1994). In contrast, service industries have not been attracted to areas with a larger industrial base. Thus, agglomeration economies do not significantly affect service industries.

The influence of the labor market, whose proxy variable is the unemployment rate, is positive in the service industry, and shows that plentiful labor increases location possibility. The results for manufacturing industries, which reveal a negative impact, suggest that deterioration in economic conditions weakens the location possibility. In addition, the results indicate that factor costs are considered more when selecting firms' locations. Higher wages decrease the expected number of new firms, and this impact is stronger for manufacturing industries than for service industries. In this sense, start-up plant location behavior is like that found in firms established in the founders' place of residence in Figueiredo et al. (2002).

Summing up, there are considerable differences about how the location determinants analyzed in this study impact start-ups in both industries, and more specifically between start-ups in manufacturing and service industries.

10.5 Conclusion

This study attempted to identify the factors affecting location patterns of new firms in Japan from the 1980s to 1990s.

One finding is that new manufacturing and service firms are not attracted by the same set of location characteristics. Manufacturing start-ups are more strongly influenced by increases in market access, lower labor costs, and a more agglomeration economic environment. In contrast, for the service industry, start-ups exhibit a greater preference for areas with a plentiful labor force and better market accessibility. Industrial agglomeration contributes to stimulating new firm formation in the manufacturing industry. While average wage is an important factor in the manufacturing industry, it is not significant in the service industry. These results indicate a marked difference in the factors that attract manufacturing start-ups and those that attract service start-ups.

Another more important finding is that market access is the factor that promotes new firm formation in both industries, though the impact on new firm formation is greater in the service industry than in the manufacturing industry. Proximity to an interregional highway is important for both industries; manufacturing industries particularly exhibit a considerably greater tendency to locate in new transportation corridors. This result suggests that transportation costs are important in the production activities of both industries. In other words, the development of transportation infrastructure may reduce travel costs between regions and increase the influence of market access.

It is well known that a reduction in transportation costs is closely related to agglomeration economies. For example, Rosenthal and Strange (2001, 2004) show that agglomeration economies attenuate rapidly with distance. Transportation improvements that bring firms closer reduce transportation and communication costs, increase the potential for interaction, and can therefore enhance the benefits of agglomeration economies (Eberts and McMillen 1999). Otsuka and Goto (2015b) show that the development of social overhead capital strengthens agglomeration economies and contributes to the rise of the competitiveness in the regional economy as a whole. Otsuka (2017) also reveals that the development of transportation infrastructure will simultaneously increase productivity and productive efficiency of regional economies.

Therefore, the findings of this study are important for regional development. The enhancement of market access, efficient transportation networks, and agglomeration economies appear to be more important than access to cheap labor in the peripheral areas, particularly for manufacturing firms. This has resulted in many cases where firms locate in the newly created transportation corridors connecting core regions, where they share opportunities to enjoy good market access and many agglomeration advantages. However, the spatial policy designed to stimulate investment in specific areas may benefit from focusing on the type of industry that is more inclined to locate in those areas. The empirical studies on agglomeration economies and transportation infrastructure have largely developed separately. Integrating these two platforms of study could help to enhance the understanding of this study's finding of the spatial organization of economic activity.

References

Audretsch DB, Fritsch M. The geography of firm birth in Germany. Reg Stud. 1994;28(4):359–65.

Bartik TJ. Small business start-ups in the United States: estimates of the effects of characteristics of states. South Econ J. 1989;55:1004–18.

Ciccone C, Hall RE. Productivity and the density of economic activity. Am Econ Rev. 1996;86 (1):54–70.

Combes PP, Gobillon L. The empirics of agglomeration economies. In: Duranton G, Henderson JV, Strange W, editors. Handbook of regional and urban economics, volume 5A. Amsterdam: Elsevier; 2015. p. 247–348.

Duranton G, Puga D. Micro-foundations of urban agglomeration economies. In: Henderson JV, Thisse JF, editors. Handbook of regional and urban economics, volume 4. Amsterdam: Elsevier; 2004.
Eberts RW, McMillen DP. Agglomeration economies and urban public infrastructure. In: Cheshire P, Mills ES, editors. Handbook of urban and regional economics, volume 3. - New York: North Holland; 1999. p. 1455–95.
Figueiredo O, Guimaraes P, Woodward DP. Home-field advantage: location decisions of Portuguese entrepreneurs. J Urban Econ. 2002;52:341–61.
Guesnier B. Regional variations in new firm formation in France. Reg Stud. 1994;28(4):347–58.
Henderson V, Kuncoro A, Turner M. Industrial development in cities. J Polit Econ. 1995;103 (5):1067–90.
Holl A. Manufacturing location and impacts of road transport infrastructure: empirical evidence from Spain. Reg Sci Urban Econ. 2004a;34(3):341–63.
Holl A. Transport infrastructure, agglomeration economies and firm birth: empirical evidence from Portugal. J Reg Sci. 2004b;44(4):693–712.
Holl A. Start-ups and relocations: manufacturing plant location in Portugal. Pap Reg Sci. 2004c;83 (4):649–68.
Keeble D, Walker S. New firms, small firms and dead firms: spatial patterns and determinants in the United Kingdom. Reg Stud. 1994;28(4):411–27.
Kieschnick MD. Taxes and growth: business incentives and economic development. Washington, DC: Council of State Planning Agencies; 1981.
Krugman P. Increasing returns and economic geography. J Polit Econ. 1991a;99:483–99.
Krugman P. History and industry location: the case of the manufacturing belt. Am Econ Rev. 1991b;81:80–3.
McCann P. Urban and regional economics. Location: Oxford University Press; 2001.
Otsuka A. Regional determinants of total factor productivity in Japan: stochastic frontier analysis. Ann Reg Sci. 2017;58(3):579–96.
Otsuka A, Goto M. Regional policy and the productive efficiency of Japanese industries. Reg Stud. 2015a;49(4):518–31.
Otsuka A, Goto M. Agglomeration economies in Japanese industries: the Solow residual approach. Ann Reg Sci. 2015b;54(2):401–16.
Otsuka A, Yamano N. Industrial agglomeration effects on regional economic growth: a case of Japanese regions, Discussion Papers 08-T-2, Regional Economics Applications Laboratory, University of Illinois, IL; 2008.
Otsuka A, Goto M, Sueyoshi T. Industrial agglomeration effects in Japan: productive efficiency, market access, and public fiscal transfer. Pap Reg Sci. 2010;89(4):819–39.
Reynolds PD. Autonomous firm dynamics and economic growth in the United States. Reg Stud. 1994;28(4):429–42.
Reynolds PD, Miller B, Maki WR. Regional characteristics affecting business volatility in the United States, 1980–1984. In: Karllson C, Johannesson J, Storey DJ, editors. Small business dynamics: international, national and regional perspectives. London: Routledge; 1994. p. 78–115.
Rosenthal SS, Strange WC. The determinants of agglomeration. J Urban Econ. 2001;50 (2):191–229.
Rosenthal S, Strange W. Evidence on the nature and sources of agglomeration economies. In: Henderson JV, Thisse JF, editors. Handbook of regional and urban economics, volume 4. Amsterdam: Elsevier; 2004.
Small and Medium Enterprise Agency. White Paper on Small and Medium Enterprise in Japan; 1999.

Small and Medium Enterprise Agency. White Paper on Small and Medium Enterprise in Japan; 2002.
Storey DJ, Jones AM. New firm formation: a labour market approach to industrial entry. Scott J Polit Econ. 1987;34(1):37–51.
Sutaria V. The dynamics of new firm formation. London: Ashgate; 2001.
Taylor MJ. Organizational growth, spatial interaction and location decision-making. Reg Stud. 1975;9:313–23.

MIX
Papier aus verantwortungsvollen Quellen
Paper from responsible sources
FSC® C105338

FSC
www.fsc.org

If you have any concerns about our products,
you can contact us on
ProductSafety@springernature.com

In case Publisher is established outside the EU,
the EU authorized representative is:
Springer Nature Customer Service Center GmbH
Europaplatz 3, 69115 Heidelberg, Germany

Printed by Libri Plureos GmbH
in Hamburg, Germany